The WILEY advantage

Dear Valued Customer,

We realize you're a busy professional with deadlines to hit. Whether your goal is to learn a new technology or solve a critical problem, we want to be there to lend you a hand. Our primary objective is to provide you with the insight and knowledge you need to stay atop the highly competitive and ever-changing technology industry.

Wiley Publishing, Inc., offers books on a wide variety of technical categories, including security, data warehousing, software development tools, and networking — everything you need to reach your peak. Regardless of your level of expertise, the Wiley family of books has you covered.

- For Dummies® – The *fun* and *easy* way™ to learn
- The Weekend Crash Course® –The *fastest* way to learn a new tool or technology
- Visual – For those who prefer to learn a new topic *visually*
- The Bible – The *100% comprehensive* tutorial and reference
- The Wiley Professional list – *Practical* and *reliable* resources for IT professionals

The book you hold now, *Windows Server 2003 Weekend Crash Course,* is your quick guide for getting up to speed with Windows Server 2003 — in a single weekend! Windows Server 2003 is Microsoft's base operating system; it lets you get maximum value out of Microsoft .NET Framework and .NET Enterprise Servers. In a single weekend, you are introduced to managing files, systems, and printers, as well as configuring security policies, managing routing, and working with remote access services. The weekend wraps up by showing you how to manage VPNs and advanced network services, as well as coverage of maintenance issues and disaster recovery.

Our commitment to you does not end at the last page of this book. We'd want to open a dialog with you to see what other solutions we can provide. Please be sure to visit us at www.wiley.com/compbooks to review our complete title list and explore the other resources we offer. If you have a comment, suggestion, or any other inquiry, please locate the "contact us" link at www.wiley.com.

Sincerely,

Richard K. Swadley
Vice President & Executive Group Publisher
Wiley Technology Publishing

15 HOUR WEEKEND CRASH COURSE

Visual

Bible

DUMMIES FOR

WILEY
Wiley Publishing, Inc.

Windows®
Server 2003
Weekend Crash Course®

Windows® Server 2003 Weekend Crash Course®

Don Jones

WILEY

Wiley Publishing, Inc.

Windows® Server 2003 Weekend Crash Course®

Published by
Wiley Publishing, Inc.
909 Third Avenue
New York, NY 10022
www.wiley.com

Copyright © 2003 by Wiley Publishing, Inc., Indianapolis, Indiana. All rights reserved.

Library of Congress Control Number: 2002100237

ISBN: 0-7645-4925-1

Manufactured in the United States of America

10 9 8 7 6 5 4 3 2 1

1B/QS/QU/QT/IN

Published by Wiley Publishing, Inc., Indianapolis, Indiana
Published simultaneously in Canada

For general information on our other products and services or to obtain technical support, please contact our Customer Care Department within the U.S. at 800-762-2974, outside the U.S. at 317-572-3993 or fax 317-572-4002.

Wiley also publishes its books in a variety of electronic formats. Some content that appears in print may not be available in electronic books.

Trademarks: Wiley, the Wiley Publishing logo, and Weekend Crash Course are trademarks or registered trademarks of Wiley Publishing, Inc. in the United States and other countries and may not be used without written permission. Windows is a trademark or registered trademark of Microsoft Corporation. All other trademarks are the property of their respective owners. Wiley Publishing, Inc., is not associated with any product or vendor mentioned in this book.

WILEY is a trademark of Wiley Publishing, Inc.

Credits

Senior Acquisitions Editor
Sharon Cox

Acquisitions Editor
Terri Varveris

Project Editor
Martin V. Minner

Technical Editor
Allen Wyatt

Copy Editor
Nancy Crumpton

Editorial Manager
Mary Beth Wakefield

Vice President and Executive Group Publisher
Richard Swadley

Vice President and Executive Publisher
Bob Ipsen

Executive Editorial Director
Mary Bednarek

Project Coordinator
Dale White

Graphics and Production Specialists
Elizabeth Brooks, Jennifer Click,
Sean Decker, Heather Pope, Erin Zeltner

Quality Control Technicians
Laura Albert, John Bitter,
Andy Hollandbeck, Susan Moritz

Permissions Editor
Laura Moss

Media Development Specialists
Marisa Pearman, Greg Stafford

Proofreading and Indexing
TECHBOOKS Production Services

Cover Design
Clark Creative Group

About the Author

With more than a decade of information technology experience, **Don Jones** is a founding partner of BrainCore.Net LLC and a world leader in the development of technical certification and assessment exams and exam delivery technologies. Don is the author of several books, including *Microsoft .NET E-Commerce Bible* and *Application Center 2000 Configuration and Administration,* and he is the coauthor of *E-Commerce For Dummies.* Don is a regular speaker at national technical conferences and provides writing and consulting services to a number of clients nationwide, including Microsoft Corporation. Don lives and travels around the country in an RV with his partner and five ferrets.

Preface

This book is for people who want to learn about Windows Server 2003, Microsoft's latest Windows-based network operating system. No experience with any prior version of Windows is required, although a familiarity with the Windows user interface is definitely helpful. You should have a basic understanding of computer networking, as Windows Server 2003 relies heavily on networking technologies. This book focuses on the many features of Windows Server 2003, including advanced topics like Terminal Services and Certificate Services. The purpose of this book is to teach you enough to begin working with Windows Server 2003 on a regular basis; only time and practice will make you an expert with such a complex product.

Who Should Read This Book

If you want to hold down a job administering servers that run Windows Server 2003, then this book is for you. If you're already familiar with Windows, but want to learn more about this version, you'll find a lot of useful information in this book, as well.

This book is designed to teach you the fundamental job tasks that most corporate network administrators need to know in just a single weekend. You'll learn through a series of very short, very focused sessions that each teach you how to accomplish a specific, key job task.

What's in this Book

This book jumps right in by showing you the various ways to install Windows Server 2003. From there, the sessions introduce the materials you're most likely to need as an administrator of Windows Server 2003 computers, especially file and print services.

Later sessions introduce more advanced topics, like Terminal Services, security, and TCP/IP. I'll walk you through all the major TCP/IP technologies, including DNS, DHCP, WINS, FTP, IIS, and more (don't worry — all of those acronyms will make sense by Saturday evening). I'll wrap up this Crash Course with really advanced topics, like Windows Clustering, troubleshooting, performance optimization, and Certificate Services.

Windows Server 2003 is a complex, full-featured operating system. No book of this size (or even three times as big) could possible teach you everything there is to know. In fact, I've been working with the Windows operating systems since 1989, and I still learn new things every day. So instead of trying to make you a guru, this book focuses on teaching you the things you need to know to administer Windows Server 2003 in a real-world work environment. Once you start working with the operating system, you'll find neat shortcuts for many tasks, learn about new features and technologies, and become more of an expert than you may imagine. That's part of the fun of Windows, and information technology in general: There's always something new to master.

Organization and Presentation

This book is organized into 30 sessions, each requiring about 30 minutes of your time. The sessions are organized as follows:

- Friday evening: Sessions 1 through 4 (about 2 hours).
- Saturday morning: Sessions 5 through 10 (about 3 hours).
- Saturday afternoon: Sessions 11 through 16 (about 3 hours).
- Saturday evening: Sessions 17 through 20 (about 2 hours).
- Sunday morning: Sessions 21 through 26 (about 3 hours).
- Sunday afternoon: Sessions 27 through 30 (about 2 hours).

As you can see, I keep you pretty busy. Of course, you don't need to follow this schedule; the book works fine at whatever pace you want to read it. You can even skip around, reading just the sessions that appeal to you. But if you're after the full Weekend Crash Course, you'll need to discipline yourself to the preceding schedule.

Each chapter includes several icons to catch your attention.

The "minutes to go" icons mark your progress within each session, so you can see how much further you have to go.

30 Min. To Go

I use Tip icons to draw your attention to best practices and other advice that can make Windows Server 2003 easier to work with.

The Note icon highlights additional information that you should be aware of or draws your attention to especially important pieces of technical information.

The Never icon alerts you to dangerous conditions that you want to avoid at all costs.

Contacting the Author

I appreciate your feedback! As a professional consultant, speaker, and author, my biggest reward is helping folks understand the complex technologies we must all work with. Please feel free to contact me with your comments and suggestions! Just visit my Web site, www.braincore.net, for contact information. I look forward to hearing from you!

Acknowledgments

Any book project can be difficult and time-consuming, and, as always, the folks that I work with at Wiley make it as smooth as possible. I read a lot of technical books, too, and Wiley's editors are among the best in the business, helping ensure that the book you hold in your hands is consistent, easy to read, and technically accurate. On this project, I'd like to thank the following editors for their diligence and hard work: Allen Wyatt of Discovery Computing, who performed the technical edit; Nancy Crumpton, the copy editor; and Martin V. Minner, the project editor. I'd also like to thank my agency, StudioB, for their continued help and support. On a more personal note, I'd like to thank Chris for an unending supply of patience through yet another major project, and my ferrets, Ziggy, Buffy, Clyde, Pepper, and Tigger, for forcing me to take a few minutes away from the keyboard to play.

Finally, I'd like to dedicate this book to all the capable professionals who've helped me and supported me in my information technology career: Jon Kilgannon, Bill Conrad, Mark Rouse, Judd Hambleton, Scott McFarland, Mike Burns, John Malenfant, John Repko, Ed Martini, Mark Scott, Chuck Urwiler, David Walls, Hugh Brown, Barbara Decker, Todd Merrell, Mary Beth Thome, Nicole Valentine, and Greg Marino. Thanks for your support, your friendship, and your professional advice through the years.

Contents at a Glance

Contents

Windows®
.NET Server 2003
Weekend Crash Course™

☑ **Friday**

☐ Saturday

☐ Sunday

Part I — Friday Evening

PART

I

Friday
Evening

Windows Server 2003 Basics

Session Checklist

✔ Windows Server 2003 editions

✔ Windows memory and processing

✔ Windows technology foundations

30 Min. To Go

Windows Server 2003 is the latest version of Microsoft's enterprise server operating system. The Windows Server 2003 family is the successor to the Windows 2000 Server family, which in turn built upon Windows NT Server. Windows Server 2003 introduces many new features and offers significant improvements to many features found in earlier Windows Server operating systems.

Before you can begin using Windows Server 2003, though, you need to understand the family of products that carry the Server name and how they differ from one another. You also have to understand their common memory and processor architecture, and some of the basic technologies that Windows Server 2003 is built upon.

The Windows Server Family

When Microsoft introduced Windows 2000 Server, they created a *family,* or series, of server operating systems. That family continues in Windows Server 2003 and consists of four separate products:

- Windows Server 2003 — Standard Edition
- Windows Server 2003 — Web Edition
- Windows Server 2003 — Enterprise Edition
- Windows Server 2003 — Datacenter Edition

Microsoft has also announced a 64-bit version of Windows Server 2003, which will be available on server computers utilizing Intel's Itanium processor or compatible processors from other companies. 64-bit editions of both Windows Server 2003 — Standard Edition and Windows Server 2003 — Enterprise Edition will be available.

 The name "Windows Server 2003" is used to refer to the entire family of server operating systems. In this book, I use the name "Windows Server 2003" when discussing features that apply to all editions, and I refer to a specific edition by name when discussing features supported only by that edition.

Each of the three Windows Server 2003 editions has specific capabilities designed to meet specific business needs, and they build upon one another. In other words, Windows Enterprise Server can do everything the standard edition can do, and more.

 Microsoft also produces a line of application servers that are collectively referred to as the "Enterprise Servers." This line includes Commerce Server, SQL Server, and Exchange Server. Don't confuse the "Enterprise Server" brand with Windows Server 2003, which is the operating system that all of the application servers run on.

Windows Server 2003 — Standard Edition

The standard edition of Windows Server 2003 provides all of the basic functionality a server operating system needs. The standard edition is intended to support small- to medium-sized businesses as a file server, application server platform, or domain controller.

SYNTAX ▶| A *file server* stores files, like Microsoft Office documents and enables users to access these files over a network. An *application server* runs application server software, such as a Web server or database server. A *domain controller* is a special type of server that centralizes security and user accounts for a business. You'll learn more about domain controllers in Session 3.

Windows Server 2003 has the following limitations:

- A maximum of four microprocessors may be used.
- No more than 4GB of memory is allowed. Of that 4GB, the operating system always reserves 2GB for its own use, allowing applications on the server to share the remaining 2GB.

Windows Server 2003 — Web Edition

Specially designed for use as a Web server, Windows Web Server provides a subset of the overall Windows Server 2003 functionality. The Web Server edition is optimized for Microsoft's Internet Information Services (IIS) Web server platform. The Web Server edition does not support some advanced services, including:

- Advanced network security features like Internet Authorization Server
- Fax services
- Terminal services

As the name implies, Windows Web Server is ideal for servers used as Internet or intranet Web servers.

Windows Server 2003 — Enteprise Edition

Windows Enterprise Server builds upon the Windows Server 2003 standard edition. It provides all of the same features and capabilities as the standard edition and adds the following:

- Support for up to eight microprocessors in a server.
- Expanded memory support that reserves only 1GB of memory for the operating system, allowing applications on the server to share the remaining 3GB.

- The ability to create clusters of two servers. You'll learn more about clustering in Session 27.

Some software applications are specifically designed to take advantage of these additional features. For example, Microsoft SQL Server 2000 is available in an "Enterprise Edition" that enables you to create clustered SQL Servers. The Enterprise Edition cannot be installed on the standard edition of Windows Server 2003 because cluster support isn't included in that edition.

Any Microsoft application server product with "Enterprise Edition" in the name may list the Enterprise Server edition of the operating system as a minimum requirement to take advantage of advanced features like clustering.

Enterprise Server is targeted toward medium to large businesses that need to run extremely powerful servers, use clustering, or run especially powerful application server software.

Windows Server 2003 — Datacenter Edition

Windows' Datacenter Server edition is the most powerful version of the operating system. Like the Enterprise Server edition, Datacenter Server builds upon the standard Windows Server 2003 edition and adds the following features and capabilities:

- Support for up to 32 processors in a single server
- Support for up to 64GB of memory
- Support for clusters of up to four servers

Microsoft designed Datacenter Server to be the most stable, reliable, and powerful version of Windows Server 2003. As such, it is also one of the most expensive. Also, Datacenter Server is the only version of Windows Server 2003 that you cannot purchase and install yourself (see the sidebar, "Where Do I Get Datacenter?")

Datacenter Server is targeted to large businesses that need the most powerful servers possible, and who also require extremely reliable servers that rarely crash and rarely need to be rebooted (aside from scheduled maintenance operations).

**20 Min.
To Go**

Where Do I Get Datacenter?

One major concern that Windows administrators have is reliability. Windows NT and, to a lesser extent, Windows 2000, have a reputation for occasionally crashing, needing to be frequently rebooted, and so forth. Microsoft has conducted numerous studies over the years to discover the reasons behind these reliability problems. Those studies determined that most operating system failures were due to hardware and device driver problems.

A *device driver* is a small software program that allows Windows to interact with a server's hardware, including its disk drives, video display circuits, modems, and so forth. Because the operating system must work closely with device drivers, they must be programmed very carefully. A small bug in a device driver can easily crash the entire operating system.

When Microsoft decided to create Windows 2000 Datacenter Server, they decided to try to eliminate all hardware and device driver problems. To do so, they created a special certification program with the industry's major manufacturers of server hardware. As a result of that program, Datacenter Server can be purchased only along with a hardware server that has been certified by Microsoft as being compatible with the operating system. So the only way to purchase Datacenter Server is to buy it preloaded on a Compaq, IBM, Dell, or other brand of server. Datacenter Server is only available on specific server models that have been rigorously tested to ensure hardware and device driver compatibility.

What's more, any future upgrades to a server running Datacenter Server must be performed by the original server manufacturer, to ensure continued operating system compatibility. If you perform your own unauthorized upgrades to a Datacenter Server, Microsoft's Product Support Services will not help you with any problems that may arise.

Windows Architecture

Like its predecessors, Windows Server 2003 is a multithreaded, multiprocessing, multitasking operating system. It has a rich set of built-in services that make it easy for software developers to create powerful applications in a relatively short period of time. Unlike older operating systems, such as Windows 3.0 and Microsoft

MS-DOS, Windows Server 2003 offers built-in memory management, task scheduling, and much more. Windows Server 2003 also offers compatibility with an enormous array of hardware devices, allowing the operating system to interact with storage devices, scanners, networks, and many other types of peripherals. All of these features fall under two categories: operating system architecture components and application architecture components.

Operating system architecture

Windows uses a layered operating system architecture, allowing different layers to handle specific functions. This approach makes Windows very flexible, allowing the operating system to run in a variety of circumstances while requiring very few changes. The three major layers of Windows' architecture are shown in Figure 1-1 and include the *HAL,* the *kernel,* and the *applications* that run under Windows.

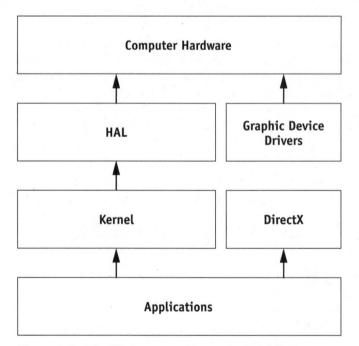

Figure 1-1   *The Windows operating system architecture*

The HAL

The Windows operating system architecture starts with the HAL, or *Hardware Abstraction Layer*. The HAL is a special piece of software that interacts directly with the hardware of a computer, including the computer's memory, processor, and various data communication devices.

The HAL can be replaced when Windows needs to run on a different type of computer. For example, Microsoft includes two HALs with Windows. One is designed for computers with only a single processor, and that HAL is fine-tuned to run best on one processor. Microsoft also provides a multiprocessor HAL, which is designed to take advantage of computers with two or more processors.

As shown in Figure 1-1, the HAL is bypassed for operations that work with the computer's graphics display. Separate drivers are provided for graphics cards; these drivers interact directly with the cards, providing faster graphics output.

The Kernel

The Windows kernel is the core of the operating system. The kernel runs on top of the HAL and uses device drivers to communicate with specific types of hardware. The kernel is responsible for running applications, drawing windows, buttons, and other elements of the graphical user interface (GUI), and so forth. In many respects, the kernel is what you think of as Windows itself.

Microsoft introduced a special set of software services called *DirectX* that communicates directly with graphics drivers. DirectX allows game programs to bypass the kernel and the HAL for very fast graphics output.

Applications

Applications are the things *you* use a server for, such as Web server software, database server software, or even Microsoft Office. Applications must be written to the Windows 32-bit API, or Application Programming Interface. This API is a special set of rules that programmers must follow in order for their applications to run on Windows. Essentially, an application uses the API to ask the kernel to perform various tasks, such as load files from disk or display graphics on a monitor. The kernel accepts applications' requests and passes them on to the HAL, which in turn translates them into the instructions understood by the computer's hardware.

Application architecture

Windows' application architecture allows the operating system to run multiple applications at the same time. Generally, each application is run in a separate *memory space,* meaning each application believes it is the only one running on the computer. If an application encounters an error and crashes, Windows can simply terminate that application's memory space. Other applications running on the server are unaffected.

Multitasking

In Windows terminology, a *task* usually represents a single software application. On a workstation computer, Microsoft Word is a task. On a server computer, an application server like Internet Information Services or Commerce Server might be a task.

**10 Min.
To Go**

Multitasking refers to Windows' ability to run multiple tasks at the same time. In reality, though, a computer's processor can't run multiple tasks at once. To enable multitasking, the Windows kernel includes a *task scheduler.* This scheduler keeps tracks of all the applications currently running on the computer and assigns each of them a *time slice.* The scheduler then instructs the computer's processor to spend a short amount of time on each task. The amount of time the processor spends on a task is determined by the task's time slice: A larger time slice means the processor works on that task longer before switching to another one.

Because modern processors are so fast, they can switch between dozens of tasks in just a few *milliseconds.* Although the computer works on only one task at a time, it switches between them so quickly and so frequently that it *seems* to be working on them all at once.

You can see the tasks the computer is working on from within Windows. Just right-click on the Task Bar and select Task Manager from the pop-up menu. As shown in Figure 1-2, the Task Manager's Processes tab shows you all the tasks the computer is running and the percentage of the processor's time that is being spent on each task.

Multithreading

Each task running under Windows is capable of running multiple *threads.* You can think of a thread as a minitask that runs within the main task. For example, Microsoft Word enables you to type a document while it prints another one and spell-checks a third. All of these operations take place in separate threads within the main Word task.

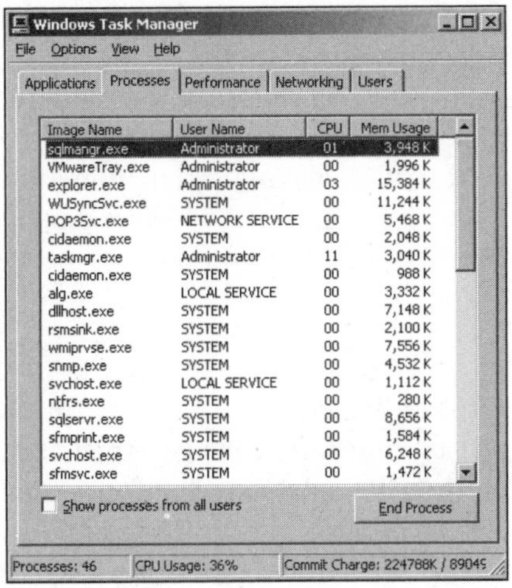

Figure 1-2   *The Windows Task Manager*

The Windows task scheduler breaks down the time slice assigned to each task and assigns the pieces to that task's threads. Each thread is then scheduled to run on the processor for the designated amount of time. Again, the processor is capable of working on only one thing at a time, but it is able to switch so fast that the computer appears to be working on multiple tasks and threads at once.

Multiprocessing

On a computer with more than one processor, Windows is truly capable of working on more than one thing at a time. The kernel's task scheduler is capable of assigning tasks and threads to a particular processor. The scheduler keeps track of how much work each processor is performing and tries to assign threads and tasks evenly, so that all processors in the computer are working at about the same rate.

As an administrator, you usually have no control over which tasks run on specific processors. Windows uses each processor in the computer as an available resource, and the scheduler makes complex decisions to determine which threads to assign to which processors. Software developers have a great deal of control over how well their applications can run on multiple processors. Some applications are written in such a way that they cannot effectively run on more than one processor. For example, an application that uses a single thread can run on only one processor because individual threads cannot be broken up between processors.

If you have an application that does not take advantage of the multiple processors in your server, contact the application's developer or manufacturer to see if a version is available that takes advantage of multiple processors.

Underlying Technologies

No operating system as large and complex as Windows Server 2003 is created entirely by one manufacturer's technologies and techniques. To create Windows Server 2003, Microsoft relied on many industry-standard technologies and used many industry techniques. Understanding these underlying technologies can help you better understand how Windows Server 2003 works "under the hood." Windows' most important underlying technologies fall into four categories: networking, security, services, and GUIs.

Networking

Windows Server 2003 provides a powerful set of networking services, allowing the operating system — and applications running on it — to communicate with other servers and applications across various types of electronic computer networks. Windows' primary networking *protocol,* or language, is TCP/IP. You have probably worked with TCP/IP before since it is also the native networking protocol used on the Internet and the World Wide Web.

You'll learn about Windows Server 2003's use of TCP/IP in Session 13.

By building Windows Server 2003 upon TCP/IP, Microsoft ensured that the operating system would be able to interact with and participate in the worldwide Internet. But, because many organizations who use Windows Server 2003 also use networking protocols other than TCP/IP, Microsoft made sure that Windows Server 2003 came with flexible networking options. In addition to TCP/IP, Windows Server 2003 can understand a variety of other network protocols, including

- IPX/SPX networks, which are common in environments that use Novell NetWare
- SNA networks, which are primarily used in conjunction with IBM midrange computers like the AS/400

- Legacy networks using DECnet, Banyan Vines, and other older network protocols

In the past, Windows included separate protocols for talking to computers like Apple Macintoshes. Today, most computers — including Macs — are capable of working with TCP/IP, so Windows no longer needs special, dedicated network protocols.

Security

While Windows Server 2003 uses an industry-standard security protocol named Kerberos (which is built upon TCP/IP), it's more important that you understand the security *concepts* the operating system uses. These concepts are built on many years of experience, and drawn from a variety of enterprise-class operating systems, including VAX and UNIX.

In Windows Server 2003, every object — such as a file, user account, printer, or other types of information — can be secured with an *Access Control List,* or ACL. The ACL lists the users who are allowed to work with the object and what actions they are allowed to perform. For example, a Word document including a list of company phone extensions might allow all of the company's users to read the file but permit only the company's receptionist to modify the file. An Excel spreadsheet containing payroll information might be visible only to members of the payroll and human resources departments. Windows uses the Kerberos protocol to determine who a user really is and then uses ACLs to determine what objects and information that user has access to.

This system of ACLs provides Windows administrators a great deal of flexibility. By carefully configuring ACLs, you can easily enable users to access the information they need to do their jobs, while protecting information that is private or confidential.

I'll introduce you to Windows security in Sessions 3 and 4.

Services

When network servers were first created, their primary task was to provide a place for users to store files that they wanted to share. As servers became more advanced, they gained the ability to run application server software, turning the servers into database servers and Web servers. As a modern, advanced operating system, Windows Server 2003 not only includes all of these abilities, but also includes many application servers built right in. These are often referred to as *services,* and they include

- Internet Information Services, which allows Windows Server 2003 to be a Web server

- Certificate Services, which allows a server to issue and authenticate digital certificates for identity authentication and encryption

- Remote Access Services, which enables remote users with modems to dial in to a Windows Server 2003 as easily as they would dial in to an Internet Service Provider (ISP)

- Domain Name Services, which allows a server to translate friendly names like www.microsoft.com into the numeric TCP/IP addresses used on the Internet

These examples are just a few of the services included with every copy of Windows Server 2003. Because Windows Server 2003 includes so many services, it offers a great value to businesses. Rather than purchasing a separate server operating system and a variety of add-on services, they can simply purchase Windows Server 2003, which includes many commonly used services right in the box, at no extra charge.

You'll learn about Windows' built-in services throughout this book, especially in the Saturday Evening sessions.

Graphical user interfaces (GUIs)

Windows Server 2003 uses a GUI, built on Microsoft's experience with Windows 3.0, Windows 3.1, Windows 95, Windows NT, Windows 2000, and every other version of Windows that has ever existed. Many of the GUI elements — such as buttons, check boxes, option buttons, and so forth — used in Windows have become industry standards.

By default, Windows Server 2003 uses the same user "Windows Classic" interface found in Windows 2000 and is shown in Figure 1-3. The "classic" user interface offers the same capabilities and features, while at the same time preserving the GUI style that many administrators are already familiar with.

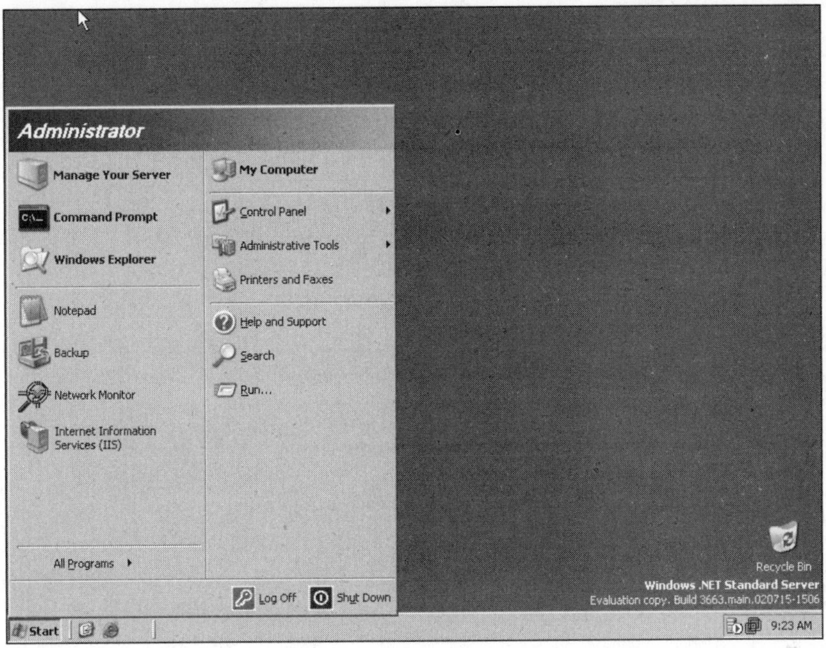

Figure 1-3   *The classic Windows GUI*

REVIEW

In this session, you learned about the four editions of the Windows Server 2003 family:

- Windows Server 2003 — Standard Edition
- Windows Server 2003 — Web Edition
- Windows Server 2003 — Enterprise Edition
- Windows Server 2003 — Datacenter Edition

You also learned about Windows' operating system and application architecture, including Windows' ability to perform multiprocessing, multitasking, and multithreading. Finally, you learned about many of the basic technologies that Windows is built on, including TCP/IP, Windows' security model, and its graphical user interface, or GUI.

Done!

Quiz Yourself

1. Which edition of Windows Server 2003 introduces the ability to create server clusters? (See "The Windows Server Family.")

2. What is the main reason Datacenter Server is the most reliable edition of Windows Server 2003? (See "Where Do I Get Datacenter?")

3. What part of Windows is responsible for interacting with a computer's hardware? (See "Operating system architecture.")

4. What part of Windows decides which tasks and threads are executed by the computer's processors? (See "Multiprocessing.")

5. What is the native networking protocol for Windows Server 2003? (See "Networking.")

Installing Windows Server 2003

Session Checklist

✔ How to perform an attended installation

✔ How to create an unattended installation

✔ How to upgrade from prior versions of Windows Server

✔ How to perform a "headless server" installation

✔ How to perform product activation

**30 Min.
To Go**

I f you've used a prior version of Windows, you'll find the Windows Server 2003 installation methods to be familiar. If not, don't worry! Windows Server 2003 is a complex operating system, but installing it is very straightforward. In this session, you'll learn about the various ways you can install Windows Server 2003, tips for saving time when you have to install Windows Server 2003 on many computers, and some of the new installation capabilities included in Windows Server 2003.

Installation Methods

Windows Server 2003 offers three basic types of installation:

- A standard CD-based installation enables you to install the operating system from a CD-ROM drive, or even from a DVD-ROM drive, if you have one.
- A network-based installation doesn't require you to have a CD-ROM drive. Instead, the installation is run from a copy of the installation CD, which is located on a networked file server.
- A RIS-based installation uses Remote Installation Services, or RIS, to install the operating system without using a CD or a copy of a CD.

Each of these three methods has specific advantages and disadvantages, which I'll cover in the next few sections. Each of these methods can be performed as an attended installation, in which you physically sit at the computer while Windows Server 2003 installs, or an unattended installation, which doesn't require any input once the installation begins.

CD-based installation

CD-based installations are the most common way to install Windows Server 2003. This type of installation requires that you physically insert a Windows Server 2003 CD-ROM into the server computer. Starting the installation depends on what kind of operating system, if any, is already running on the computer:

- If the computer doesn't have an operating system, insert the Windows Server 2003 CD-ROM and then reboot the computer. The computer prompts you to "Press any key to boot from CD-ROM." When you see that prompt, press a key to begin a Windows Server 2003 attended installation.
- If the computer already has a Windows operating system installed, inserting the CD-ROM should automatically display the Windows Server 2003 Installation menu. You'll be able to start the installation process only if the computer is running a Windows Server operating system, like Windows 2000 Server and you want to perform an upgrade. I'll show you how to perform an upgrade later in this session.

  If you want to perform an unattended installation, or specify installation options, just cancel the Installation menu and leave the CD-ROM in the computer. You'll be able to start an unattended or attended installation, which I'll describe a bit later in this chapter.

- You can also boot the computer using an MS-DOS floppy disk that contains CD-ROM drivers for the computer. This technique enables you to start the Windows Server 2003 installation process and specify installation options, such as the option for an unattended setup.

CD-based installations are most often used for an attended installation. CD-based installations are fast because the installation software can read data from a CD-ROM very rapidly. However, CD-based installations limit the number of computers you can install at a time because you must have a CD-ROM for each. Many companies prefer not to use CD-based installations because they run the risk of damaging the Windows Server 2003 CD-ROMs.

If you have access to a CD-R or CD-RW drive, you can create a copy of the Windows Server 2003 CD-ROM. You are permitted to create the copy only if you already own an original CD-ROM, and you are still bound by the terms of the Windows Server 2003 license agreement when you use the copy. Creating a copy is a good idea if you plan to perform CD-based installations and don't want to risk damaging your original Windows Server 2003 CD-ROM.

Network-based installation

A network-based installation is made possible when you copy the contents of the Windows Server 2003 CD to a networked file server and then make the copy available over the network. You start the installation process by launching the winnt.exe or winnt32.exe program. As I'll describe later in this chapter, you can specify options to start an attended or unattended installation.

Network-based installations are usually slower than a CD-based installation because computers can't copy files across a network as quickly as they can from a CD-ROM. However, because multiple computers can access a network at the same time, you can start the installation process on many servers at once. This capability makes network-based installations well suited for unattended installations, in which you install Windows Server 2003 on many computers at once.

The number of servers you can install at the same time depends on the capacity of your network. High-bandwidth networks like Fast Ethernet allow more servers to access the installation files; lower-bandwidth networks like regular Ethernet slow down more quickly as additional servers use the network to copy the installation files.

RIS-based installation

Windows 2000 Server included RIS to help install Windows 2000 Professional on workstation computers. Windows Server 2003 extends the capabilities of RIS, so that you can use RIS to install Windows Server 2003 as well as workstation operating systems.

RIS is not included in Windows Web Server.

RIS is a special type of network-based installation. It requires a Windows Server 2003 running the RIS server software, and either special software or special network interface cards (NICs) in the computers you want to install Windows Server 2003 on. RIS also requires advanced preparation before you can begin an installation. A complete description of how RIS works is beyond the scope of this book. In fact, RIS could take up a book all by itself! Here's a brief overview of how you can use RIS to install Windows Server 2003:

1. You start by performing a CD- or network-based installation of Windows Server 2003 on a sample computer. The sample computer's hardware should closely resemble the hardware of the other computers you want to install Windows Server 2003 on.

2. After your sample computer has been set up, you use special software included with Windows Server 2003 to prepare a *RIS image*. A RIS image is essentially a copy of the sample server.

3. The RIS image is placed on a RIS server. The server must be running Windows Server 2003 and the RIS server software (which is included with Windows Server 2003). The RIS image must be configured so that the server recognizes it as being available.

4. The computers you want to install the image on should have PXE-compatible NICs. PXE-compatible NICs have the ability to look for a RIS server when the computer boots, instead of trying to boot from the computer's hard disk or CD-ROM. When the computer boots, the NIC locates the RIS server on your network and enables you to select the image you want to install.

5. Once you select an image, the RIS server copies it to the computer. After the copy is complete, the computer reboots and a shortened version of the installation routine executes to finish installing Windows Server 2003.

If your computers don't have PXE-compatible NICs, you can still use RIS. You have to create a bootable floppy disk with the RIS client software. The Windows Server 2003 documentation describes how to create a bootable RIS floppy disk.

RIS installations can be attended or unattended. In an attended installation, you answer a few questions after RIS copies the image and reboots the computer. In an unattended installation, RIS copies the image, reboots the computer, and completes the Windows Server 2003 installation by itself.

RIS installations are useful for installing Windows Server 2003 on a large number of computers at once, when those computers must contain the same Windows Server 2003 configuration options. RIS is also useful for creating a standardized Windows Server 2003 configuration, which can then be deployed to new server computers that are added to your network.

Creating RIS images and configuring a RIS server can be complex because the exact configuration of your environment will dictate the configuration options. The Windows Server 2003 documentation contains details on setting up a RIS server and creating RIS images that will work on your network.

**20 Min.
To Go**

Performing an Installation

Once you've decided what type of installation you want to perform, you need to decide *how* you will perform it. Windows Server 2003 gives you two choices: attended installation and unattended installation.

Attended installation

In an attended installation, you must remain at the computer while Windows Server 2003 is installed. You have to select various installation options and provide configuration information in the Setup Wizard, including

- The name of the new server
- Which network protocols that the Setup Wizard will install
- Which optional software components that the Setup Wizard will install
- The date, time, and time zone of the server

- The product ID number, which is usually printed on a label affixed to the Windows Server 2003 CD-ROM jewel case (assuming you purchased Windows Server 2003 through a retail channel; if you didn't, see the sidebar, "Activation Keys and Product IDs").

The one installation option you *must* have is the product ID number. You must provide a valid product ID number in order to install Windows Server 2003. If you have lost your product ID number, you need to contact Microsoft for a replacement.

You can begin an attended setup by running the Setup Wizard directly:

- For a CD-based installation, run `winnt32.exe` if the computer is already running a version of Windows. If the computer has been booted using a DOS floppy disk, run `winnt.exe`. Both executables can be found in the `i386` subfolder on the Windows Server 2003 CD-ROM.

- For a network-based installation, run `winnt32.exe` or `winnt.exe` from the network copy of the Windows Server 2003 CD-ROM.

- For a RIS-based installation, start the installation process normally, using your RIS boot floppy or a PXE-compatible NIC. A special Mini Setup Wizard automatically runs after the RIS image has been copied and the computer has been rebooted.

You usually can accept the default selections during an attended installation. Even if you forget to select a particular optional software component, you can always add it later.

Activation Keys and Product IDs

Microsoft sells two different types of Windows Server 2003 packages: A retail package and a volume license package. Retail packages are sold through regular retail channels, such as computer stores. Those packages come with a product ID, which is used to activate the operating system after you install it. Each product ID can be used to activate only one copy of Windows Server 2003, so you can't reuse them.

Volume license packages are distributed to customers who have a volume license agreement with Microsoft. These packages include a volume license ID instead of a product ID. Typically, volume license packages do not require activation.

> Make sure you're using the right ID when you install Windows Server 2003. You can't use a volume license ID with a retail package, and you can't use a product ID with a volume license package. Companies will usually purchase volume license packages, which allow you to distribute Windows Server 2003 to a number of computers without having to individually activate each one.

Installation options

When you start the installation process by running `winnt32.exe` or `winnt.exe`, you can specify one or more options to customize the installation process. To specify an option, simply include it when running the Setup Wizard. For example, to specify the `/dudisable` option, just run `winnt32.exe /dudisable` or `winnt.exe /dudisable`.

There are many different installation options, and the Windows Server 2003 documentation includes a complete list. The most important options are

- `/checkupgradeonly`. This option is available only when you run `winnt32.exe`; it is not available with `winnt.exe`. This option tells the Setup Wizard to check your computer for Windows Server 2003 compatibility and display a report of any possible compatibility problems. Windows Server 2003 is not installed when you specify this option.

- `/dudisable`. This option disables Windows Dynamic Update. Normally, Dynamic Update connects to the Internet during the setup process and downloads any updated files that may be needed on your computer. Use the `/dudisable` option when you aren't connected to the Internet or when you don't want the Setup Wizard to spend time checking for updates.

- `/makelocalsource`. This option tells the Setup Wizard to copy the contents of the Windows Server 2003 CD-ROM to the computer's hard drive, and then install using that copy. This option enables you to remove the CD-ROM from the computer after the installation process starts.

Installation options are useful for controlling the behavior of the installation process because they enable you to override the process' default behaviors to suit your environment. Installation options are also the key to performing unattended installations.

Unattended installation

Attended installations can be time-consuming because they require you to physically enter so many pieces of information. When you are setting up several computers, manually entering server names, product ID numbers, and other information for each computer can become tedious. In an unattended installation, you can create special text files called *answer files*. Answer files contain the configuration information the Setup Wizard needs, allowing the Wizard to install Windows Server 2003 without requiring you to be present.

Creating an answer file

Windows Server 2003 includes a sample answer file in the i386 folder of the Windows Server 2003 CD-ROM. The file is named unattend.txt, and you can customize it to create your own answer file. Windows Server 2003 also includes a special utility called the Setup Manager, which enables you to use a graphical interface to specify setup options and create an answer file.

The sample answer file looks something like this:

```
[Unattended]
Unattendmode = FullUnattended
OemPreinstall = NO
TargetPath = *
Filesystem = LeaveAlone

[UserData]
FullName = "Your User Name"
OrgName = "Your Organization Name"
ComputerName = *
ProductKey= "JJWKH-7M9R8-26VM4-FX8CC-GDPD8"

[GuiUnattended]
; Sets the Timezone to the Pacific Northwest
; Sets the Admin Password to NULL
; Turn AutoLogon ON and login once
TimeZone = "004"
AdminPassword = *
AutoLogon = Yes
AutoLogonCount = 1
```

```
[LicenseFilePrintData]
; For Server installs
AutoMode = "PerServer"
AutoUsers = "5"

[Display]
BitsPerPel = 8
XResolution = 800
YResolution = 600
VRefresh = 70

[Identification]
JoinWorkgroup = Workgroup
```

**10 Min.
To Go**

As you can see, the answer file format is pretty easy to figure out. By providing the appropriate information, you can prevent the Setup Wizard from requiring any manual input from you during the installation, effectively enabling you to start the installation and then walk away.

The answer file's format must be exactly right, or the installation process will fail. Using the Setup Manager, which is included in the \Support\Tools **folder of the Windows Server 2003 CD-ROM, provides an easy way to create answer files without worrying about the correct format.**

Using an answer file

You have to tell the Windows Server 2003 installation process to use an answer file, if you've prepared one. winnt.exe and winnt32.exe both provide an installation option that enables you to specify an answer file. Imagine that your answer file is located in a text file named myanswers.txt, located on the computer's C:\ drive in a folder named unattended. You would use the installation option /unattend:c:\unattended\myanswers.txt.

You specify the unattended installation option just as you would any other installation option. In fact, you can combine the unattended option with other installation options, such as /dudisable or /makelocalsource, to completely customize the installation process.

Upgrading from Prior Versions of Windows

Windows Server 2003 can perform an upgrade if your computer is already running Windows NT Server 3.51, Windows NT Server 4.0, or Windows 2000 Server. You cannot perform an upgrade on a computer running Windows 9x, Windows NT Workstation, or Windows 2000 Professional.

An upgrade retains all of the applications, configuration options, and settings on your computer, so you don't have to reconfigure the computer after the upgrade is complete. To start an attended upgrade, simply insert the Windows Server 2003 CD in your computer and select "Install Windows Server 2003" from the menu that automatically displays. To perform an unattended upgrade, first create an answer file. Then, run `winnt32.exe /unattend`. You do not need to specify an answer file for an upgrade because Windows Server 2003 retains the configuration of your existing operating system.

You can perform an upgrade using a CD-based or network-based installation. However, you cannot perform an upgrade using a RIS-based installation because the RIS image overwrites your existing operating system without preserving its configuration.

You may want to perform a *clean install* instead of an upgrade. A clean install erases your computer's previous operating system and performs a new installation of Windows Server 2003. Clean installations are useful if your computer's existing operating system is misconfigured or if you are experiencing problems with the operating system that a fresh version of Windows Server 2003 could correct. To perform a clean install, simply follow the directions for a regular attended or unattended installation. If the Setup Wizard asks you whether or not you want to upgrade your existing operating system, select No.

Product Activation

Beginning with Windows Server 2003, Microsoft requires all operating system installations to be *activated*. Activating the product registers it with Microsoft. If you do not activate Windows Server 2003 within an allotted time period (usually 30 days), it will refuse to function.

The operating system automatically prompts you to activate when it is started for the first time. Automatic activation requires you to have a live Internet connection. If you do not have an Internet connection, Microsoft provides a phone number you can call to perform a manual activation.

Product activation is tied to the product ID number you provide to the Setup Wizard when you install Windows Server 2003. Each product ID number may be used only to activate a specific number of Windows Server 2003 installations. The exact number of activations depends on the Windows Server 2003 license you purchased.

If your company has a Select Agreement or Open License Agreement with Microsoft, you may be provided with a special bulk product ID. That product ID bypasses product activation, enabling you to install as many copies of the operating system as your agreement permits.

Once a product ID has activated its maximum number of Windows Server 2003 installations, it no longer works. To prevent your product ID numbers from becoming overused, make sure you obtain a unique product ID number for each copy of Windows Server 2003 you install (unless your company has a special bulk product ID number under a Microsoft agreement).

Do not share your product ID numbers with other individuals or organizations. Microsoft uses product ID numbers and product activation to combat piracy. Your software license does not permit you to share your product ID numbers, and doing so may lead to legal problems.

Headless Servers

Many companies prefer to keep their servers in secure, environmentally controlled data centers. With the computers safely locked away, there is really very little need for them to have keyboards, monitors, or mice. As you will learn throughout this book, Windows Server 2003 can easily be managed remotely from an administrator's desktop computer.

Certain key functions of a server do require a monitor, keyboard, and mouse. For example, working with the computer's built-in BIOS configuration usually must be done from the *console,* or the server's physical keyboard. Working with newer server hardware, though, Windows Server 2003 allows even BIOS configuration and other "low-level" tasks to be conducted remotely. In fact, Windows Server 2003 is designed so that it can be installed and operated in a computer that has neither a mouse, monitor, keyboard, or even video card. Servers operating without those usually critical components are called *headless servers.*

Windows Server 2003 supports CD-based, network-based, and RIS-based installations on headless servers. Headless server installations can be performed only on server hardware that is compatible with Windows Server 2003's headless server capabilities; you should consult your hardware vendor for compatibility information. Once your server hardware has been configured to operate in a headless server mode, Windows Server 2003 installation should be conducted as you would with any other server.

Done!

REVIEW

In this session, you learned about the various installation methods supported by Windows Server 2003:

- CD-based
- Network-based
- RIS-based

You also learned about attended and unattended installations, how to create answer files for unattended installations, and how to start both attended and unattended installations. You learned about Windows Server 2003's ability to upgrade your computers' existing operating systems, and you learned about the product activation required by Windows Server 2003. Finally, you learned about Windows Server 2003's new "headless server" installation capabilities.

QUIZ YOURSELF

---

1. What are the three ways you can install Windows Server 2003? (See "Installation Methods.")
2. How do you initiate a CD-based installation? (See "CD-based installation.")
3. What two commands can be used to initiate a network-based installation? (See "Network-based installation.")
4. What special type of network interface card (NIC) is required to perform an installation using RIS? (See "RIS-based installation.")
5. What are two ways to create an answer file for use in an unattended installation? (See "Creating an answer file.")
6. What operating systems can be upgraded to Windows Server 2003? (See "Upgrading from Prior Versions of Windows.")

Managing Users and Groups

Session Checklist

✔ How to add local users and groups

✔ How server security works

✔ How to configure local account policies

✔ How to configure security auditing

**30 Min.
To Go**

Windows Server 2003 includes powerful security features, enabling you to control who can use a server and exactly what they can do with it. Windows Server 2003 also allows many servers to work together in a *domain,* sharing security information and making it easier for users to work with a large number of servers at once.

In this session, you'll learn about Windows Server 2003's local users and groups, its capabilities for managing user and group accounts, and how to configure security auditing so you can see what people are doing with your server.

Server Security

Windows Server 2003 can play different roles on a network, depending on your security requirements:

- As a *standalone server,* Windows Server 2003 maintains its own user accounts and groups. These accounts determine who can use the server. Standalone servers don't share security information with each other. If a user wants to use two different standalone servers, he must have a user account and password on each.

- As a *domain controller,* Windows Server 2003 maintains user accounts and groups that can be shared with other servers. This collection of users and groups is called a *domain* and enables users to access multiple servers with a single user account and password. In Windows Server 2003, domains are handled by Active Directory, which you'll learn more about in the next session.

- As a *member server,* Windows Server 2003 maintains its own user accounts, just like a standalone server. Member servers can also use the user and group accounts in an Active Directory domain. This capability means member servers can grant access to users with a domain account or users with a local server account.

Windows Server 2003's flexible security architecture makes it suitable for a wide range of computing environments. For example, small companies with only one or two servers can use standalone servers, which require very little administrative effort to maintain. Larger organizations can have an Active Directory domain, which provides central control of user accounts and makes it easier to work with a large number of servers. Larger organizations usually have a mix of domain controllers, which store the domain's user accounts, and member servers, which often contain resources that users access with their domain user accounts. Very large organizations may have several different domains, allowing different divisions of the company to maintain their own user accounts, while still sharing resources and servers with each other.

In this session, I focus on the security used by standalone servers and member servers. In the next session, I describe Active Directory and show you how domain controllers work.

Local Users and Groups

The key to server security is users and groups. A *user*, or *user account*, represents a real person who needs to use the resources on a server. In addition to granting access to the server, users and groups are also used to control exactly what people can do once they gain access to the server. As you will learn in Session 6, access to the files and folders on a server is controlled by specifying which users and groups are permitted to access each file or folder.

Users

User accounts are configured with several pieces of information:

- A user name, or user ID, which uniquely represents and identifies the account — for example, "JohnL," "DJones," or "RhondaHinz." User names are often an abbreviation of the user's full name, which makes it easier for the user to remember.

- A proper name, which is the user's full name. While Windows Server 2003 doesn't actually care about the user's full name, it's a useful piece of information that can help administrators easily identify user accounts.

- A password, which is a series of numbers, symbols, and letters. Passwords are intended to be a secret that only the user and the server know. When a user provides the correct password, the server is assured that the user is who they claim to be.

- Account properties, which define special information about the user. For example, account properties may indicate whether or not a user is allowed to access a server only during business hours. Account properties may also be used to temporarily lock users out, preventing them from accessing the server even if they have the correct password.

Managing users

**20 Min.
To Go**

Windows Server 2003 enables you to create user accounts using the Computer Management application (assuming you are logged on to the server with a user account that has the authority to create user accounts). The application is located in the Administrative Tools folder, which can be accessed from the Start menu. Once the application is opened, just expand the Local Users and Groups folder. As shown in Figure 3-1, you can manage users by selecting the Users folder.

You should get into the habit of managing your Windows Server 2003 computers from a workstation running Windows XP Professional. Doing so is more efficient than going to the server's keyboard, so I'll show many management screen shots — such as Figure 3-1 — from the Windows XP point of view.

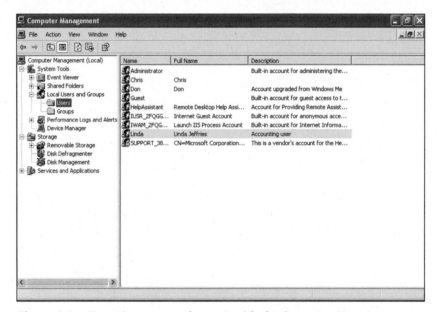

Figure 3-1   *Managing users and groups with the Computer Management application*

The Computer Management application has a Graphical User Interface (GUI) that makes it very easy to manage user accounts and groups. Generally, you can modify a user account just by right-clicking it with your mouse and selecting the appropriate task from the pop-up menu. For example, to create a new user, right-click the Users folder and select New User from the pop-up menu. Fill in the new user's user name, password, and other information, and you're finished!

Use the Computer Management application to create new user accounts, modify old ones, or delete user accounts that are no longer used. Some common tasks that you might perform using the Computer Management application include

- Changing users' passwords when they forget them
- Locking and unlocking user accounts to control access to the server
- Creating new user accounts and deleting old ones

Built-in users

Windows Server 2003 also includes two built-in user accounts with special capabilities:

- **Administrator.** The "super user" of the server. Administrator can do anything on the server and cannot be locked out. You supply the password for the Administrator account when you install Windows Server 2003. You cannot delete the Administrator account, but you can rename the account and change the account password.

- **Guest.** Intended for users who want to access the server but don't have user accounts on the server. When you install Windows Server 2003, the Guest account has a blank password and is disabled, preventing it from being used. You can rename the Guest account and change its password. Because the Guest account usually does not have a password, anyone can use it to access your server. To prevent anyone from accessing your server without authorization, leave the Guest account disabled unless you have a specific reason not to.

Many hackers try to break into a computer by guessing the password of the Administrator or Guest accounts. You can prevent hackers from using the Guest account by disabling it; you can make it harder for hackers to break into the Administrator account by renaming it.

Groups

Most of the time, you do not want to permit individual users to access the files, folders, and other resources on a server. Instead, you can permit several users to access those resources. Groups are designed to help you organize your users, making it easier to grant access to several users in one step.

What groups should you create?

Groups often reflect the organization of your company. For example, you might create groups to represent each department in your company: accounting, human resources, operations, and so forth. Those groups can then contain the user accounts that represent the members of those departments.

Try to create groups that represent the groups of people you will assign permissions to. If a couple of people need access to a particular file, create a user group. Add the appropriate user accounts to the group, and grant the group access to the file. It's usually easier to assign permissions on a file or folder to a group even if the group contains only one user. That way, if you ever delete the user account (either on purpose or by accident), the group will still have permission to the file or folder. You can just add other user accounts to the group as necessary to permit users to access the files or folders.

I show you how to assign file and folder permissions to groups and users in Session 6.

Managing groups

Groups are managed with the Computer Management application. The `Local Users and Groups` folder expands to reveal a `Groups` folder, which you can select to see the groups that have been created. As shown in Figure 3-2, groups can contain as many users as necessary. Individual user accounts can be placed in more than one group, and those users gain the capabilities of *all* the groups they belong to. Groups cannot, however, include other groups; they can contain only user accounts.

Figure 3-2 *Managing group membership*

To create a new group, just right-click the Groups folder and select New Group from the pop-up menu. Fill in the group's name, and use the buttons to add and remove user accounts from the group's membership list.

You can manage the group membership for a particular user by modifying that user account's properties. This feature enables you to quickly add a user to several groups, without having to modify all of the individual groups one at a time.

Built-in groups

Windows Server 2003 includes several built-in groups that have special capabilities. Any user account placed into one of these built-in groups automatically has the special capabilities associated with that group. The built-in groups include

- **Administrators.** Members of this group can perform any action on the server. The built-in Administrator account is automatically a member of this group.

- **Server Operators.** Members of this group can perform tasks such as shutting the server down, controlling access to files and folders, and so forth.

- **Print Operators.** Members of this group can manage the printers that may be attached to a server. They can control who is allowed to use a printer, delete print jobs, and add new printers to the server.

- **Backup Operators.** Members of this group are allowed to read any file or folder on the server, for the purpose of copying those files and folders to backup tapes. This capability enables Backup Operators members to partially bypass the normal security on a file, so that they can make a safe copy of the file in case it is accidentally modified or deleted.

Never place users into any of the built-in groups without first considering the special capabilities the users will gain. Be especially careful of placing users into the Administrators group, as they will be able to perform any action on the server.

The built-in groups should never be renamed or deleted. If you don't want anyone to have the special capabilities of a particular group, simply remove all of the user accounts from the group. The groups themselves don't have passwords, so they cannot be broken in to by hackers.

Local Account Policies

Windows Server 2003 enables you to customize the behavior of your user accounts by configuring special account policies. You work with policies by using the Local Security Policy application, which is in the Administrative Tools folder on the Start menu. After you launch the Local Security Policy application, expand the Account Policies folder. As shown in Figure 3-3, you'll see two subfolders: Password policy and Account Lockout policy.

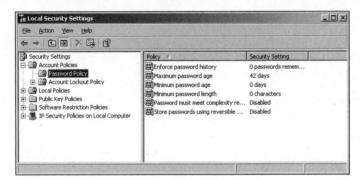

Figure 3-3   *Managing local account policies*

Password policies

Password policies control how your users' passwords are treated. You can modify the policy settings by simply double-clicking the policy and filling in the appropriate information. The most commonly used password policies are

- **Enforce password history.** This policy tells Windows Server 2003 to remember the passwords your users have used in the past. Users are not permitted to reuse old passwords. Instead, they have to use new passwords whenever they change their passwords. You can configure how many old passwords are remembered.

- **Maximum password age.** You can configure the maximum number of days that users can keep their passwords. Once that number of days has passed, users are required to change their passwords.

- **Minimum password age.** You can configure the number of days users must wait before changing their passwords again.

- **Minimum password length.** Short passwords are easy for hackers to guess. You can help make passwords more secure by requiring that they be at least a certain length. Common minimum lengths are between six and ten characters, with longer passwords being harder for hackers to guess than shorter passwords. Of course, longer passwords are also harder to remember, so don't make the minimum password length longer than ten characters. Of course, users are always welcome to use passwords that are longer than the minimum.

By combining the previously listed policies, you can ensure that your users have fresh passwords at all times. For example, you might configure a password history of 12, a maximum password age of 30 days, and a minimum password age of 25 days, ensuring a brand-new password every month.

Well-planned password policies ensure that your users' passwords are hard to guess and are changed frequently, the two key factors that help prevent hackers from guessing users' passwords and breaking into your servers.

Remember that password policies are configured individually on each standalone and member server. If users have accounts on multiple servers, they will probably use identical passwords, so make sure your servers' password policies are also identical.

Account Lockout policies

**10 Min.
To Go**

If a hacker is trying to break into your system by guessing a user's password, she will often try times. Windows Server 2003 keeps track of how many times an invalid password is used with a user account and can be configured to lock out the user account to prevent any further attempts at password guessing. This configuring is performed using the Account Lockout policies in the Local Security Policy application.

Just like Password policies, the Account Lockout policies can be modified by double-clicking the appropriate policy and filling in the required information.

The important Account Lockout policies are

- **Account lockout threshold.** This policy determines how many times Windows Server 2003 enables someone to try to access a user account with the wrong password. After the threshold has been passed, the account is locked out. For example, by setting this policy to 3, you can be assured that user accounts are locked out after the third wrong password is tried.

  Don't set this policy too low, or users may find their accounts locked out just because they mistyped their passwords. On the other hand, setting this policy too high allows a hacker several attempts to guess the password. A good setting for this policy is between three and five attempts.

- **Account lockout duration.** This policy determines how long an account remains locked out. You can specify a value in hours, or you can specify zero to leave the account permanently locked out.

Once an account is locked out, you can use the Computer Management application to unlock it. As shown in Figure 3-4, locked-out user accounts are displayed with a special icon. Simply right-click the account, select Properties from the pop-up menu, and clear the Account Is Locked Out check box to unlock the account.

Linda Properties

General | Member Of | Profile

Linda

Full name: Linda Jeffries

Description: Accounting user

☑ User must change password at next logon
☐ User cannot change password
☐ Password never expires
☐ Account is disabled
☑ Account is locked out

OK   Cancel   Apply

Figure 3-4   *Unlocking a user account*

Tip

Passwords are case-sensitive. If users keep locking themselves out by typing the wrong password, check to see that the CAPS LOCK key on their computer is off. Also, make sure the users know their passwords. If necessary, use the Computer Management application to change a forgotten password.

Security Auditing

You may need to keep track of who is using your server and what they're doing on it. Windows Server 2003 maintains a Security Event Log, which you can view with the Event Viewer application. The Event Viewer can be found in the Computer Management application. Once the application loads, select the Security folder to see any security events, as shown in Figure 3-5.

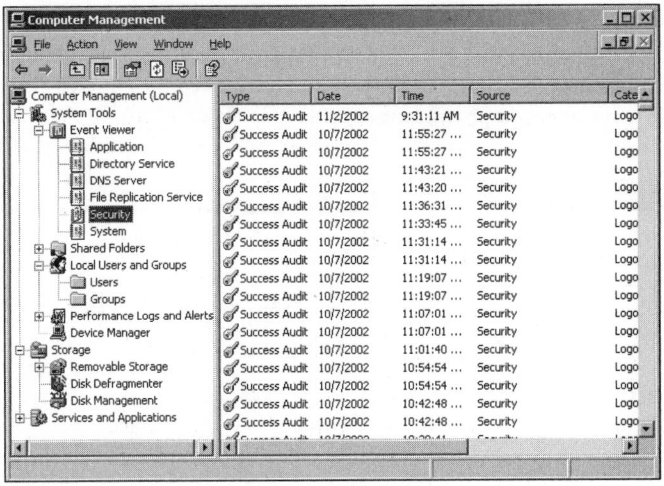

Figure 3-5　　*The Security Event Log*

By default, Windows Server 2003 does not automatically report on common security events. However, you can use the Local Security Policy application to configure Audit policies, which allows Windows Server 2003 to add entries to the Security Event Log for specific events. The Audit policies include:

- **Audit logon events.** This policy tells Windows Server 2003 to create Security Event Log entries whenever someone attempts to access the server.

- **Audit account management.** This policy audits the creation, modification, or deletion of user and group accounts.

- **Audit object access.** This policy allows Windows Server 2003 to audit file and folder access, helping to keep track of what files and folders are being accessed by users.

- **Audit policy change.** This policy audits any changes to the local security policies, so you can see if another user has changed the policies you have defined.

The Audit policies can be configured to audit only successes, only failures, or both. Successes occur when a user is permitted to perform an event, such as logging on with the correct password. Failures occur when a user is denied an event, such as attempting to log on with the incorrect password.

Auditing requires Windows Server 2003 to perform extra work. Be careful to audit only the events necessary to meet your needs. Enabling all of the auditing events may have a negative impact on your server's performance.

Done!

REVIEW

Windows Server 2003 has a very flexible security architecture. In this chapter, you learned how Windows Server 2003 can play different roles on a network:

- Standalone server
- Domain controller
- Member server

You also learned that standalone servers and member servers can have their own user and group accounts and that those servers come with several accounts built right in. You learned how to create your own users and groups, and you learned how to control user accounts by defining a server's local account policies. Finally, you learned how to use security auditing to keep tabs on how your servers are being used and by whom.

QUIZ YOURSELF

1. What are the names of the built-in Windows Server 2003 user groups? (See "Local Users and Groups.")

2. What are the names of the built-in Windows Server 2003 users? (See "Local Users and Groups.")

3. How can you control the minimum length of passwords used by local users? (See "Local Account Policies.")

4. How do you enable security auditing in Windows Server 2003? (See "Security Auditing.")

Using Active Directory

Session Checklist

✔ How to design an Active Directory domain

✔ How to promote a server to be a domain controller

✔ How to manage domain users and groups

**30 Min.
To Go**

Managing user accounts on individual servers may seem great, but with too many servers in your environment, it can quickly become a nightmare. When new users join your organization, you have to create accounts for them on *every* server. When users want to change their passwords, they have to do so on *every* server. Active Directory is intended to make those problems disappear by providing a centralized place for user and group accounts (and other information). In this session, you'll learn when to use Active Directory, how to plan an Active Directory domain, and how to implement and manage a domain.

Active Directory is a *very* complex topic. While you'll be able to learn the basics in this 30-minute session, you'll find entire books dedicated to Active Directory planning, implementation, or management. If you'll be using Active Directory a lot, be sure to read more on the subject.

Why Use Active Directory?

In an environment with more than a few servers, you quickly grow tired of managing local users and groups on those servers. Standalone and member servers have no way of sharing their users and groups with one another; each server has a completely independent list of local users and groups. This behavior presents several difficulties:

- You have to create user accounts on each server when someone joins your organization and remove those accounts when someone leaves.
- Users have to provide a user name and password each time someone accesses resources on a different server.
- When it's time to change users' passwords, users must do so on each server.

Active Directory provides a central list of users and groups, which is called a *domain*. When users log on to a domain, using a domain user account, they are immediately recognized by all the servers who are members of that domain. Active Directory thus provides major advantages over using local user and group accounts in an environment with many servers:

- You only have to create user accounts once — in the domain.
- Users only provide their user names and passwords once — when they log on to the domain.
- When they change their passwords, users only do so once — in the domain.

Active Directory does have a couple of disadvantages. The major disadvantage is the requirement to have special servers called *domain controllers*. Domain controllers are responsible for maintaining the domain's list of users and groups. DCs also keep track of which computers are members of the domain, and domain controllers share the user and group account list with member computers.

A minor disadvantage is that Active Directory can be complex, especially in large environments. A poorly planned Active Directory installation can be slow, unreliable, and difficult to manage. In order for Active Directory to work smoothly, you need to understand how it works, and you need to spend time planning to make Active Directory fit your organization's needs.

How Active Directory Works

Active Directory is built around special servers called domain controllers, or DCs. Any Windows Server 2003 can be made into a DC, either in a brand-new domain or in an existing domain. DCs all contain a copy of the domain database, which is often referred to simply as "the directory." The directory contains all of the domain user and group accounts, as well as configuration information about the domain itself.

A domain can contain multiple DCs. In fact, it's a good idea to have at least two DCs in every domain. That way, if one experiences a hardware failure or other problem, the second DC can keep the domain up and running. All of the DCs in a domain use a process called *replication* to ensure that each DC has the same domain information as the others.

In order to log on to the domain, users must be using a workstation operating system that supports Active Directory, such as Windows 2000 Professional or Windows XP Professional. The workstation itself must also belong to the domain, an option usually configured when the workstation operating system is installed. Users simply provide their domain user name and password, and the workstation communicates with a DC to make sure the user name and password match. If they do, the user is officially logged on to the domain and can begin accessing resources on the domain's member servers and DCs.

Domain requirements

Active Directory DCs must be running Windows 2000 Server, Windows Server 2003, or a later version of the Windows Server operating system. Active Directory also requires a Domain Name Service (DNS) server, although you can install and run a DNS server on one or more of your DCs, if necessary.

Your domain also requires a name. Usually, the name of your domain is a registered Internet-type domain name, such as wiley.com. Your DNS server must be *authoritative* for that domain name, which means it must be able to accept new name entries for the domain, and provide name resolution for all names contained within the domain. Your DNS server must also support two special features:

- SRV records, which allow a DNS server to keep track of network servers that offer special functionality, like Active Directory domain controllers

- Dynamic updates, which allow computers to insert their name information into a DNS server automatically, rather than requiring an administrator to manually update the DNS database

 The DNS server software included with Windows Server 2003 meets Active Directory's requirements when properly configured. I'll show you how to configure DNS in Session 14.

Domain structure

A domain is really nothing more than a special kind of database, and all databases have a structure. In the case of Active Directory domains, the structure is hierarchical, or tree-like, much like the "tree" of folders on your computer's hard drive.

The domain itself is the "root" of the tree. The "branches" are called *organizational units,* or OUs. OUs function much like the folders on your hard drive, helping to organize the objects in the domain. In the case of your hard drive, folders help organize files; in Active Directory, OUs help organize users, groups, and computers. For example, an OU named Accounting might contain all of the domain users who work for your company's accounting department. Figure 4-1 shows an example Active Directory tree.

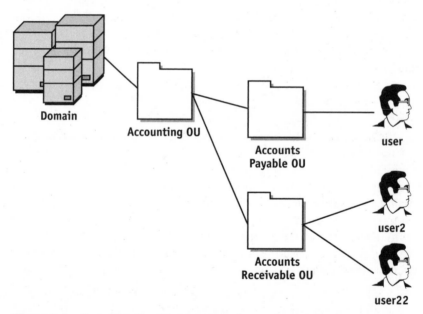

Figure 4-1 *Sample Active Directory domain*

OUs enable you to apply special security and configuration settings to every user, group, and computer within the OU. For example, you might configure the Accounting OU so that users within the OU can log on only during regular business hours, or you might require those users to maintain special desktop settings.

Session 11 introduces you to the various security and configuration policies you can apply to an OU.

Planning a Domain

**20 Min.
To Go**

Planning a domain can be a difficult task. You can simplify the task by focusing on two important questions:

- Who will manage the user and group accounts?
- What users share common security and configuration requirements?

In this section, I explore the various answers you might have for these two questions, and show you how they can lead to an effective Active Directory domain design.

Laying out domains

Smaller organizations can usually use a single domain because all of their users and groups are managed by a single group of individuals (usually the information technology department). Larger organizations, however, may have users whose accounts are managed by different groups, such as corporate divisions or departments. In those cases, multiple domains may be required.

Introducing World Metro Bank

Throughout the remainder of this book, I use the fictional World Metro Bank as an example of how Windows Server 2003 can be used. World Metro Bank is a large international bank with a North American headquarters in New York and a European headquarters in Paris. They have branch offices throughout North America and Europe. Some branch offices are large, with hundreds of tellers, loan officers, and other employees. Others are smaller, with only a few tellers. The bank also has a new insurance division, which operates out of San Francisco and has only 100 employees. While the insurance division is owned by World Metro Bank, it is managed independently of the bank.

Because World Metro Bank has such a variety of requirements in their organization, you're likely to find some that match those of your organization. By studying the decisions that World Metro Bank makes, you'll have some help judging what to do in your own company.

Answer the question "Who will manage the user and group accounts?" Once you know the answer, you'll know how many domains you need: one for each group of people who will manage some of your user accounts.

Single domains

The easiest configuration is a single domain. The domain has a name, such as worldmetrobank.com. Every user and group within the domain is managed by a single individual or group of individuals. World Metro Bank's new insurance division is an ideal candidate for a single domain because it is relatively small and all of its users are managed by the division's information technology (IT) department.

 Size is rarely a factor in deciding to use a single domain. Enormous corporations with many thousands of users can have a single domain if all of their users and groups are managed by some central individual or department.

Domain trees

Large organizations usually distribute the management of their user and group accounts. In those distributed situations, a domain tree with parent and child domains is often appropriate.

For example, World Metro Bank's North American headquarters has an IT department that manages the user accounts for headquarters employees. Each major region of the country has a regional service office, which has an independent IT department that manages the user accounts for that region's employees. All of the regional offices report to headquarters. In this instance, headquarters might create a top-level, or *root,* domain named worldmetrobank.com. Each regional office would then be assigned a child domain, such as west.worldmetrobank.com and east.worldmetrobank.com. Figure 4-2 shows how the domains are related to one another.

Each of the domains is managed by a separate IT department. However, all of the domains *trust* one another, meaning users in one domain can access resources in the other domains. That trust is *transitive,* meaning that because the West region trusts headquarters, and because the East region also trusts headquarters, both East and West implicitly trust one another. This implicit transitive trust is shown by a dotted line in Figure 4-2.

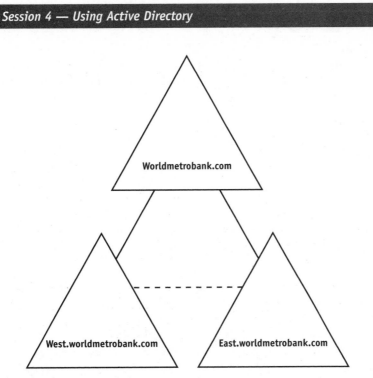

Figure 4-2 *World Metro Bank's domain tree*

Forests

World Metro Bank's European division is an independent entity, with its own head-quarters, regional service offices, and so forth. The European division uses the root domain metrobank-euro.com, with child domains named uk.metrobank-euro.com and fr.metrobank-euro.com.

Users in the European and North American divisions sometimes need to access information located in the other division. To accommodate this need, a manual trust is created between the two root domains, as shown in Figure 4-3. This trust creates a *forest*, consisting of the two trees that trust each other.

Deciding on OUs

Once you've decided what domains you'll have, you need to decide what OUs those domains will contain. You can look at the political organization of your company as a guideline for creating OUs, but remember that the primary purpose of OUs is to organize users who have common security or configuration requirements.

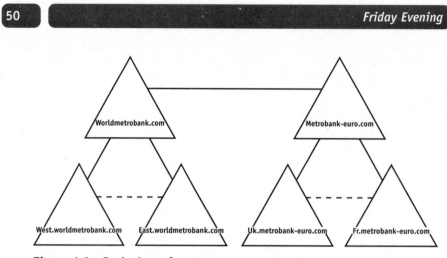

Figure 4-3　*Designing a forest*

For example, Metro World Bank's North American headquarters includes hundreds of employees in various departments. Each department has an administrative assistant who is responsible for performing tasks like resetting user passwords. That capability can be provided by breaking each department's users into separate OUs and granting the assistants password-reset and other permissions on the appropriate OUs.

In the regional service offices, all of the employees share identical security and configuration requirements, so only a single OU is required.

Your OU structure is not permanent. You can create new OUs, delete old ones, and move users between OUs as necessary to accommodate your organization's needs.

Making a Domain Controller

After (and only after) you've decided how many domains you'll have, and what their names will be, should you make your first DC. The first DC on your network is for a root domain, such as World Metro Bank's worldmetrobank.com domain. Subsequent DCs can be added to that domain or can be used to create new child domains, such as east.worldmetrobank.com.

To create a domain controller, install Windows Server 2003 on a computer. Then, open the Start menu and select Run. Type dcpromo.exe and click OK. The Domain

Controller Promotion Wizard walks you through the process of promoting the server to be a domain controller.

If you don't already have a compatible DNS server on your network, the Wizard offers to install the Microsoft DNS Server software on the new DC. You should allow it to do so if the new DC will also be the DNS server for the new domain.

**10 Min.
To Go**

After you provide the Wizard with your new domain name and other information, it installs Active Directory on your server and then restarts the server. Active Directory installation can take a long time, especially when you're adding a new domain controller to an existing domain. Be patient, have a cup of coffee, and let the Wizard do its work.

Running dcpromo.exe **on a system that already serves as a domain controller demotes the controller to a standalone server.**

How Many DCs Do You Need?

Every domain (both root and child domains) should contain at least two domain controllers, to ensure that the domain continues running even if one server fails. Beyond that, you should carefully consider how many other DCs you need in each domain and where those DCs will be located.

Generally, you want to place a DC on the same local area network as any large number of users. Doing so makes it easier and faster for those users to log on, since they'll have a DC right on the same network. Especially large groups of users may need more than one DC to handle the task of logging everyone on.

DCs perform other special functions, such as providing a *global catalog* that enables users to locate domain resources more easily. You can determine which DCs provide these special functions. Although a complete description of how to do so is beyond the scope of this session, you can find many good books on Active Directory design and implementation that provide all the details.

Managing Domain Users and Groups

Once your domains are up and running, you can start creating OUs, domain user accounts, and domain group accounts. Domain users and groups work just like local users and groups, which you learned about in Session 3. However, instead of using the Computer Management application, you use the Active Directory Users and Computers application, shown in Figure 4-4.

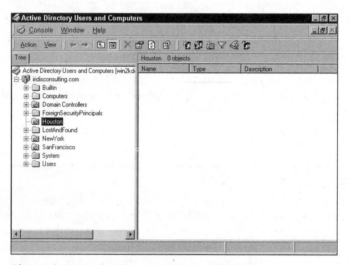

Figure 4-4 *Active Directory Users and Computers*

Active Directory Users and Computers enables you to create, edit, delete, and reorganize OUs, users, and groups in the domain. The application is installed along with Active Directory and can be found in the Administrative Tools folder on the Start menu.

Active Directory includes several built-in groups and offers three different types of groups. The built-in groups include

- **Domain Administrators.** This domain group has full control over the domain. This group is similar to the local Administrators group included on each server.

- **Enterprise Administrators.** This domain group has full control over an entire forest.

The types of groups used within Active Directory are

- **Domain local groups.** These groups can be used only by members of a domain and can contain domain user accounts and domain global groups. For example, you generally assign file and folder permissions to domain local groups.

- **Domain global groups.** These groups can be used by all domains within a tree and can contain only domain user accounts. You usually place users into domain global groups to organize them and then place domain global groups into domain local groups. Because permissions are assigned to domain local groups, users gain access to resources through their nested group membership. I explain this concept in more depth in Session 6.

- **Universal groups.** These groups can be seen by all members of a forest. These groups are used only occasionally and can contain users and other universal groups.

Done!

REVIEW

In this chapter, you learned how Active Directory can be a useful addition to your network, and how it can save time and headaches for both yourself and your users. You learned the basics of how Active Directory works, and how to plan an Active Directory domain. You also learned how to promote a server to be a domain controller, and how to manage the users and groups in a domain.

QUIZ YOURSELF

1. Why would you want to use Active Directory? (See "Why Use Active Directory?")

2. What process allows domain controllers to synchronize their copies of the directory? (See "How Active Directory Works.")

3. How do you change a member server to a domain controller, or vice-versa? (See "Making a Domain Controller.")

4. Several top-level domains that trust one another form a what? (See "Planning a Domain.")

5. What application is used to manage Active Directory users and groups? (See "Managing Domain Users and Groups.")

Friday Evening
Part Review

1. What are the four editions of Windows Server 2003, and what are their major differences?

2. What does the term *multitasking* mean?

3. What are three methods you can use to install Windows Server 2003?

4. How would you set up and start an unattended upgrade of Windows Server 2003 using a CD-ROM?

5. What capability allows Windows Server 2003 to run on servers that have no mouse, monitor, keyboard, or video card?

6. What are the built-in local users included with Windows Server 2003? How about the built-in users installed with Active Directory? What can these users do?

7. What are some of the built-in local groups included with Windows Server 2003? How about the built-in groups installed with Active Directory? What can these groups do?

8. How can you determine who has been logging on to your servers and accessing resources?

9. How can you force users to select passwords with at least ten characters?

10. How can you prevent users from changing their passwords and then immediately changing back to their old passwords?

11. What are the three roles a server can play on your network?

12. What is the difference between a standalone server and a member server?

13. When is a single domain appropriate for an organization?

14. Why might an organization choose to include all of their users in a single organizational unit (OU)?

15. How can two independent domains be brought together into a forest?

16. What must a DNS server provide in order to be compatible with Active Directory?

17. How can you remove Active Directory from a domain controller and make it a standalone server again?

18. What is the best method or methods to install Windows Server 2003 on a dozen identical computers that are attached to your network?

19. What advantages does Active Directory offer over using local user accounts on standalone servers?

20. What must you do to reactivate a user who has mistyped her password too many times and has become locked out?

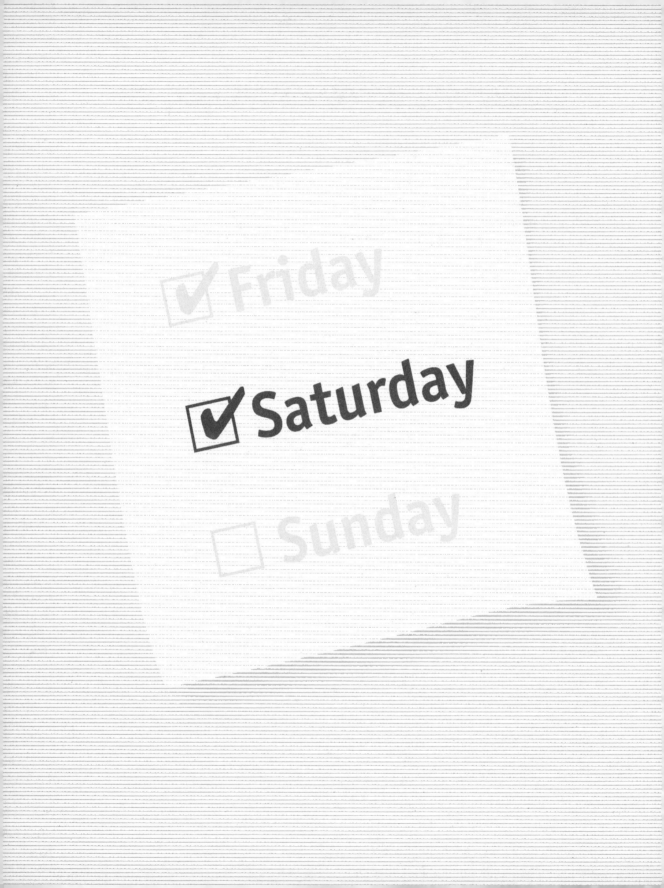
☑ Friday

☑ Saturday

☐ Sunday

Part II — Saturday Morning

Session 5
Managing Disks, Files, and File Systems

Session 6
Managing File Sharing and File Security

Session 7
Managing the Distributed File System

Session 8
Advanced File Management

Session 9
Managing Printers and Faxes

Session 10
Managing Terminal Services

Part III — Saturday Afternoon

Session 11
Configuring Security Policies

Session 12
Using the Security Configuration Manager

Session 13
Networking with TCP/IP

Session 14
Managing the Domain Name System Service

Session 15
Managing the Windows Internet Name System Service

Session 16
Managing the Dynamic Host Configuration Protocol

Part IV — Saturday Evening

Session 17
Managing Internet Information Services

Session 18
Managing Web Sites

Session 19
Managing Routing and Remote Access Services

Session 20
Managing the Internet Authentication Service

PART

II

Saturday Morning

Managing Disks, Files, and File Systems

Session Checklist

✔ How to configure disk drives

✔ How to use software fault tolerance

✔ How to select a file system and format disks

✔ How to optimize disk performance

30 Min. To Go

O ne of the primary purposes of any operating system is to help manage the mass-storage devices in your computer, and Windows Server 2003 is no exception. It provides powerful and flexible features that enable you to get the most from the hard drives installed in your computer, and in this session you'll learn all about Windows Server 2003 disk management, file systems, and disk optimization. You'll also learn about Windows Server 2003's built-in fault tolerance features, which can help keep a failed hard drive from becoming a nightmare.

Disks, Partitions, and Drives

Windows Server 2003 is designed to automatically recognize all of the hard disks installed in your computer, and it refers to each one as a *disk*. The first hard drive is referred to as disk 0, the second as disk 1, and so forth. All new disks are referred to as *basic disks,* which means they can contain a limited number of partitions and cannot be used for special features like fault tolerance (which I'll discuss later in this session).

Once partitions have been created on a disk, they are assigned drive letters by the operating system. These drive letters represent *logical drives.* Drive letters A and B are reserved for the first two floppy disk drives in your computer; the first hard drive partition is usually lettered C, the next one D, and so on. CD-ROMs and other types of drives also receive drive letters. Drive letters are the primary way of accessing the contents of a drive. All of the folders and files on a drive are referenced by their location on a specific drive letter. Figure 5-1 shows an example of the drive letter assignments given to hard disks, floppy disks, and CD-ROM drives on a typical server.

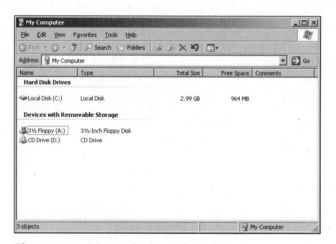

Figure 5-1   *Drive assignments in a computer*

Disk Management

Windows Server 2003 includes a special application to help you manage the disks and drives on your computer. The application is located within the Computer Management application, which is located in the Administrative Tools folder on the Start menu. After launching Computer Management, select the Disk Management item to see the disks and drives attached to your computer. A typical server's Disk Management is shown in Figure 5-2.

Breaking Up Disks with Partitions

When you install Windows Server 2003, it enables you to create at least one *partition* on one of your disks. Partitions are used to break large hard drives into smaller segments. In the past, partitions were a necessity because many operating systems could only handle hard drives that were smaller than 2GB in size. Larger drives had to be divided up so that the operating system could deal with the smaller sections. Windows Server 2003 is capable of dealing with disk drives in excess of 1,000GB, so partitions aren't usually necessary.

All disks must have at least one partition in order for the operating system to use them; you'll normally create a single partition that encompasses all of the available space on a disk.

Figure 5-2   *Disk Management*

Disk Management includes only hard drives, CD-ROMs, and other drives; floppy drives are not shown.

The server in Figure 5-2 has one hard drive and a CD-ROM. The hard drive has been divided into four partitions, and three of those partitions have been assigned drive letters. The CD-ROM has also been assigned a drive letter.

Partitions without an assigned drive letter cannot be used to store files and folders.

You can use Disk Management to accomplish several important tasks:

- To create a new partition, right-click the empty area of a hard disk and select Create Partition from the pop-up menu.

- To change the drive letter assigned to a CD-ROM or partition, right-click it and select Drive Letters from the pop-up menu.

- To convert a basic disk to a *dynamic disk,* which supports more partitions as well as special features like fault tolerance, right-click the disk and select Convert to Dynamic Disk from the pop-up menu.

- To remove a partition, right-click it and select Delete from the pop-up menu.

Never change the drive letter of a partition or delete a partition without carefully considering the consequences. Changing a drive letter or deleting a partition may break applications that have already been installed, or it may cause permanent loss of applications or data.

Fault Tolerance

Unfortunately, hard drives can sometimes break. When they do, all of the information on that hard drive is often lost. Modern hard drives can be enormous, and when one breaks, you can lose an enormous amount of data. Windows Server 2003 helps prevent such losses by providing two levels of software-based fault tolerance: mirroring and RAID 5.

Windows Server 2003's fault tolerance features are also found on special disk controller cards, which are often installed in servers. These controllers provide much faster and more efficient fault tolerance, so you should use them instead of Windows Server 2003's software-based fault tolerance whenever possible.

Mirroring

20 Min. To Go

Mirroring allows two identically sized partitions, located on separate disks, to automatically duplicate one another. Both partitions become a *mirror set,* which means they always contain the same content and appear to the operating system as if they were a single partition. Mirror sets use only one drive letter.

If one of the disks in a mirror set fails, the other one continues operating, and no data is lost. Disk Management gives you the tools necessary to work with mirror sets:

- To create a mirror set, select an empty, unformatted area of a dynamic disk. Hold down the Ctrl key and select another unformatted partition of the same size. Right-click one of the disks and choose New Volume from the pop-up menu. On the New Volume dialog box, choose Mirror Volume.

- To break a mirror set, right-click one of its partitions and choose Break Mirror from the pop-up menu. The first partition retains the drive letter that was assigned to the mirror; the other partition becomes a normal logical drive, although it will contain the same content as the first.

- If one of the drives in a mirror set fails, replace the affected disk. Break the mirror, and then re-create the mirror using the new disk.

Saving information to a mirror set is somewhat slower than saving to a normal partition because Windows Server 2003 must write the saved information to both parts of the mirror set.

RAID 5

RAID is an acronym that stands for Redundant Array of Inexpensive Devices. That's a fancy way of saying disks are fairly inexpensive, and using several of them together (the array) can help improve fault tolerance. Each of the several different RAID "levels" has different features. Mirror sets, in fact, are also referred to as RAID 1 on some operating systems.

On Windows Server 2003, RAID 5 arrays consist of at least three partitions of equal size. You create a RAID 5 array in much the same way that you create mirror sets: Select all of the areas you want to include in the volume, right-click one, and select New Volume from the pop-up menu. On the New Volume dialog box, select RAID 5 Volume.

Remember that RAID 5 volumes can be created only by using identically sized empty areas of dynamic disks. If you want to include a basic disk in a RAID 5 volume, you must first convert the disk to a dynamic disk.

In a RAID 5 array, the operating system saves data to all of the array partitions at once, dividing saved information between them. The operating system also calculates *checksum data*, which is derived by performing a mathematical operation on the saved data. This checksum data allows the operating system to re-create missing data, and the checksum data is also spread across the partitions in the array.

If one disk in a RAID 5 array fails, the checksum data from the remaining drives is used to recreate the data that was stored on the failed disk. Until the failed disk is replaced, the checksum data is used to recalculate the missing data, as if the disk had never failed. Once the disk is replaced, the checksum data is used to rebuild the data on the new disk. If two or more disks in the array fail, then all of the data on the array is lost.

RAID 5 arrays also slow down the process of saving data a bit, although not as much as mirror sets. On the other hand, RAID 5 arrays actually speed up the process of reading data because all of the disks in the array work together to deliver data to the operating system.

The greatest disadvantage to RAID 5 arrays is that some of your available disk space is sacrificed to store the checksum information. In any RAID 5 array, your total disk space equals the space available on all but one of the disks in the array. For example, in an array with five 10GB disks, you have a total of 40GB of available space. The other 10GB is used to store checksum data. Most administrators feel the tradeoff of disk space for fault tolerance is a good one, and you'll find that most servers use RAID 5 arrays.

File Systems

Once you've configured the disks and partitions in your computer, including any fault tolerance features you choose to use, you need to select a file system. File systems are used to organize the data on a drive into files and folders. Windows Server 2003 supports several different file systems, each with different features:

- **FAT16.** The FAT16 file system is compatible with older operating systems like MS-DOS and Windows 95. FAT16 is an inefficient file system and causes wasted space on modern, large hard drives. Use FAT16 only if the file system needs to be accessed by older operating systems.

- **FAT32.** The FAT32 file system is more efficient than FAT16 and is compatible with Windows 98 and Windows Me (as well as later versions of Windows 95). FAT32 does not provide the ability to assign security permissions to files and folders, does not support encryption or compression, and is less efficient than NTFS.

- **NTFS.** The NTFS file system is the best file system to use with Windows Server 2003. It is very efficient, supports compression, encryption, and security permissions, and is compatible with Windows 2000 and Windows NT 4.0 Service Pack 4 and higher. You should use the NTFS file system unless you have a specific reason not to.

Windows Server 2003 enables you to format almost any type of disk, including removable disks like floppy disks, with these file systems. The one exception is CD-ROM and DVD-ROM discs, which are always formatted with their own special file systems.

The only reason to select a file system other than NTFS is usually on a computer that contains two operating systems. In those cases, you should select a file system that both operating systems can work with.

Once you've selected a file system for a partition, you need to *format* the partition with the file system. Formatting is a process that organizes the partition and allows the operating system to begin saving data to it. Use Disk Management to format partitions by right-clicking the partition, selecting Format from the pop-up menu, and then selecting the appropriate file system from the dialog box.

Formatting a large partition can take a long time, no matter which file system you select. The partition cannot be used until the formatting process is complete, so be prepared to be patient!

Disk Optmization

**10 Min.
To Go**

Windows Server 2003 offers additional capabilities to improve the performance of the disks in your computer. Most hard drives have pretty standard capabilities for transferring data to the operating system, so once you've installed top-of-the-line drives in your computer, you have to look at optimization methods to improve the performance of those drives.

Using disks carefully

Carefully planning how the disks in your computer are used can help improve disk performance. The key is to not overburden any one disk with too much work. For example, suppose your computer contains four hard drives. You could use one hard drive for the operating system files and another hard drive for user data files. The remaining two drives might be saved for future expansion. That scenario sounds good, but the user data drive would be doing an awful lot of work if you have a lot of data on it.

A better solution is to use one drive for the operating system files and make a RAID 5 array from the remaining three drives. You'll achieve much better performance because all three drives can share the load of the user data, rather than dumping all of the work on one drive.

Many administrators insist on at least five drives in every server. The first two drives are configured as a mirror and used to store the operating system files. The mirror ensures that the operating system is protected from the failure of a single drive. The remaining drives are made into a RAID 5 array, which provides great performance and fault tolerance.

Whenever possible, use a hardware disk controller to create mirror sets and RAID 5 arrays. Because the disk controller has its own dedicated processors to handle your data, it offers much better performance than Windows Server 2003's software-based fault tolerance features.

Stripe sets for better performance

Earlier in this session, you learned that RAID 5 volumes save data a bit slower than a regular volume because the operating system must calculate and save checksum information along with the data. Windows Server 2003 supports a special type of volume called a *stripe set,* which is very similar to RAID 5 in the way it works. As with a RAID 5 volume, stripe sets spread data across several identically sized disks, which speeds up the process of reading data. Unlike RAID 5, stripe sets do not calculate checksum information. This means they can save data very quickly. However, because they lack checksum information, stripe sets do not provide fault tolerance. And, because the data on a stripe set is spread across the disks in the set, if one disk should fail, all of the data on the stripe set will be lost.

World Metro Bank

In a large organization like the World Metro Bank (our fictional case study for Windows implementation), you're likely to find a number of different drive-usage scenarios.

For example, each branch office will probably include a Windows Server 2003 computer that contains the office's files and provides shared printing for the office's users. That file server might include a number of disk drives in a RAID 5 array, which would be used for storing shared files. The server might also include two large hard disks in a mirror set, which would be used for the operating system files.

World Metro Bank would likely choose to use hardware-based RAID 5 arrays and mirror sets because of the increased performance offered by the hardware drive controllers.

Part II — Saturday Morning
Session 5

Stripe sets without checksum information are sometimes referred to as RAID 4 arrays or as stripe sets without parity. *Parity* is a term used to refer to the checksum data a RAID 5 array uses.

Stripe sets are useful for storing less important data that needs to be accessed quickly but can be easily restored from a CD-ROM or a tape backup if necessary. To create a stripe set, select the empty areas of two or more dynamic disks, just as you would to create a RAID 5 array. Then, right-click one of those areas and select New Volume from the pop-up menu. On the New Volume dialog box, select Stripe Set Volume.

Do not store critical data on a stripe set, unless that data is regularly backed up. Remember, if only one of the disks in the stripe set fails, all of the data in the stripe set is lost.

Done!

REVIEW

In this chapter, you learned about Windows Server 2003's organization of the disks in your computer, including basic disks and dynamic disks. You learned how to create partitions on a disk, select a file system for the partition, format the partition, and assign a drive letter to the partition. You also learned about Windows Server 2003's software fault tolerance features, including the ability to create mirror sets and RAID 5 arrays by using the Disk Management application. Finally, you learned some tips for optimizing the disks in your computer, such as striped sets.

QUIZ YOURSELF

1. What kinds of disk fault tolerance does Windows Server 2003 offer? (See "Fault Tolerance.")

2. What three main file systems does Windows Server 2003 support? (See "File Systems.")

3. What are the advantages of the NTFS file system? (See "File Systems.")

4. How can you change the drive letter associated with a specific partition? (See "Disk Management.")

5. When a new drive is added to a computer, what type of disk does Windows Server 2003 configure it as? (See "Disks, Partitions, and Drives.")

Managing File Sharing and File Security

Session Checklist

✔ How to protect files with file security

✔ How to make files available to network users

✔ How to protect files with share security

✔ How to best manage file and share security

**30 Min.
To Go**

A s its name implies, Windows Server 2003 is a network server operating system. That means your servers primarily are used by users who connect to the server via a network, rather than by users who log on to the server itself. As a network operating system, Windows Server 2003 provides powerful, flexible features that enable you to determine who may access your files and what they can do with them.

File Security

The basis of Windows Server 2003's file security system is the NTFS file system because only the NTFS file system supports file-level security. On any volume formatted with NTFS, every single file and folder includes an Access Control List, or ACL. The ACL is basically a list of users and groups who are permitted to access the file or folder, and a list of the actions those users may perform.

File permissions are available only on NTFS volumes. Volumes formatted with the FAT16 or FAT32 file systems cannot use file permissions.

Managing permissions

File and folder permissions are managed from within Windows Explorer. Simply right-click any file or folder (or a group of files and folders), and select Properties from the pop-up menu. Then, select the Security tab, as shown in Figure 6-1.

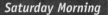

Figure 6-1   *File permissions dialog*

The Security tab enables you to specify the users or groups that should have access to the file or folder. On the tab, you can do the following:

- You can select users and groups from the local users and groups on your computer. However, keep in mind that domain controllers don't have local users and groups.

- If your computer is a member of a domain, you can also select users and groups from the domain. On a domain controller, this option is your only one.

- You can select more than one user or group and assign different permissions to each.

Figure 6-2 shows the dialog box used to select users and groups from the local computer or from the domain.

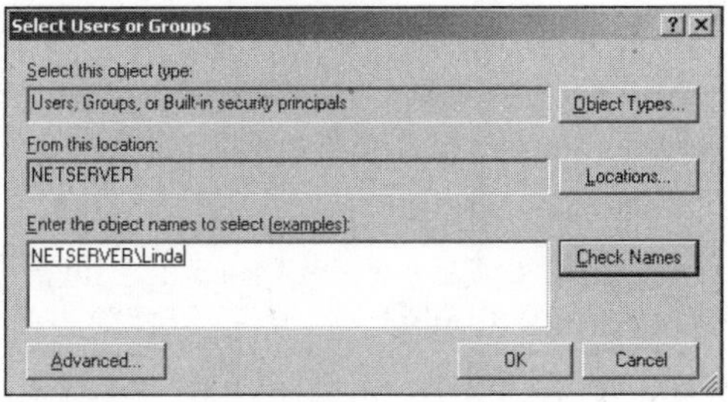

Figure 6-2 *Selecting users and groups*

Permission types

Once you select the users and groups you want, you need to assign their actual permissions to the file or folder. There are several basic permissions:

- **Full Control.** Allows the user to perform any action on the file. Full Control includes all of the other possible permissions.
- **Modify.** Allows the user to change the contents of the file or delete it. However, the user cannot change the permissions on the file. This permission includes Read, Read & Execute, and Write permissions.
- **Read.** Permits the user to examine the file but not change or delete it.
- **Read & Execute.** Allows the user to load the file into memory (in the case of an executable file) and run it. This permission is appropriate for applications.
- **Write.** Allows the user to change the contents of the file.
- **List Folder Contents.** This permission applies only to folders and never to files. This permission allows a user to see what other files and folders are in a particular folder.

What's in a Permission?

The basic permissions for file security — Full Control, Modify, Read, and so forth — aren't the only permissions you can assign. Windows Server 2003 also supports "special permissions," which provide a finer degree of control over how files and folders are used.

Windows Server 2003 enables you to assign or deny special permissions by clicking the Advanced button on the Security tab. On the Advanced Security Settings dialog box, you can set all of the special permissions:

- **Read Attributes** and **Write Attributes.** Allow a user to modify file and folder attributes, such as Hidden or Read-Only.

- **Read Extended Attributes** and **Write Extended Attributes.** Allow a user to read and write the extended attributes of a file. These attributes differ depending on the file type and may include information like the file's author, the file's subject, and so forth.

- **Create Files.** Applies only to folders and allows users to create new files within a folder. Likewise, **Create Folders** allows new folders to be created.

- **Write Data.** Allows users to overwrite the contents of a file, while **Append Data** only allows users to add to a file's contents.

- **Delete Subfolders and Files.** Applies only to folders and allows a user to delete the subfolders and files in a folder.

- **Change Permissions.** Allows a user to modify the permissions on a file.

- **Take Ownership.** Allows a user to make herself the owner of a file.

Some of these special permissions are included in the regular file permissions (Read, Write, Full Control, and so forth). Working with the special permissions directly enables you to customize exactly how a file or folder can be used.

Assigning permissions

Each of these permissions can be assigned in one of three states:

- **Allow.** Gives the permission to the user.

- **None.** Doesn't assign any permission to the user. However, users may gain permission through membership in another group (more on this in a bit).

- **Deny.** Prevents the user from gaining the permission through any means.

**20 Min.
To Go**

Imagine that you work for World Metro Bank and have a user named Linda. Linda belongs to a group named Accounting. If you allow the Accounting group Read permission to a file, Linda gains Read permission through her membership in the group — she doesn't need explicit permission on the file. You can deny Linda Read permission on the file, which prevents her from accessing the file even though the rest of the Accounting group can do so. In that type of scenario, the file's Security tab might look like the one shown in Figure 6-3.

SUS Properties	? X

General | Sharing | Security | Web Sharing | Customize |

Group or user names:

- Administrators (NETSERVER\Administrators)
- CREATOR OWNER
- Linda Johnson (NETSERVER\Linda)
- SYSTEM
- Users (NETSERVER\Users)

[Add...]   [Remove]

Permissions for Linda Johnson	Allow	Deny
Full Control	☐	☐
Modify	☐	☐
Read & Execute	☐	☑
List Folder Contents	☐	☑
Read	☐	☑
Write	☐	☐

For special permissions or for advanced settings, click Advanced.   [Advanced]

[OK]   [Cancel]   [Apply]

Figure 6-3   *Setting up Allow and Deny permissions*

A Deny permission always overrides any other permissions.

Ownership and permissions

The creator of a file is considered to be its owner, and the owner of a file always has Full Control over the file, even if he isn't specifically listed on the Security tab. In addition to the permissions I described earlier, you can assign two special permissions to files:

- **Take Ownership.** This permission gives users the right to become the owners of a file. By default, the Administrators group always has Take Ownership permission over all files on the computer.

- **Change Permissions.** This permission gives users the ability to change the list of groups and users who can access a file and to change the permissions on a file.

Both of these special permissions are included in the Full Control permission I described previously.

Understanding inheritance

Windows Server 2003 supports *inheritance* in file and folder permissions. Inheritance means that a file or folder doesn't have to have permissions applied to it. Instead, the file or folder picks up the permissions from the folder it is contained in.

For example, suppose you create a folder named Documents and apply security permissions to it. By default, any other subfolders you create within Documents, as well as any files contained within Documents or those subfolders, have the exact same permissions as the Documents folder itself. You can assign different permissions to subfolders, and those permissions combine with the ones on the parent. The actual permissions on any file or folder are a combination of its own explicit permissions and the ones inherited from its parent folder.

You might not always want inheritance to work, though. To continue the example, suppose you create a subfolder named Private under the Documents folder. You might want the permissions on Private to be completely different from those on Documents. Also, you might not want any future changes to the permissions on Documents to "fall through" to the Private folder through inheritance.

To block inheritance, modify the Security properties on the folder (like Private) that should have different permissions. Click the Advanced button on the Security tab to display the Advanced Security Settings dialog box, as shown in Figure 6-4.

Uncheck the "Inherit from parent the permission entries that apply to child objects" check box. Windows Server 2003 prompts you to copy the parent's permissions or remove them completely.

- If you want use the parent folder's permissions as a starting point, select Copy. Then, modify the permissions to meet your needs.

- If you want to start with a clean slate, select Remove. Then, assign the appropriate permissions.

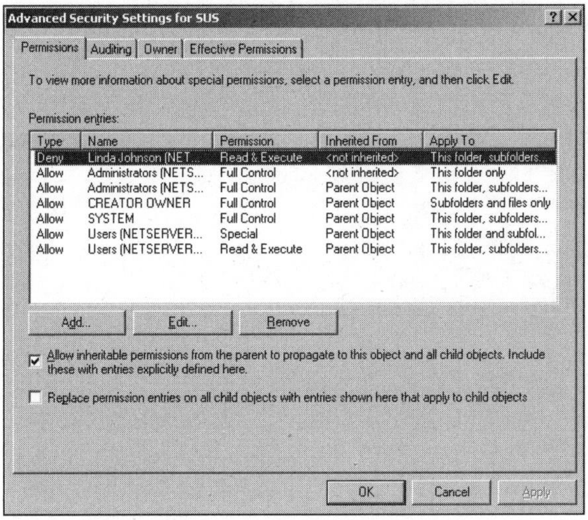

Figure 6-4 *Advanced Security Settings*

Inheritance can be very tricky to figure out. Windows Server 2003 helps by always showing you the current combined permissions on a file or folder in the Security tab. Permissions gained through inheritance are grayed out, indicating that you cannot modify them directly. This behavior enables you to easily identify permissions applied directly to the file or folder, and permissions that were inherited from the parent folder.

Sharing Files

Once you've secured your files and folders by using file permissions, you can make them available to the other users on your network. You start by *sharing* one or more folders on your server. Sharing makes the folder and its contents available to network users.

To share a folder, right-click it and select Properties from the pop-up menu. Then click on the Sharing tab and select the "Share this folder as" radio button, as shown in Figure 6-5.

Figure 6-5 depiction omitted

Figure 6-5   *Sharing a folder*

You must provide a *share name,* which is the name users will use to access the folder. The share name may be different from the folder name, or it may be the same, depending on your needs.

Once a folder has been shared, users can access it by using a *UNC path.* UNC stands for Universal Naming Convention, and a UNC path is a standardized way of accessing shared resources on a network. UNCs begin with two backslash characters, followed by the name of the server hosting the shared resource. The server name is then followed by a single backslash and the name of the shared folder. So, if a server named Server01 is hosting a shared folder name Documents, the UNC would be \\Server01\Documents.

UNCs are not case-sensitive, so you don't have to worry about mixing up uppercase and lowercase letters.

Accessing shared folders

Windows desktop operating systems, such as Windows 98, Windows Me, Windows 2000 Professional, and Windows XP, make it easy to use UNCs to access shared resources. For example, you can select Run from the Start menu, type a UNC, and click OK. The designated shared folder appears in an Explorer window, enabling you to work with the files in the shared folder.

Mapping drive letters

**10 Min.
To Go**

Many users find it difficult to remember UNCs, especially when they have to remember a lot of them. On the other hand, most users are comfortable working with drive letters, since the hard drives on their computers already use drive letters (such as C:\ and D:\). Windows operating systems enable users to *map* a UNC to a drive letter. Mapping assigns a drive letter to a specific UNC, enabling the user to open the UNC just as if it were a hard drive or CD-ROM on her computer.

To map a drive letter to a UNC on Windows XP Professional:

1. Open the Start menu.

2. Right-click My Computer and select Map Network Drive from the pop-up menu.

3. On the Map Network Drive dialog box, shown in Figure 6-6, type the UNC the drive letter should map to and select the drive letter you want to use.

Figure 6-6   *Mapping a drive letter to a UNC*

4. If you want the drive letter to automatically remap to the same UNC every time the you log on, check the "Reconnect at logon" checkbox.

5. Click OK.

Most other Windows operating systems follow the same procedure, although My Computer may be located on the desktop rather than on the Start menu.

Part II — Saturday Morning
Session 6

Share Security

Shared folders can have their own permissions, called *share permissions*.
Remember, files on a FAT16 or FAT32 volume cannot have file permissions. If you
want to share files on a FAT16 or FAT32 volume, then share permissions offer the
only means of limiting user access to the files.

**Share permissions can be applied to any shared folder. It does
not matter what file system is used to store the files within the
shared folder.**

When you create a new shared folder, it starts out with the special Everyone
group having Read permission on the share. You can modify the share permissions
by clicking the Permissions button on the Sharing tab, as shown in Figure 6-7.

Figure 6-7   *Share permissions*

Shared folders have only three types of permissions:

- **Full Control.** Allows users to take any action with the shared files.
- **Change.** Allows users to modify the shared files.
- **Read.** Allows users to read the shared files. This is the default permission
  assigned to new file shares.

What's the Everyone Group?

Windows Server 2003 contains several "special" groups that you won't see in User and Group management or in the Active Directory Users and Computers application. The most important of these special groups is *Everyone*. The Everyone group represents literally everyone; that is, any user who connects to the server. The Everyone group contains all other users and groups.

When a shared folder is sharing files that are located on an NTFS volume, *the share permissions and file permissions combine.* The most restrictive combination of the share and file permissions take effect. For example, suppose you have a file named Private.doc, located in a shared folder named Documents. Private.doc has NTFS file permissions assigned, granting Read permissions to the Domain Users user group. The Documents shared folder has the default share permissions, granting Full Control to the special Everyone group. The *effective* permissions on the file, or the permissions that users will encounter, is the most restrictive combination of the two. In this example, the Domain Users group will have Read permissions, despite the more lenient permissions on the shared folder.

Other special groups include:

- **System.** Represents the operating system itself.
- **Interactive Users.** Represents any user logged on to the server's console.
- **Network Users.** Represents any user accessing the server from across the network.

Best Practices for File Security

With so many options for file and share security, it's easy for things to get out of control. World Metro Bank has chosen to follow the industry best practices regarding file security:

- Always assign permissions to domain local groups (or to local groups if you're not in a domain).
- Place users into domain global groups.
- Place domain global groups into domain local groups (or local groups) to assign permissions to the users in the global groups.

- Only use share permissions when you need to control access to files on a FAT16 or FAT32 partition.

- When sharing files on an NTFS partition, only use NTFS file permissions. Combining file and share permissions makes it difficult to troubleshoot any security problems you may encounter.

- Allow inheritance to work whenever possible. Try to organize your folders so that you don't have to block inheritance. Blocking inheritance can lead to tricky situations when it comes time to troubleshoot access problems.

- If you do need to assign different permissions to a file or folder, block inheritance before doing so. If you don't, the file or folder will still inherit permissions from its parent folder and combine those with the permissions you apply directly. This situation makes it very difficult to troubleshoot the file permissions if a user has trouble accessing the file or folder.

Done!

REVIEW

In this chapter, you learned how permissions can be applied to files and folders, and how those permissions can be inherited from parent folders. You also learned how to share files to make them available on your network, and how to use share security to protect shared files. Finally, you learned important best practices for file security, including the best ways to use inheritance and user groups to control access to files.

QUIZ YOURSELF

1. What permission allows a user to read, write, and change permissions on a file? (See "Permission types.")

2. How can you make files accessible to users on the network? (See "Sharing Files.")

3. In what order should you place users in groups and assign file permissions? (See "Best Practices for File Security.")

4. When it is appropriate to use share security over file security? (See "Share Security.")

5. How can you tell which file permissions have been inherited from a file's parent folder? (See "Understanding inheritance.")

Managing the Distributed File System

Session Checklist

✔ How the Distributed File System works

✔ How to create a Distributed File System root server

✔ How to add nodes and replicas to a Distributed File System root

✔ How to manage the Distributed File System

**30 Min.
To Go**

As you learned in Session 6, you share folders in order to make their contents available to users on your network. Those users can access the shared folders by using Universal Naming Convention paths, or UNCs. Many users have difficulty remembering UNCs, though, and so the Windows operating systems enable those users to map drive letters to UNCs. The drive letters enable users to access shared resources as if the resources were on the users' local computers.

Many users may run out of drive letters, though. After all, there are only 26, and several of those are used for the user's local drives — floppy drives, CD-ROM drives, and so forth. When users run out of drive letters to map, they're stuck with having to remember UNCs.

Windows Server 2003 offers a way to make UNCs easier with the Distributed File System (DFS). In this session, you'll learn how DFS works, how to set it up, and how to use it to make your network resources easier to access and more reliable.

How DFS Works

Without DFS, users must access shared resources in a *server-centric* fashion. In other words, they have to know what server a resource is on because UNCs all start with a specific server name. Remembering which server has which resources is the hardest part about using UNCs, especially since many organizations tend to use hard-to-remember server names like SRNYNET01 or PHLFS034.

DFS is designed to hide the server-centric view of network resources. In a DFS system, users have to remember only two things: the names of the DFS server and of the DFS *root*. You can name the DFS root anything you like. DFS enables you to create a single virtual network resource that brings together all of the shared folders on all of your servers.

 You'll have to select a Windows Server 2003 to act as the DFS server. Choose a server with an easy-to-remember name, so that users will have an easier time remembering what UNCs to use.

Building a tree

DFS works by building a tree. The start of the tree is the DFS root, which is simply an easy-to-remember name that you make up. You might use the name of your company, for example, which is easy for users to remember.

You build the rest of the tree by adding *links*. A link is a single shared folder located on another computer. You provide the name of the link, which does not have to be the same name as the shared folder.

For example, suppose you have several file servers in your organization, each with several shared folders, as shown in Table 7-1.

Table 7-1 *Sample File Servers and Shared Folders*

Server Name	Shared Folder
NYFS001	Documents
NYFS001	Applications

Server Name	Shared Folder
NYFS001	ConfidentialOps
SFFS002	Documents
SFFS002	UserFiles
SFFS002	ConfidentialHR

The set of sample servers and shared folders in Table 7-1 offers many difficulties for users:

- The server names are difficult to remember, although the names probably have significance to your organization's network administrators.

- One shared folder name is used twice, making it difficult for users to remember which Documents shared folder they need to use.

- Confidential documents are stored on two different servers under two different shared folder names, making it difficult for users to remember which UNC to use.

DFS can make this sample situation easier for users. Imagine that you set up a DFS server named Corporate and create a DFS root named Files. You could then add each of the shared folders shown in Table 7-1 as nodes in the DFS tree. The UNCs for those nodes might look something like this:

- \\Corporate\Files\Documents\NY (a link for \\NYSF001\Documents)

- \\Corporate\Files\Documents\SF (a link for \\SFFS002\Documents)

- \\Corporate\Files\Applications (a link for \\NYSF001\Applications)

- \\Corporate\Files\Confidential\Ops (a link for \\NYSF001\ ConfidentialOps)

- \\Corporate\Files\Confidential\HR (a link for \\SFFS002\ ConfidentialHR)

- \\Corporate\Files\UserFiles (a link for \\SFFS002\UserFiles)

As you can see, DFS enables you to construct a well-organized tree. What's more, users can browse the tree on their computers, navigating their way to the correct shared folder. Users no longer have to worry about what server they need to access because the DFS server offers all of the information in an easy-to-use location.

Notice that DFS paths can be sort of virtual. For example, \\Corporate\Files\ Documents doesn't map to any shared folders. But the two subnodes, NY and SF, do map to shared folders. Documents is referred to as a *virtual link* because it exists not to map to a shared folder, but rather to provide organization to the DFS tree.

Virtual nodes are a great way to organize shared folders that contain related content but are located on different servers. Virtual nodes enable users to browse to the shared content more easily, without worrying about all of the actual servers involved.

Providing references

20 Min. To Go

The DFS server doesn't store the files that your users access — the files remain on their original servers. DFS simply provides a *reference* to users' computers. The reference process works like this:

1. A user types a UNC (or browses to one) that is on the DFS server — for example, \\Corporate\Files\UserFiles.

2. The DFS server receives the request and looks up the UNC in the DFS tree.

3. The DFS server retrieves the actual shared folder UNC from the DFS tree and returns that UNC to the user's computer.

4. The user's computer directly accesses the UNC provided by the DFS server.

DFS does these steps transparently, so the user doesn't even realize it is happening. This behavior provides DFS with several advantages:

- The DFS server doesn't actually have to do much work, so a relatively small DFS server can serve an entire organization.

- If you have to move the files in a shared folder to another server, you don't have to tell your users. You simply have to update the link mapping in the DFS tree, and DFS provides users' computers with the new reference.

- DFS can even provide references to non-Windows shared folders, such as the shared volumes created on a Novell NetWare server.

- Users who have already mapped drive letters to UNCs can continue using them because DFS doesn't "break" the original shared folder UNCs.

DFS also includes a few caveats you should be aware of:

- Because users' computers are receiving a reference from DFS, they must be able to directly access the UNC DFS provides. For example, if DFS provides a reference to a NetWare server's shared volume, the users' computers must have the client software necessary to access a NetWare server.

- DFS has no effect on permissions. The permissions on the shared folder, as well as any permissions on the files themselves, continue to operate normally.

- Users' computers have to support the DFS referral behavior. Windows 98, Windows Me, Windows 2000, Windows XP, and Windows Server 2003 all feature built-in support for DFS. Windows NT 4.0 supports DFS if Service Pack 4 or later is installed. Windows 95 requires you to install special DFS client software, which is available from Microsoft.

Creating a DFS Root

You can create two types of DFS roots on a Windows Server 2003 computer:

- **Standalone.** A standalone DFS root runs on a Windows Server 2003 computer. The root exists only on that computer.

- **Domain-based.** A domain-based DFS root is stored in Active Directory. A member server may still act as the DFS server, but because the DFS tree itself is stored in Active Directory, it is protected by Active Directory's own fault tolerance features.

To create a new DFS root on a server:

1. Open the Distributed File System console, which is located under the Administrative Tools program group on the Start menu.

2. Right-click the Distributed File System item in the left pane of the console and select New Root from the pop-up menu.

3. Select the type of root you want to create (standalone or domain-based).

4. Enter the name of the server that will become the DFS server. The default server name is the name of the server you are running the DFS console on.

5. Either select an existing file share on the server or create a new one. This file share becomes the root share in the DFS tree. It does not need to contain any files.

6. Select a name for the DFS root. You're finished!

After creating the root, the DFS console appears as shown in Figure 7-1.

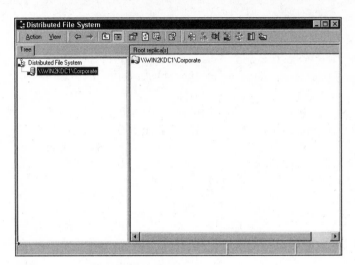

Figure 7-1 *The DFS console*

Adding DFS Links and Targets

After creating your DFS root, you can begin adding links. DFS also enables you to add multiple shared folders for a single link, creating multiple targets. Multiple targets can be used to load-balance user requests across several identical shared folders.

Adding links

To add a new link to the DFS tree, right-click the DFS root in the DFS console. Select New Link from the pop-up menu to display the New Link dialog box, as shown in Figure 7-2.

When you create a new link, you must provide the following information:

- The name of the link.
- The complete UNC path to the shared folder that the link represents.
- The number of seconds clients will cache the DFS referral. Whenever a client receives a DFS referral to a shared folder, the client saves, or caches, that referral for the specified number of seconds. By caching the referral, the client can return to the shared folder again without having to get a new reference from DFS.

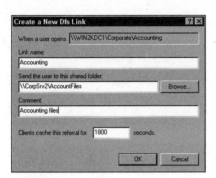

Figure 7-2   *Adding a DFS link*

Remember to make your link names logical and easy to remember, so that users can use the DFS tree more easily.

After creating the new link, it appears in the DFS console. The link includes only a single target: the UNC you provided when you created the link.

Adding targets

Once you've created a link, you can add multiple targets to it. You should add multiple targets only if each one contains the exact same files and folders as the others. When clients request a referral for the link, DFS refers them to only one of the targets.

Using multiple targets is a great way to help spread the burden associated with popular files on your network. For example, you may have a set of documents that are frequently accessed by your organization's users. You could store one copy of the documents on one server and force that server to handle all of the users who want to read the documents. The server may not be able to handle the load, though, and will begin to respond slowly. The solution is to copy the documents to one or more additional servers, placing the documents into shared folders. You can then add those shared folders as targets in the DFS link. DFS automatically distributes the incoming referral requests across all of the targets associated with the link, distributing the workload.

Do not configure a link with multiple targets if users will be modifying the files in the shared folders. DFS does not automatically copy the changes made in one shared folder to the others, and so the targets will no longer contain identical content.

DFS and Replication

Domain-based DFS trees can use Active Directory's File Replication Service (FRS) to help synchronize the content of multiple targets. While this may seem like a great way to enable users to modify documents that are contained in a multiple-target DFS link, you'll find that FRS has serious limitations.

- FRS cannot merge changes made to files. Imagine that you have created a DFS link with two targets. Both targets contain a file named Phones.doc. Sally accesses the DFS link and is referred to the first target, while Bob accesses the DFS link and is referred to the second target. Both Bob and Sally modify Phones.doc at the same time and save their changes. FRS overwrites one copy of Phones.doc with the other, causing either Bob or Sally to lose their changes.

- FRS can only copy files that are not in use. If users have a file open in an application, FRS is unable to copy or overwrite the file.

- FRS is inefficient when handling large files and can impact server performance when it tries to copy them.

I recommend that you use multiple targets only when users will not change the content of the shared folders. You can learn more about FRS' capabilities in Windows Server 2003's online help.

Managing DFS

**10 Min.
To Go**

In addition to creating new DFS roots and links, the DFS console enables you to perform many day-to-day administrative tasks relating to DFS:

- To delete a DFS link target, right-click the target and select Delete from the pop-up menu.

- To filter the links that are displayed (making it easier to find the one you want), right-click the DFS root and select Filter Links from the pop-up menu. Then, enter the number of links to show or the name of the links to show.

- To temporarily prevent users from receiving referrals to a specific target, right-click the target and select Disable/Enable Mapping from the pop-up menu. This action does not disconnect users who are currently using the target's shared folder. To reenable the target, simply repeat the procedure.

World Metro Bank

How will the World Metro Bank use DFS? In such a large organization, with so many offices and so many file servers, DFS becomes a critical part of the bank's plan to make their network resources easily accessible to their users.

A Windows Server 2003 at both the American and European headquarters will host a DFS root. Major file shares from each branch office will be represented as DFS links. For example, the Houston branch office would keep its loan files in \\WMB-USA\Files\Houston\Loans, which is much easier to remember than the actual server and share name: \\USAHOU465\LoanFiles.

Users' personal files will be addressed in DFS, too. A user named Charles might access his files by connecting to \\WMB-USA\Users\Charles. No matter what office Charles moves to, his personal files will always be accessible at that UNC, even if his files are moved to a different file server in the company.

The bank also plans to use DFS to load-balance access to common documents. Four file servers will be set up at the American headquarters, each with identical content. DFS will be used to load-balance access to that content. Only network administrators will be able to post changes to the load-balanced documents, and those administrators know to copy new files to all four servers. Users will be granted only Read permissions to the documents, preventing them from making any changes.

You can use the DFS console to manage DFS roots on other servers, too. Just right-click the Distributed File System item in the console and connect to a DFS server. This technique enables you to manage multiple DFS servers from one place.

REVIEW

In this chapter, you learned how the Distributed File System (DFS) can be used to create a representation of your network's files and folders that is not server-centric. You learned how to create a DFS root, how to add DFS links to the root, and how to add multiple targets to DFS links. You also learned how multiple targets are used by DFS to load-balance access to shared files and folders. Finally, you learned how to perform day-to-day DFS administrative tasks using the DFS console.

Quiz Yourself

1. What happens when a DFS server receives a client request for a particular UNC? (See "How DFS Works.")

2. How can you configure DFS to load-balance access to shared folders across multiple identical copies of the folder? (See "Adding targets.")

3. How can you make the DFS tree more fault tolerant, so that the failure of the DFS server will not necessarily result in the loss of the DFS tree data? (See "Creating a DFS Root.")

4. How does DFS enable clients to access shared folders on non-Windows servers? (See "Providing references.")

5. What should you do in DFS if you need to move a shared folder to a different server? (See "Providing references.")

Advanced File Management

Session Checklist

✔ How to compress files on a hard disk

✔ How to encrypt and decrypt files on a hard disk

✔ How to manage disk space using quotas

**30 Min.
To Go**

Windows Server 2003 offers a number of advanced file management features, which can help organizations use their servers' hard disks more efficiently and safely. In this session, you'll learn how to use file compression to save hard disk space. You'll also learn how to use file encryption to protect the files stored on a server. Finally, you'll learn how to use disk quotas to limit the amount of disk space individual users can utilize on a server.

File Compression

Windows Server 2003 has the ability to compress files stored on any NTFS volume. When compression is used, files take up less space on disk. The operating system automatically decompresses files that are being accessed, so client computers don't need to have any special compression software installed. The operating system also recompresses files that are changed and then saved, ensuring that the file uses as little disk space as possible.

New versions of Windows (including Windows Me and Windows XP) have a feature called Compressed Folders, which are special folders whose filenames have a .zip extension. Compressed Folders do not use Windows file compression; they are actually ZIP archive files, identical to the kind created by third-party applications like WinZIP. Windows Server 2003 is capable of working with Compressed Folders.

Performance impact of compression

Windows Server 2003 requires extra time when a user accesses a compressed file. The operating system has to decompress (and recompress, if the file is changed and then saved) the file. The performance impact required to decompress a single file is very small, but if a large number of users are attempting to access a large number of compressed files, the additional work performed by the server becomes quite noticeable and can make the server seem unusually slow to respond.

Hard disks are becoming larger and less expensive every day. Whenever possible, you should upgrade the hard disks on your servers if they are full, rather than use compression.

I recommend using compression if you need to make extra disk space on a server while you are waiting for new hard disks to be shipped.

Compression is most commonly used on files that are not used very often. For example, when you install a Windows Service Pack, the Service Pack's installation saves copies of the files it replaces. Those copies are compressed, which means they take up as little disk space as possible. Because the files are accessed only if you decide to uninstall the Service Pack, the server's performance isn't negatively impacted.

Other files that might be eligible for compression include:

- Last year's accounting files, which aren't regularly needed but still must be available at a moment's notice.

- Old customer files, which might be needed in an emergency but are otherwise seldom used.

- Other archived data, which is accessed often enough to keep it on the server, but usually less than once or twice a week.

If you have archived data that is accessed less than once a month, consider burning the data onto a CD. The CD provides a permanent copy of the data, and the data no longer takes up hard disk space on the server.

How to use compression

Windows Server 2003 makes it easy to enable compression. You can compress a single file, a group of files, a folder, or a group of folders, by following these steps:

1. Select the files or folders that you want to compress.
2. Right-click a selected file or folder and select Properties from the pop-up menu.
3. Click the Advanced button to display the Advanced Attributes dialog box.
4. Check the "Compress contents to save disk space" check box, as shown in Figure 8-1.

Figure 8-1   *The Advanced Attributes dialog box*

5. Click OK. If you are compressing a folder, Windows Server 2003 asks if you want to apply the compression to the files and folders contained within the folder you selected. Select the appropriate option.

Windows Server 2003 may require several minutes to compress the files and folders you selected. When they are compressed, their filenames are displayed in an alternate color, alerting you to the fact that they are compressed.

By default, Windows Server 2003 displays the names of compressed files and folders in blue. You can change that color by selecting Folder Options from the Tools menu in Windows Explorer.

You can uncompress files by performing the same procedure and simply clearing the compression check box on the Advanced Attributes dialog box.

You can uncompress files only if the hard disk contains enough free space to store the uncompressed files.

Rules for compressed files and folders

Windows Server 2003 allows the compression attribute to be applied to files and folders. When you move and copy files and folders, Windows Server 2003 may change the compression attribute. When deciding how to handle compressed files and folders, Windows Server 2003 follows these rules:

- Compressed files remain compressed if they are moved to a new location on the same volume. Compressed files moved to a different volume take on the compression attribute of the folder they are placed into.

- Compressed files that are copied always take on the compression attribute of the folder they are copied to. The original file remains compressed.

- Compressed folders follow the same rules as compressed files.

Notice that the treatment of the compressed file is closely related to whether it is being copied or moved. For example, imagine that you have a folder named C:\Archive, which contains a file named Resources.xls. Both the file and the folder are compressed. Your server also has a folder named C:\Active, which is not compressed, and a second hard disk named D:\ which uses the FAT32 file system. Here's how Windows Server 2003 would treat them if they were moved or copied:

- If Resources.xls is moved to another folder on C:\, it remains compressed.

- If Resources.xls is copied to C:\Active, the new copy is uncompressed, but the original file remains compressed.

- If Resources.xls is moved to the D:\ drive, it is uncompressed because the FAT32 file system does not support compression.

- If Resources.xls is copied to the D:\ drive, the original file remains compressed, but the copy on D:\ is uncompressed.

Remember, only the NTFS file system supports file compression. If you want to compress files on any other file system, use the Compressed Folders feature or a third-party archiving application like WinZIP.

File Encryption

20 Min. To Go

Many organizations store confidential information on their servers, and they may need to ensure that only authorized users can access those files. Of course, NTFS file permissions provide a great way to restrict access to files and folders, as you learned in Session 6. However, some organizations may be under legal or governmental restrictions that require even stronger security.

For the strongest possible file protection offered by the operating system, Windows Server 2003 provides the Encrypting File System (EFS). EFS uses digital encryption keys to encode files so that only the owner, and users the owner designates, can access the files. Windows Server 2003 uses the strongest encryption methods available and provides a way for organizations to recover files that were encrypted by employees who have left the company.

Some countries have laws regarding the encryption of files. International versions of Windows Server 2003 may contain weaker encryption routines, or no encryption capabilities at all, in compliance with international and local laws.

Performance of encryption

Similar to the extra time required for file compression, Windows Server 2003 requires extra time to encrypt and decrypt files. If a large number of users attempt to access a large number of encrypted files, the server may seem slow to respond. Generally, only especially sensitive files are encrypted, so the negative performance impact of encryption is minimal.

One way to further minimize the performance overhead of encryption is to encrypt only individual files. When you encrypt a folder, Windows Server 2003 automatically encrypts the files within that folder, as well as any new files added to the folder. The folder itself isn't encrypted; it is simply marked so that future files placed within it will be automatically encrypted. While that's a nice feature, users have a tendency to forget about the work on the server and just dump large numbers of files anywhere, whether or not they need encryption. If you encrypt only files, then Windows Server 2003 won't automatically encrypt new files placed into the same folder, and you can prevent unnecessary performance overhead due to encryption.

You should also consider how your users utilize encrypted files. For example, when Microsoft Word opens a document, it creates one or more temporary files. If the original file is encrypted, but the folder containing the file is *not* marked for encryption, then the temporary files will be unencrypted — exposing their contents for all to see. In that kind of situation, it makes sense to encrypt the folder, so that any temporary files will also be protected.

How to use encryption

You can encrypt files and folders using the same procedure you use to compress them (see "How to use compression" earlier in this session). The Advanced Attributes dialog box also contains a check box labeled "Encrypt contents to protect data." Checking that check box encrypts the files or folders you've selected.

 You cannot apply both compression and encryption to the same files or folders. If you select one option, the other is automatically cleared. You have to choose one or the other.

When you encrypt a file, Windows Server 2003 asks if you want to encrypt only the file, or if you want to encrypt the file and its parent folder. Select the appropriate option to complete the encryption process.

By default, only the user who encrypts a file can decrypt it. So, while it is a common practice for administrators to compress files for their users, the users have to encrypt their own files. Once a file is encrypted, not even an administrator can access it.

 By default, the names of encrypted file and folder are displayed in green. You can change the color by selecting Folder Options from the Tools menu in Windows Explorer.

After you encrypt a file, you can view its Advanced Attributes again and click the Details button next to the encryption check box. The Encryption Details dialog box, shown in Figure 8-2, enables you to specify other users who can decrypt the file. You can also see (but not modify) a list of users who can act as Data Recovery Agents, which are users authorized to decrypt the file on behalf of your organization.

Encryption Details for C:\Documents and Settings\Administrator\My D...   ✕

Users Who Can Transparently Access This File:

User Name	Certificate Thum...
Administrator(Administrator@NETSERVER)	4939 B49B 954...

[Add...]   [Remove]   [Backup Keys]

Data Recovery Agents For This File As Defined By Recovery Policy:

Recovery Agent Name	Certificate Thum...

[OK]   [Cancel]

Figure 8-2 *Managing an encrypted file*

Users on the "allowed" list can access encrypted files transparently, as if they were not encrypted at all. Users on the Recovery Agents list must take special steps to decrypt a file, and they must save a decrypted copy in order to access the contents of the file.

Rules for encrypted files and folders

Encryption follows the same rules for moving and copying as file compression (see "Rules for compressed files and folders" earlier in this session). Encrypted items that are moved on the same volume retain their encryption; items moved to a different volume, or copied, take on the encryption attribute of their new folder.

Remember that only the user who encrypts a file (or users they permit) can decrypt it. This rule often trips me up when I'm trying to move files to a different volume or copy the file. Because those operations may require the file to be decrypted, they can be performed only by a user with permission to decrypt the file.

Recovering encrypted files

Domain administrators define recovery agents using domain security policy. These agents are added to the "recovery agents" list of all encrypted files on all computers that belong to the domain. The agents can decrypt any encrypted file. To do so, they must back up the encrypted file, restore it to a secure computer, log on as a recovery agent, and decrypt the file.

World Metro Bank

World Metro Bank has decided to make good use of the Encrypting File System. Users in the bank are encouraged to encrypt sensitive files that contain confidential customer information, such as loan documents. Once a customer loan is complete, the encrypted files are backed up to tape for archival purposes and removed from the file servers.

Should the files ever be needed, they can be restored from tape, and either decrypted by the original loan officer or decrypted by one of the bank's designated Recovery Agents.

Encrypted file recovery is usually performed only if the original, encrypting user has left the organization, has somehow lost her digital encryption certificate (which is usually managed automatically by her workstation operating system), or if a law enforcement agency requests that the file be decrypted.

Encrypted file recovery can be a complicated task, depending on the configuration of your organization's domains. Read the Windows Server 2003 documentation thoroughly before attempting to recover encrypted files.

Disk Quotas

**10 Min.
To Go**

One of the most common uses for Windows Server 2003 is as a file server: a central repository where users can store their data files. Unfortunately, users often forget to clean up old files, they save many copies of the same file, and they do other things that result in a lot of server disk space being consumed. Sure, hard disks are getting bigger and less expensive every day, but no company wants to pay for disk space that's being wasted.

Disk quotas were created to help manage how users utilize server disk space. You can define quotas, which assign specific space limitations (called *thresholds*) to specific users. The thresholds apply for an entire volume, and users who exceed the threshold can be cut off — preventing them from using any more disk space.

Quota warnings are sent using the Windows Messenger service and appear as a small pop-up dialog box on users' computers. Users' computers must be running the Messenger service (which is installed and started by default) in order to receive quota warnings.

Using disk quotas

You have to enable disk quotas on a per-volume basis, and they can be enabled only on volumes that use the NTFS file system. To enable disk quotas, right-click the volume in Windows Explorer, and click on the Quota tab. As shown in Figure 8-3, checking the "Enable Quota management" check box makes the rest of the tab's options available to you.

Figure 8-3 *Enabling quota management*

The Quota tab has several options. Here's what they do:

- **Deny disk space to users exceeding quota limit.** Check this check box to prevent users from using any more disk space once they exceed their quota threshold.

- **Limit disk space to.** This option enables you to specify the maximum amount of disk space each user can utilize on the volume.

- **Set warning level to.** This option warns users that they are approaching their quota limit when they reach the designated utilization level. This option should be set at a lower level than the "Limit disk space to" option.

- **Logging options.** The two logging options cause Windows .NET Server 2003 to create an Event Log entry whenever a user exceeds the warning limit you set or when they exceed their quota limit.

The options on the Quota tab are the defaults and apply to all users who do not have a specific quota entry. If you leave the "Do not limit disk space to" option selected (the default), only those users with a specific quota entry are limited.

Only files that a user owns count against that user's quota. By default, users own the files they create. Administrators (or anyone with the correct permissions) can take ownership of a file; when they do so, the file then counts against *their* quota.

To create a quota entry, click the Quota Entries button. The Quota Entries dialog box, shown in Figure 8-4, enables you to review existing entries, edit them, and create new ones.

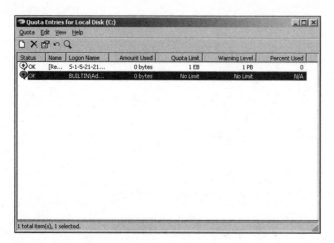

Figure 8-4 *Quota entries*

To create a new quota entry, select New Quota Entry from the Quota menu. Enter the user names (you cannot use groups) that the new quota will apply to. Then, enter the maximum amount of disk space and a warning level for those users. Keep the following facts in mind:

- Quota entries override the default settings, which you specify on the Quota tab.

- Windows Server 2003 creates a default quota entry for Administrators, specifying no limit. Applying a limit to Administrators can cause Windows Server 2003 to malfunction.

- Any users who do not have a specific quota entry will use the default quota, which you specify on the Quota tab.

- If you set a default quota on the Quota tab, you can exempt specific users by creating a "No limit" quota on the Quota Entries dialog box and including the appropriate user accounts in the quota entry.

- Quotas are created on a per-volume basis. If your server has multiple volumes, and you want the same quotas on each volume, you have to create them on each volume. The Quota Entries dialog box enables you to export quota entries to a file. You can then import those entries from the file into another volume's Quota Entries dialog box.

You can use the Quota Entries dialog box to see which quota entries have reached a warning level and which ones have been exceeded. Checking the dialog box every so often is a great way to keep tabs on your users' disk use.

Disk quotas and compression

What if your users compress some of their files? The files use less disk space, but the users may need to uncompress the files some day. To avoid problems when users uncompress their files, Windows Server 2003 uses the *uncompressed* file size in quota calculations, regardless of how much disk space the file is actually using.

This behavior may cause some confusion with your users. They can use Windows Explorer to see that the compressed files aren't using the entire amount of space allotted in their quota, yet they may be receiving warning messages that their quota is approaching its limit. You need to educate your users and explain that the uncompressed file size is used in quota calculations.

Done!

REVIEW

In this session, you learned how to use file compression to compress files so that they use less disk space than they normally would. You also learned how to use file encryption to protect sensitive files and how to recover encrypted data if necessary. You also learned how to use disk quotas to limit the amount of disk space users can fill up on your servers.

QUIZ YOURSELF

1. What happens if you move a compressed file to a different hard disk? (See "Rules for compressed files and folders.")

2. What happens if you mark a folder for encryption and then create a new Notepad file in that folder? (See "How to use encryption.")

3. Can you encrypt and compress a file at the same time? (See "How to use encryption.")

4. What types of restrictions can you apply using disk quotas? (See "Disk Quotas.")

5. How does file compression interact with disk quotas? (See "Disk quotas and compression.")

Managing Printers and Faxes

Session Checklist

✔ How to set up printers

✔ How to set up fax services

✔ How to share printers and faxes

**30 Min.
To Go**

I n Sessions 6, 7, and 8, you learned how to use various Windows Server 2003 technologies for file sharing, one of the most common uses of any network server operating system. One of the other common uses for a network server is to share printers, enabling all of the users on your network to use a common set of print devices. Windows Server 2003 extends its print-sharing capabilities to include fax sharing, enabling the users on your network to easily send faxes from the desktops via a properly configured Windows Server 2003.

In this session, you'll learn how to install and configure printers and print sharing, set up Fax Services, and share fax devices with the users on your network.

Setting Up Printers and Print Devices

Windows Server 2003 is a Plug and Play operating system, which makes it relatively easy to add new hardware like print devices. Windows Server 2003 also supports older, non-Plug and Play printers, so you can continue using the print devices your company already owns.

Installing print devices

If you attach a Plug and Play print device to your system using either a Universal Serial Bus (USB) or parallel cable, Windows Server 2003 automatically detects the print device and prompts you to insert the Windows Server 2003 CD or a CD provided by the print device's manufacturer. Windows Server 2003 installs the necessary printer drivers, automatically sets up a printer, and the new print device is ready to go.

Printer Terminology

Whenever a printer is connected to a network file server, several software and hardware components are involved. In order to keep things straight, you need to become accustomed to the terminology used to refer to those components:

- A *print device* is a physical piece of hardware that produces printed output on sheets of paper. Print devices can take the form of laser printers, inkjet printers, dot-matrix printers, and so on.

- A *printer,* in Windows terminology, is a software queue managed by a server. Because a print device can print only one thing at a time, a printer lines up the items that need to be printed and feeds them to the print device one at a time. Administrators can change the order of the items in a printer, allowing important print jobs to be sent to the print device more quickly than less important print jobs.

  Applications always print to printers, which queue the print job until the print device is ready to handle it.

- A *printer driver* is a software component that knows how to communicate with a print device. In order for Windows to use a print device, you must install a matching printer driver. The print device's manufacturer usually provides a printer driver for Windows Server 2003, and the Windows Server 2003 CD includes printer drivers for many popular print devices.

Some manufacturers provide specific, step-by-step instructions for installing a print device for use with Windows Server 2003. Always follow those instructions. Some manufacturers also provide additional software to help their print devices work more efficiently; see the manufacturer's documentation for details on using the software.

If you have a non-Plug and Play print device attach it to your Windows Server 2003 computer. Then, follow these steps:

1. Open the Start menu, and click on Printers and Faxes.
2. Double-click the Add Printer icon to launch the Add Printer Wizard.
3. Follow the instructions provided by the Wizard. Depending on the type of print device you attach, you may need to provide:
   - The port the device is attached to, such as LPT1
   - A name for the new printer
   - The manufacturer and model of the print device
   - Other device-specific settings
4. The Wizard may prompt you to insert the Windows Server 2003 CD, or a manufacturer-provided CD, in order to install printer drivers.
5. The Wizard installs the necessary drivers and automatically creates a printer that represents the new print device.

Networked Print Devices

Many large organizations use networked print devices, rather than attaching print devices directly to a Windows Server 2003 computer. Networked print devices connect directly to your network and act as a self-sufficient print server. For example, many Hewlett-Packard laser printers offer an HP JetDirect option, which allows the laser printer to become a networked print device.

Technically, the users on your network could send print jobs directly to the networked print device. However, most organizations like to take advantage of Windows Server 2003's printer management features and create a printer on a Windows Server 2003 computer. The printer accepts print jobs from users and then sends them to the networked print device.

Follow the manufacturer's instructions for creating a printer on Windows Server 2003 that represents a networked print device.

Configuring printers

Once you have installed your print devices and created the necessary printers in Windows Server 2003, you can configure the printers to match your environment's needs. Printers are configured by right-clicking the printer's icon and selecting Properties from the pop-up menu. Windows displays the Printer Settings dialog box, shown in Figure 9-1:

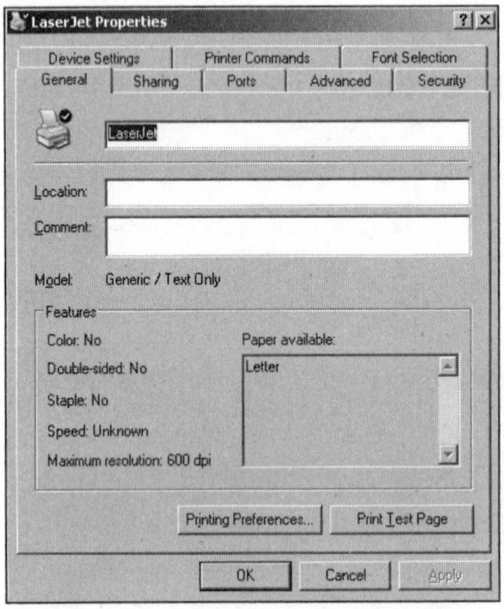

Figure 9-1 *Printer Settings dialog box*

Here are some of the things you can configure a printer to do:

- **Only print during specified hours.** The printer accepts print jobs during all hours but holds them until the hours you specify. One use for this feature is to have large print jobs printed to a special "nighttime" printer, which holds jobs until the evening hours. You can create a second printer pointing to the same print device that accepts normal-sized print jobs during the day for immediate printing.

- **Configure a printer pool.** This configuration allows one printer to point to multiple identical print devices. Incoming print jobs are accepted by the printer and sent to the least busy print device in the pool. This feature allows a bank of print devices to handle print jobs, helping produce printed output more quickly in a busy environment.

**20 Min.
To Go**

- **Modify a printer's priority.** If more than one printer points to the same print device, each printer can be assigned a priority. Print jobs in printers with higher priorities are directed to the print device first. When no high-priority jobs are left, printers with a lower priority are allowed to use the print device.

Sharing Printers

After you have created and configured your printers, you can share them. Just as sharing a folder makes it available to network users, sharing a printer enables network users to send print jobs to that printer. To share a printer, just right-click its icon and select Sharing from the pop-up menu. You can specify a share name, which is the name users will have to use to connect to the printer.

When you share a printer, you can specify permissions that control who is allowed to print to the printer, who is allowed to control jobs on the printer, and so forth.

As shown in Figure 9-2, the Sharing dialog box also enables you to install non-Windows Server 2003 printer drivers on your server.

Figure 9-2   *Installing additional printer drivers*

Part II — Saturday Morning
Session 9

World Metro Bank

World Metro Bank plans to use networked print devices in all of its offices and set up printers on each office's Windows Server 2003 computer. Each office will include one dot-matrix print device for each teller window and will also include three laser print devices. The laser print devices will be configured as a printer pool, so that users printing to the associated printer can get their output as quickly as possible.

When a Windows XP client computer tries to print to a printer being shared by a Windows Server 2003, the Windows XP client does not have to install any printer drivers. Instead, it uses the drivers available on the server. Windows Server 2003 printer drivers are also compatible with client computers running Windows 2000. If you have client computers running Windows 95, Windows 98, Windows Me, or Windows NT 4.0, you can install the printer drivers for those operating systems on your Windows Server 2003. When the client computers connect to the shared printer for the first time, they can download the drivers right from the server, rather than prompting their users to provide a manufacturer's printer driver on CD or floppy disk.

Other operating systems' printer drivers aren't installed normally. Instead, they must be copied to a special folder on the Windows Server 2003. Read the Windows Server 2003 documentation for details on how to perform this special type of installation.

Setting Up Fax Services

Windows Fax Services is a separate piece of software that must be installed from the Windows Server 2003 CD. To install Fax Services:

1. Select Control Panel from the Start menu.
2. Double-click Add/Remove Programs on the Control Panel.
3. Click the Add/Remove Windows Components icon.
4. Locate the Fax Services item on the list, as shown in Figure 9-3. Place a checkmark next to the Fax Services item.
5. Click OK, and Windows Server 2003 installs Fax Services.

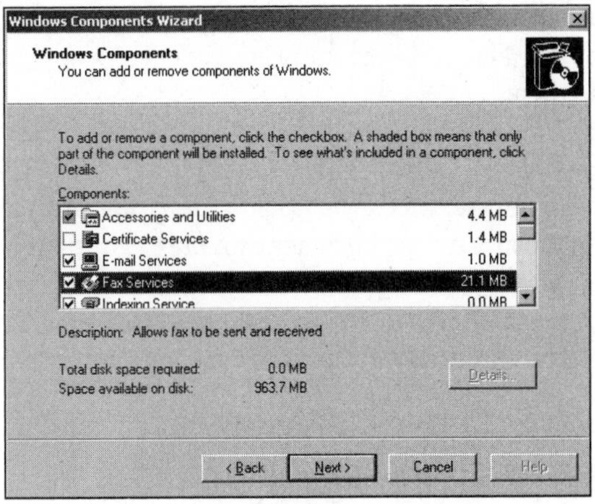

Figure 9-3   *Installing Fax Services*

6. Click OK to close the Add/Remove Programs application and then close the Control Panel window.

What's a Fax Device?

The most common form of fax device is a fax modem. Many notebook computers include built-in fax modems, and most aftermarket modems sold today have built-in fax capabilities. Windows Server 2003 automatically recognizes most new fax modems and prompts you for the correct device driver CD.

Windows Server 2003 also supports compatible fax boards. These boards don't support the dual fax/modem functionality of less expensive fax modems, but they do offer multiline, high-efficiency fax capabilities. Brooktrout is one company that manufactures dedicated fax boards that are compatible with Windows Server 2003. Their fax boards are available in two-line, four-line, and larger versions, allowing Windows Server 2003's fax printer to send multiple faxes at once.

When purchasing a dedicated fax board, you must be extremely careful to select a model that includes a Windows Server 2003–compatible device driver. Visit the Windows Hardware Compatibility List at `www.microsoft.com/windows` for a list of fax devices that Microsoft has tested for Windows Server 2003 compatibility.

Fax Services immediately recognizes any compatible fax devices that are already installed in your computer. You can also add Plug and Play fax devices at any time, and Fax Services will recognize them.

When a fax device is present in your computer, Fax Services creates a special printer called "Fax Printer." You can print documents to this printer, and Windows prompts you for a destination fax number and cover page information. After filling out the information, Fax Services converts the document to a fax and sends it.

You can manage the faxes in your system by using the Fax console. To access the Fax console, open the Start menu. Under the All Programs folder, point to Accessories, then Communications, and then click on Fax Console. The Fax console is shown in Figure 9-4.

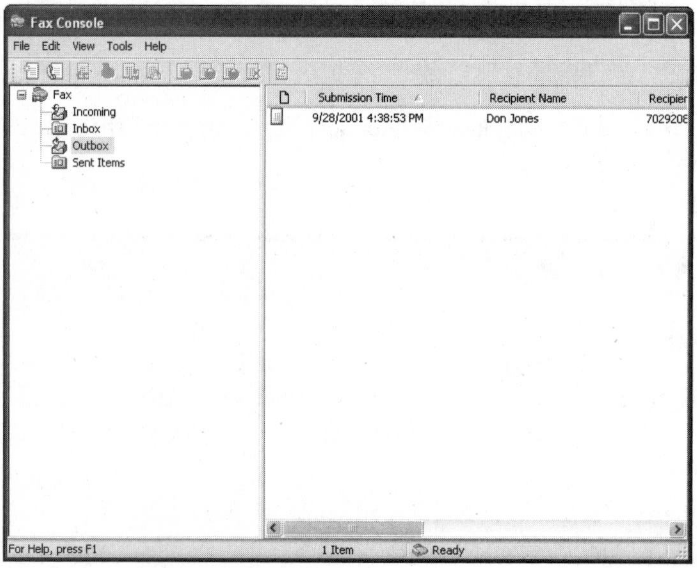

Figure 9-4 *The Fax console*

The Fax console enables you to configure your fax device, set default options (such as the default cover page), and manage faxes that are currently in progress.

Sharing Fax Devices

Windows Server 2003' fax printer can be shared like any other printer, enabling network users to "print" to a server's fax printer. This feature enables Windows

Server 2003 to act as a basic fax server, providing a centralized place for users to send faxes from their desktop computers.

10 Min. To Go

Want a REAL Fax Server?

Windows Server 2003's fax-sharing functionality is new, but fax servers have been around for a long time. One popular Windows-based fax server is RightFax. But now that Windows Server 2003 has built-in fax server capabilities, why would anyone purchase a product like RightFax?

Full-fledged fax servers like RightFax cost thousands of dollars and provide plenty of extra features to justify the price. For example:

- Most fax servers can automatically route faxes to the fax server nearest the recipient, automatically saving you long-distance phone calls without requiring your users to take extra steps.

- Fax servers can also receive faxes, and use character recognition (CR) technologies to route incoming faxes to the appropriate individual's e-mail box.

- Fax servers enable you to create standard documents, like sales brochures, and attach them to outgoing faxes. This feature makes it easy for sales organizations to send standard documents to customers.

- Fax servers usually use dedicated high-speed fax boards, allowing them to send and receive faxes much more efficiently, with less performance impact on the host server, than Windows Server 2003's built-in fax-sharing capability.

Windows Server 2003's fax-sharing capabilities are suitable for very small businesses that only need to send faxes through the server; larger organizations that also need to receive and automatically route faxes are better off investigating products like RightFax.

World Metro Bank plans to implement a fax server product like RightFax. By strategically installing fax servers throughout their organizations, Bank employees will be able to send many faxes for the cost of a local phone call, no matter where the fax actually originates from.

Fax sharing offers wonderful opportunities to save money in your organization. For example, suppose your organization has offices in several major cities, and each office is connected by a wide area network (WAN) connection. If you place a Windows Server 2003 in each office, install a fax device in each server, and connect each fax device to a local telephone line, you can actually save money on faxes! Simply have your users connect to all of the fax devices and then "print" to whichever fax server is closest to the fax recipient.

For example, a user in New York could connect to the Boston fax server and print a document that is to be faxed to a Boston-based recipient. Although the fax was technically printed in New York, it would be faxed by the Boston fax server — a local phone call, instead of a long-distance call from New York. This type of setup requires your users to select the right fax server, but it can result in big savings for your organization.

Done!

REVIEW

In this session, you learned about the various terms used to refer to printers and print queues within Windows Server 2003. You learned how to set up, configure, and share print and fax devices, and how to perform advanced configuration options like printer pooling. You also learned about different types of fax devices supported by Windows Server 2003, and you learned how to configure Windows Server 2003 to act as a fax server for your organization.

QUIZ YOURSELF

1. If your environment includes Windows 98 client computers, how can you ensure that those clients are able to print to the printer you share on your Windows Server 2003 computer *without* requiring additional CDs or floppy disks? (See "Sharing Printers.")

2. In a busy environment, how can you combine several identical print devices so that they balance your organization's printing workload between them? (See "Configuring printers.")

3. How do you allow Windows Server 2003 to recognize fax devices installed on your computer? (See "Setting up Fax Services.")

4. How do users on your network send a fax using a shared fax device on a Windows Server 2003? (See "Sharing Fax Devices.")

Managing Terminal Services

Session Checklist

✔ How Terminal Services works

✔ How to set up Remote Administration mode

✔ How to set up Application Server mode

✔ How to set up Terminal Services licensing

**30 Min.
To Go**

Windows Server 2003 includes a special feature known as Terminal Services. The feature was originally introduced in Windows NT 4.0 Terminal Server Edition and incorporated into the main Server product in Windows 2000. Windows Server 2003 offers a number of improvements in Terminal Services, making it one of the product's most important features. In this session, you'll learn all about Terminal Services, including how it works and how you can set it up on your own servers.

What Is Terminal Services?

Terminal Services gives Windows Server 2003 the ability to act as a *terminal server*. A terminal server uses a centralized computing model, rather than the distributed computing model you are probably accustomed to.

For example, in a traditional distributing computing environment, client and server computers both run complex operating systems, like Windows XP and Windows Server 2003. Client and server computers are both powerful computers, each fully capable of performing complex tasks on their own. In this environment, client computers are often referred to as *smart clients* or *fat clients* because they are fully functional computers capable of running applications.

How Terminal Services Works behind the Scenes

Under the covers, Terminal Services works quite differently from products like pcAnywhere. Most remote control products only allow a single user to control the remote computer, and they are designed to enable users to remotely control their office computers from home, making it easier to work from home. Most remote control products transmit the user's keystrokes and mouse clicks from the client computer to the remote computer, and transmit entire graphic images of the remote computer's screen back to the client for display.

Terminal Services is designed for multiple users, in effect splitting the server into multiple processes, as shown in Figure 10-1. Each process contains a single user's desktop, enabling multiple users to control the server without knowing that other users are doing the same thing. Using graphic images for the screen display would be incredibly inefficient for multiple users, so Terminal Services takes a different approach.

Windows applications draw their buttons, icons, windows, and other graphic elements by simply asking the operating system to do so. All Windows operating systems include a Graphics Device Interface, or GDI, which allows applications to tell the operating system what kind of things to draw on the screen — buttons, check boxes, windows, and so forth. Terminal Services intercepts the requests sent to the GDI by applications and transmits those requests from the server to the client computer. The client computer's Terminal Services software receives the GDI requests and executes them on the client computer, reproducing the exact screen elements requested by the application. The GDI requests are also carried out on the server, so that the applications running on the server can function properly.

In a centralized computing environment, the client computers are often *dumb terminals,* or *thin clients.* In this environment, the client computers don't need to be anything more complex than a monitor, mouse, and keyboard, with a very small operating system. Thin clients can also be implemented as special thin-client software running on a traditional smart client. In a centralized computing environment, the client doesn't actually do any work. In fact, it's not even responsible for drawing the user's desktop graphics and icons! All of the work is done on the server, and the image of the desktop, along with the image of any applications the user is running, are transmitted to the thin client or dumb terminal.

You may be familiar with remote control products like pcAnywhere. These products are a good example of how Terminal Services work. A Terminal Services client essentially is remotely controlling the Terminal Services server. All of the work takes place on the server. The client simply sends the user's keystrokes and mouse clicks to the server, and the server sends the screen image back to the client for display. The big difference between Terminal Services and products like pcAnywhere is that Terminal Services enables more than one user to remotely control the server at once. Each user has her own desktop, and Terminal Services makes it seem as if each user is the only one remotely controlling the computer. Figure 10-1 illustrates how Terminal Services works.

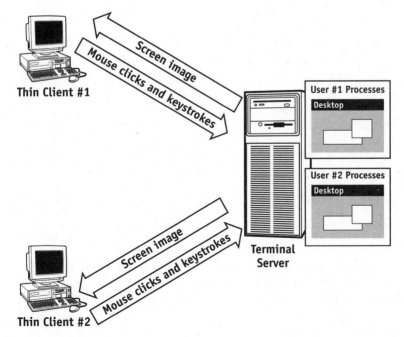

Figure 10-1   *How Terminal Services works*

Terminal Services Capabilities

When you think of all the things a computer has to do in order to run an application, you start to realize how complex Terminal Services has to be. For example, applications can do all of the following tasks when running on a computer:

- Print documents to a print device that is attached to the computer
- Play sounds through the computer's speakers and sound card
- Access the storage devices, like hard disks and CD-ROM drives, on the computer
- Access the communications ports, such as serial ports, on the computer

When an application is running on a Terminal Services server, the application doesn't realize that it's being controlled by a user on a totally different computer. The application believes that it's running entirely on the Terminal Server and, by default, uses the resources on that server, which can present problems for applications:

- Documents print to the printer attached to the Terminal Services server, rather than to a printer that is physically close to the user.
- Sounds play on the server, not on the user's computer.
- Only the server's storage devices are accessible, although the user's documents might be on his computer instead of on the server.
- Only the server's communications ports are available, although the user might have devices attached to her client computer's communications ports.

Terminal Services provides special capabilities to overcome these potential problems. Users connect to a Terminal Services server by using special Terminal Services client software. This software is included with Windows Server 2003 and can be installed on any computer running Windows 3.1, Windows 95, Windows 98, Windows Me, or Windows NT. Windows XP comes with client software, which is called Remote Desktop Connection. Windows CE also comes with Terminal Services client software. The client software works with the Terminal Services server to provide *map-back* capabilities:

- When a user connects to a Terminal Services server, the server attempts to create printers that match the printers configured on the user's client computer. So long as the server contains the correct printer drivers, this

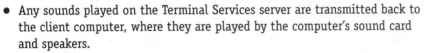

automatic printer mapping results in the user's printer appearing on the server. When the user prints documents to those printers, Terminal Services transmits the print job to the printers on the user's client computer, which then takes care of printing the documents on the user's print devices.

**20 Min.
To Go**

- Any sounds played on the Terminal Services server are transmitted back to the client computer, where they are played by the computer's sound card and speakers.

- The storage devices on the user's client computer are mapped to drive letters on the Terminal Services server. For example, the user's local C:\ drive might appear as the Z:\ drive on the Terminal Services server, allowing applications running on the server to access data on the user's client computer.

- Any applications that attempt to access the server's communications ports are redirected to the client computer's communications ports.

Windows Server 2003 includes version 5.1 of the Terminal Services software, and Windows XP includes version 5.1 of the client software. Earlier versions of the client software can provide only printer map back; sound, storage, and communication port map back is not provided by earlier versions.

Why Use Terminal Services?

Terminal Services is a great way for users to remotely work on company projects. For example, many client-server applications run very slowly over dial-up connections because the dial-up connection simply can't handle the amount of data the application needs to transmit. If the application is running on a Terminal Services server, though, the application has a full-speed local area network (LAN) connection, which can handle the data. The user's dial-up connection must carry only the Terminal Services data (keystrokes, mouse clicks, and screen images), which is much smaller. Figure 10-2 illustrates a dial-up application environment. Laptop computer #1 runs much faster because it is running the application through Terminal Services. Computer #2 is slower because it is running the application itself, and the application's data must travel over a slow dial-up connection.

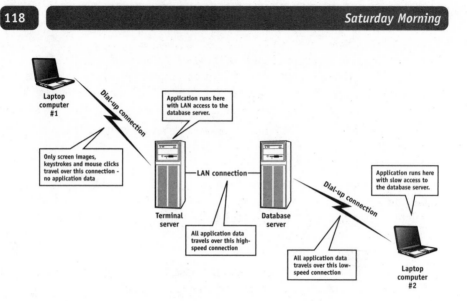

Figure 10-2 *Terminal Services as a dial-up application server*

Terminal Services also makes it easier for administrators to maintain their servers. Imagine that you're the network administrator in an organization with four branch offices. When you need to work on the servers in your own office, it's easy enough: Just stroll into the computer room and log on to the server's console. But what if you need to work on the servers in other offices? You can either drive (or fly) to the office, or get someone in the office to log on for you and follow your instructions. With Terminal Services, you can remotely control the server, just as if you were standing right in front of it.

Remote Administration with Terminal Services

Windows Server 2003 automatically installs Terminal Services in Remote Administration mode — you don't have to do anything extra. Remote Administration mode enables members of the server's Administrators group to remotely control the server, just as if they were standing in front of it. Up to two administrators can connect at once. The administrators simply have to install the Terminal Services client software on their client computers.

Remember, when a server is joined to a domain, the Domain Admins user group is added to the server's local Administrators group. So Domain Admins have the ability to log on to Terminal Services for remote administration.

When two remote administrators are connected to the same server, they both see their own desktops and can control the machine independently. They don't see one another moving the mouse, opening windows, and so forth. However, it is possible for them to *shadow* each other.

Shadowing enables an administrator to see what another remote user is doing, and even allows the administrator to control the other user's mouse and keyboard in Terminal Services. This feature is designed to enable administrators to look "over the shoulder" of a user and help them resolve any problems they might be having.

To use shadowing, you must be logged on to the same Terminal Services server as the user you want to shadow. You must be logged on remotely; you cannot shadow if you are logged on to the server's console. Once you're logged on, follow these steps:

1. Open the Terminal Services Administrator application, which is located on the Start menu under the `Administrative Tools` folder.

2. Locate the Terminal Services session that you want to shadow. Sessions are listed with the name of the user who initiated the session, making it easy to locate the right one.

3. Right-click the session and select Shadow from the pop-up menu. Depending on how Terminal Services is configured, the other user may have to click on a dialog box giving you permission to shadow him.

A separate window opens, displaying the other user's session. You and the other user will see the same thing. Either one of you can move the mouse or type using your keyboards.

Application Server Mode

Although Remote Administration mode is certainly useful, application server (also called *AppServer*) mode is where Terminal Services really shines. AppServer mode enables users to connect to Terminal Services and run applications.

You have to install separate software in order to run Terminal Services in AppServer mode. The software is included on the Windows Server 2003 CD, and you can install it by following these steps:

1. Open the Start menu, and then open the Control Panel.

2. Open the Add/Remove Programs utility.

3. Click on Add/Remove Windows Components.

4. In this list of Windows components, place a checkmark next to Terminal Services, as shown in Figure 10-3.

![Windows Components Wizard screenshot. Windows Components. You can add or remove components of Windows. To add or remove a component, click the checkbox. A shaded box means that only part of the component will be installed. To see what's included in a component, click Details. Components list: Remote Installation Services 2.0 MB (checked), Remote Storage 3.5 MB (checked), Terminal Server 0.0 MB (checked, highlighted), Terminal Server Licensing 0.9 MB (unchecked), UDDI Services 6.7 MB (checked). Description: Configures this computer to allow multiple users to run one or more applications remotely. Total disk space required: 0.0 MB. Space available on disk: 963.7 MB. Buttons: Back, Next, Cancel, Help.]

Figure 10-3   *Installing Terminal Services*

5. Click OK. Windows reminds you of restrictions regarding user applications, which I discuss next. Click Next.

6. Decide what kind of Terminal Services security you want. Full Security mode does not enable user applications to access the server's Registry or sensitive areas of the hard disk. Older applications may require this type of access in order to work correctly; if you are installing that type of application, select Relaxed Security mode.

7. Wait while Windows installs Terminal Services and provide the Windows Server 2003 CD-ROM if Windows asks for it.

When you install Terminal Services for Application Server mode, you must also install at least one licensing server on your network. I discuss licensing servers later in this chapter.

Install Terminal Services only on a computer that doesn't have any user applications (like Microsoft Office) installed. When you install Terminal Services, any existing user applications no longer function. They must be uninstalled and then reinstalled using special techniques I discuss next.

Setting up applications

Applications running on a Terminal Services server have some restrictions on how they behave. For example, many applications create temporary files in a folder named C:\Temp. That won't work under Terminal Services because many different users might be using the application at once, and their temporary files could get mixed up.

Some applications, such as Microsoft Office XP, take special steps when you install them on a server that is running Terminal Services in AppServer mode. Other applications require that you take special installation steps to ensure Terminal Services compatibility. Those special steps generally involve running an application compatibility script, which modifies the application after you install it to ensure compatibility with Terminal Services.

Microsoft includes several compatibility scripts with Windows Server 2003 (for a complete list, refer to Windows Server 2003's online help). Microsoft often makes additional scripts available for download from the Windows Web site.

**10 Min.
To Go**

You can install most applications using the Add/Remove Programs utility on the Control Panel. Older applications' setup routines may fail using that method; if they do, take the following steps:

1. Open a command-line window.

2. Type change user /install and press Enter.

3. Install the application using its regular Setup routine. Be sure to install the application on an NTFS volume.

4. Type change user /execute and press Enter.

5. Run any appropriate application compatibility scripts.

After installing an application, log on to Terminal Services remotely as a regular user (one who is not an administrator) and test the application thoroughly.

Setting up users

You can decide which users have access to Terminal Services and modify the conditions under which they can connect. Simply use Active Directory Users & Computers, and open a user's properties, as shown in Figure 10-4.

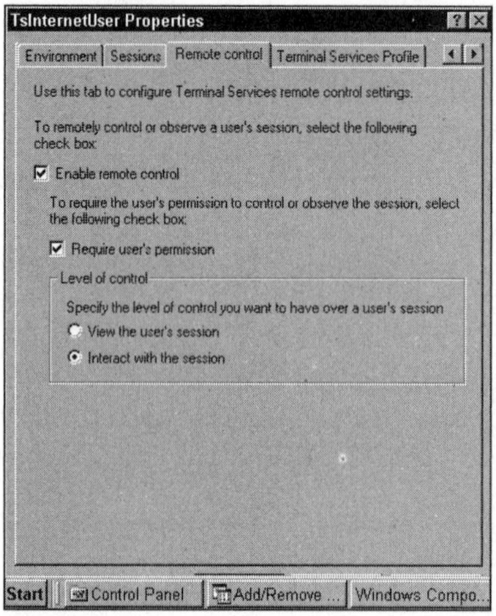

Figure 10-4 *Terminal Services user properties*

Installing Client Software

Windows XP is the only Windows operating system to date that includes a Terminal Services client, called Remote Desktop Connection. The Windows Server 2003 CD includes Terminal Services client software for 32-bit and 16-bit Windows operating systems, and Microsoft provides a free downloadable client for Windows CE.

Users with Windows-based computers must have client software in order to connect to Terminal Services. You install the client software by simply running the Setup program for the appropriate version.

Many organizations use dumb terminals, also called WinTerminals, that have the client software built-in. These terminals are much less complex (and less expensive) than a full computer, and usually require little or no administrative effort to set up and maintain. However, dumb terminal users perform all of their work on Terminal Services. Users with Windows-based computers can use a combination of Terminal Services and their own computers' capabilities.

You can adjust the following properties on a per-user basis:

- Whether or not a user is permitted to log on to Terminal Services
- How long a user may remain connected once logged on
- How long the user may remain idle before Terminal Services disconnects him
- How long disconnected sessions remain active before Terminal Services logs the user off. A user can disconnect and then reconnect later, and her session will still be up and running. When a user logs off, her session is terminated.
- How many active sessions a single user may have at once.

You can set these properties on a per-user basis. You can also provide default values for most of these properties using the Terminal Services Manager application.

Terminal Services Licensing

Terminal Services does not have any special licensing requirements when running in Remote Administration mode, because Remote Administration mode is designed so that only two administrators can remotely control a single server. However, once you install Terminal Services for AppServer mode, Terminal Services operates for only 90 days without a Terminal Services Licensing Server.

You can install Terminal Services Licensing on any Windows Server 2003. Simply follow the same procedure for installing Terminal Services: Open Add/Remove Programs, click on Add/Remove Windows Components, and place a checkmark next to Terminal Services Licensing.

Licensing servers keep track of how many Terminal Services Licenses you have purchased. Each license allows a single user to log on to Terminal Services. All of the Terminal Services servers on your network can share a single Licensing server; the Licensing server distributes licenses to the other servers as users attempt to log on. When a user logs off, her license is released and can be reused when another user attempts to log on. However, when all of the licenses are depleted, no additional users are allowed to log on to Terminal Services.

When your company purchases Terminal Services licenses, you must activate those licenses using Microsoft's Web site and the Terminal Services Licensing application, which is installed on Licensing servers. The activation process registers your licenses with Microsoft and makes them available for your Licensing server to distribute.

Part II — Saturday Morning
Session 10

World Metro Bank

World Metro Bank plans to use Terminal Services in Remote Administration mode to administer its servers, allowing the bank to physically secure the servers in a locked room and aggressively limit access to that room.

The bank also plans to use Terminal Services in Application Server mode, providing bank employees with the ability to work on corporate applications from home. By using Terminal Services, the bank can be sure that a wide variety of home computers can be used to access the company applications, rather than providing employees with the high-end computers necessary to run those applications.

Finally, the bank plans to use Windows terminals instead of computers in their customer service divisions. Customer service representatives run only a single database application, which runs fine on Terminal Services. By using terminals instead of regular computers, the bank will save hundreds of thousands of dollars in hardware costs alone, especially since terminals rarely require hardware upgrades.

Once you activate a license, it becomes tied to a specific Licensing server. Make sure you perform regular backups of the Licensing server to prevent the licenses from becoming lost in a hardware failure. If you do lose your licenses, you must contact Microsoft to reactivate them.

The procedure for activating a license differs depending on how you purchased it; consult the instructions included with the license, or the Windows Server 2003 online help, for complete details on license activation.

Done!

REVIEW

In this session, you learned how Terminal Services works, and how it can be used in an enterprise environment. You learned how to install Terminal Services in AppServer mode, and how to use Terminal Services for remote server administration. You also learned about Terminal Services licensing, and how to install applications on a Terminal Services server running in AppServer mode.

QUIZ YOURSELF

1. How long can you use Terminal Services in Remote Administration mode before you need to install a Licensing server? (See "Terminal Services Licensing.")

2. What security mode should you select for older applications that need access to the Windows Registry? (See "Setting up applications.")

3. How many administrators can connect to a server running Terminal Services in Remote Administration mode? (See "Remote Administration with Terminal Services.")

4. What determines how many users can connect to Terminal Services in AppServer mode? (See "Terminal Services Licensing.")

5. What information is transmitted between a Terminal Services server and client? (See "How Terminal Services Works behind the Scenes.")

6. What map-back capabilities does a Terminal Services 5.0 client feature? (See "Terminal Services Capabilities.")

PART

II

Saturday Morning
Part Review

1. What file system supports file and folder permissions?
2. What file system is compatible with Windows Server 2003 and Windows 98?
3. How can you make the files on a Windows Server 2003 computer available to users on the network?
4. How can you control access to files that are located on a FAT32 volume?
5. What is the minimum number of hard disks required for a RAID 5 array?
6. What are the two components of a UNC?
7. What does DFS stand for?
8. How do you add new UNCs to DFS?
9. How does DFS enable you to load-balance access to shared files?
10. How can you compress an encrypted file?
11. Who can access an encrypted file?
12. How can you prevent users from using too much disk space on a server?
13. If a user compresses a file, how does it count against his disk quota?
14. How does a printer relate to a print device?
15. How can you control the hours that users can print documents?
16. How does Terminal Services send screen images to a client?
17. Who is allowed to log on to Terminal Services in Remote Administration mode?

18. How long will Terminal Services operate in AppServer mode without a Licensing server?

19. What map-back capabilities are provided by the Terminal Services 5.1 client software?

20. How can users send faxes using a centralized Windows Server 2003 computer?

PART

III

Saturday
Afternoon

Configuring Security Policies

Session Checklist

✔ How security policies work

✔ How to configure local security policy

✔ How to configure domain security policy

✔ How to manage security policies

**30 Min.
To Go**

O ne of the primary functions of a network operating system like Windows
Server 2003 is to enforce security. Older versions of Windows were capable of
maintaining a high level of security, if properly configured. Unfortunately,
their security configuration settings were scattered throughout a dozen different
applications, making it difficult for administrators to configure their servers
properly.

Windows 2000 introduced centralized security configuration through the use of
policies, and Windows Server 2003 expands on the use of policies to administer
servers.

Most organizations have written policies in place detailing how the organization's private information should be handled. Likewise, Windows Server 2003's
policies provide a written description of how the server treats various security

features. And, just as the CEO of a company can modify that company's written policies, an administrator can modify the policies of a server to fit the needs of an organization or situation.

In this session, you'll learn what policies are and how they work. You'll also learn the difference between local and domain security policies, and you'll learn about some of the most important policies supported by Windows Server 2003.

How Security Policies Work

Windows Server 2003's policies act as a list of rules, instructing the operating system how to perform certain tasks, whether or not to require certain actions, and so forth. In fact, you've already learned about two types of Windows Server 2003 policy: account policy audit policy, which I discussed in Session 3.

The policies I discuss in this session are much like those in Session 3 because they act as configuration options for the operating system. These policies are *not* like another type of policy you may have heard about: group policies. Group policies are beyond the scope of this book, although I've included some basic information about them in the sidebar entitled "Group Policies," in this session.

Policies work because they are built into the core Windows Server 2003 operating system. Whenever Windows Server 2003 is asked to perform certain tasks, or allow certain actions, it checks to see if the appropriate policy is configured to support or allow the task or action.

Other software applications can add their own policies, which they can check before performing certain tasks or allowing certain actions. For example, installing Terminal Services on a Windows Server 2003 (a topic I discussed in Session 10) adds policies relating directly to Terminal Services, which an administrator can configure to customize the behavior of that software.

Local and Domain Security Policies

Security policies exist on all Windows Server 2003 computers, whether or not they belong to a domain. For example, in Session 3, you learned about the account policies that a server uses to determine the minimum length of passwords, the maximum age of a password, and so forth. In Session 4, you learned that some of those same policies can be configured on a domain controller to affect an entire domain.

Group Policies

Windows Server 2003 is well known for another type of policy: group policies. Like the security policies I discuss in this session, group policies act as configuration options and rules. However, group policies are primarily designed to configure and control users and their computers, rather than to provide global control over basic aspects of a server or an entire domain.

For example, you can create a group policy that specifies the picture shown on each user's desktop. That policy can be applied to a domain, a site, or an organizational unit (OU) within Active Directory and affects all users and computers contained within the domain, site, or OU.

Other types of group policies enable you to automatically install new software applications on users' computers, prevent users from changing drive letter mappings, and so forth. Group policies are a great way to reduce the cost of administering a large organization because they enable you to create centralized configurations that are then distributed to your users.

Unfortunately, group policies are also extremely complex because they support a hierarchy of inheritance, precedence, and combination. The very flexibility that makes group policies so useful also makes them complex enough for their own book, and if you're interested in learning more about group policies, I recommend you purchase such a book. One title you might find helpful is the *Active Directory Bible,* published by Wiley.

Part III — Saturday Afternoon
Session 11

Security policies exist on local servers, where they are enforced by the server itself. Security policies also exist in Active Directory domains, and those policies are enforced by all servers and client computers that are members of the domain.

Managing local security policy

Local security policy is managed using the Local Security Policy application, shown in Figure 11-1. Simply double-click any policy to modify its setting.

Figure 11-1   *The Local Security Policy application*

The security policies on a local computer are organized into four basic groups:

- **Account policies.** Control how user accounts and passwords are treated. You learned about these policies in Session 3.

- **Audit policies.** Determine the activities that the operating system monitors and logs to the Security Event Log. You learned about these policies in Session 3.

- **User rights assignment policies.** Control the special actions users can perform on the server. I discuss these policies in this session.

- **Security options.** Control the operation of Windows Server 2003's security features. I discuss these policies in this session.

Additional policies enable administrators to customize different aspects of the server's security. Some of these policies will be discussed in later sessions; others are beyond the scope of this book, although you can find more information on them in Windows Server 2003's online help. The additional policy categories are

20 Min. To Go

- **Public key policies.** By default contains only the policy for Encrypted Data Recovery Agents. As you learned in Session 8, designated agents have

the ability to decrypt data on a server. The Encrypted Data Recovery
Agents policy contains the digital certificates used by the recovery agents
to perform decryption.

**Do not delete the default recovery certificate from the policy. If
you do, you will be unable to recover any encrypted data without
the user name and password of the user that originally encrypted
the data.**

- **Software restriction policies.** Added by Terminal Services when it is
  installed in AppServer mode, which I discussed in Session 10. Only two
  policies are available, and only the default policy is in effect. You originally configure the default policy by selecting the software security mode
  when you install Terminal Services.

- **IP security policy.** Controls the network-level security provided by the
  IPSec protocol. IPSec allows servers to automatically encrypt data sent
  between two specific locations, treat certain protocols in a special fashion,
  and so forth. A discussion of IPSec is beyond the scope of this book,
  although I provide a brief discussion of it in Session 19.

Managing domain security policy

Domain security policy is also managed with the Local Security Policy application,
on any domain controller in the domain. The name of the application in this case
is a little confusing because you're not really modifying the security policy of an
individual server, as the name implies; you're modifying the policy for the entire
domain.

The trick is that an Active Directory domain controller doesn't have very many
private configuration options. Active Directory replicates most of a domain controller's configuration options to all of the other domain controllers in the domain,
or it disables the local configuration entirely.

For example, you cannot create local users and groups on a domain controller
using the Computer Management application. Once Active Directory sets itself up,
Computer Management disables the Users and Groups folder because Active
Directory's database overwrites the server's local user and group database. And,
while the server's local security policy can still be managed using the Local
Security Policy application, any changes you make automatically replicate to the
local security policy of your other domain controllers.

Pick one domain controller that you'll use to make security pol-icy changes. Make sure your fellow administrators use the same computer. Otherwise, you could each make conflicting changes on two different domain controllers, and Active Directory would determine which change "sticks" and becomes domain policy.

Domain policy vs. local policy

Security policies don't combine or inherit. If you configure local security policies on a domain controller, all your other domain controllers pick up the same policies through Active Directory replication. However, your member servers do not inherit the new policies.

For example, suppose you modify domain policy so that passwords must be at least ten characters long, and must be changed every 30 days. All domain user accounts would be subject to the new policies, and the policies would replicate to all domain controllers, which would enforce them. The policies would not in any way affect the password configuration for local user accounts created on member servers, unless you manually edited the local security policy on each member server as well.

Managing policies on a large number of individual servers is very time-consuming. In the next session, I'll introduce you to the Security Configuration Manager, which can help automate the task of managing local computer policies.

Usually, user accounts are created only in the domain, and so the configuration of local security policy on member servers isn't an issue. However, some local security policies that are designed to protect servers should be implemented on *all* of your servers, and you need to be aware that simply changing domain policy isn't sufficient. I'll point out a few of these critical security policies in the next section.

Using Security Policies

Since security policies define the "rules of the road" for your servers' secure operation, you should take some time to review the available policies and configure them to meet the security needs of your organization. In this section, I'll address some of the most important security policies and give you recommendations for using them to implement a reasonably secure environment.

Always remember that security comes at a cost of some kind. We're all familiar with the cliché television comedy in which the urban apartment-dweller has to unlock fifty deadbolts to open his door and gets locked out when he loses just one of the fifty keys. Some security policies make your servers more secure but may make working with those servers less convenient, or even make the servers less accessible than your organization desires. Be sure you understand the ramifications of any policy you implement so that the policy won't negatively affect your organization's operations.

Make policy changes one at a time and then review their effect on your operations. If things stop working correctly, you'll know exactly which policy to change back.

Account and audit policies

Account policies are divided into two groups: password policies, which control the length, age, and other parameters of users' account passwords, and lockout policies, which control when a user's account is locked out and how long it stays that way.

Audit policies determine which operating system events, like logging on or accessing a file, are logged to the Security Event Log.

I discussed the account and audit policies in Session 3.

User rights assignment policies

Try to log on to a Windows Server 2003 that is a domain controller using a regular user account (an account that isn't an Administrator). You can't! That's because regular users don't have the *right* to log on to a server's console. Only domain administrators have that *right*.

Just as the Bill of Rights guarantees American citizens certain freedoms, Windows Server 2003's user rights assignment policies guarantee certain capabilities to users and groups. Unlike the Bill of Rights, though, you can modify user rights with the click of a button. Here are some of the most important user rights:

- **Access this computer from the network.** This right enables users to connect to a server to retrieve a list of shares. Users must have this right before they can access any shared files or printers on a server. By default, the special Everyone group has this right.

- **Allow logon through Terminal Services.** This right enables a user who connects to Terminal Services to log on to the server. By default, only members of Administrators and Remote Desktop Users have this right.

- **Backup files and directories.** This right enables a user to read files and folders only for the purpose of writing them to a backup device. By default, members of the Administrators and Backup Operators groups have this right.

- **Deny access to this computer from the network.** Anyone with this "right" isn't allowed to connect to the computer. This is one of a half-dozen "reverse rights," or "nonrights" that Windows Server 2003 supports. This right overrides the "Access this computer from the network" right. If you have both rights, you can't access the computer from the network.

- **Log on locally.** This right determines who can log on at the server's console by physically standing in front of the server and typing on its attached keyboard. The default user groups with this right are different on domain controllers and member servers.

- **Remove computer from docking station.** I mention this right because it's one that doesn't usually apply to Windows Server 2003. However, because Windows Server 2003 and Windows XP share a common code base, they have the same user rights. You may run into a few user rights that, like this one, don't make sense; keep in mind that they may apply more to the Windows XP product line and are just in Windows Server 2003 because they're part of the family.

- **Shut down the system.** This is a right you'll want to manage carefully, since you don't want just anyone shutting down a server. This right goes along with another one named "Force shutdown from a remote system," which enables remote users to force the server to shut itself down.

- **Take ownership of files and other objects.** Anyone with Full Control permissions on a file can take ownership of it, but members of the Administrators group can *always* take ownership of a file, even if the group has no other permissions on the file. That capability comes from this user right, which includes the Administrators group by default.

**10 Min.
To Go**

> The user rights' default users and groups change when a server joins a domain and when a server is promoted to a domain controller. Be sure to verify your servers' user rights whenever you make one of those changes.

Security options policies

The security options policies are a collection of miscellaneous security options that enable you to make your Windows Server 2003s more secure (a process known as *hardening*). I'll cover some of the key policies and give you recommendations for using them.

- **Accounts.** Four policies start with "Accounts:" and you should set all of them. They are

  - **Administrator account status.** This policy determines whether or not the built-in Administrator account is enabled, which, by default, it is. If you can disable this policy (thereby rendering the Administrator account useless), then you should do so because the Administrator account is one of the first ones a hacker tries to attack. Make sure that you have another user account with administrative rights, though, so that the disabled Administrator account doesn't prevent you from managing your servers.

  - **Guest account status.** Disabled by default, this policy allows you to enable the Guest account. I don't recommend that you do because the Guest account is usually a hacker's second target in an attack.

  - **Rename administrator account.** If you must leave your Administrator account enabled, name it something else by configuring this policy. Hackers won't be able to attack the user name "Administrator" any more, which will slow them down.

  - **Rename Guest account.** You should definitely configure this policy, even if your Guest account is disabled. Renaming the account removes an obvious target for hackers.

- **Devices: Restrict CD-ROM access to locally logged-on user only** and **Devices: Restrict floppy access to locally logged-on user only.** These two policies, disabled by default, prevent network users from accessing the contents of the server's CD-ROM or floppy drive. Many administrators share their servers' CD-ROM drives, so the first policy should usually be left disabled. However, floppy drives are often a source of computer viruses. Enabling the second policy prevents network users from accessing the contents of the server's floppy drive, stopping a potential virus.

- **Interactive logon: Do not display last user name.** When enabled (it's disabled by default), this policy clears out the name of the previously logged-on user when you try to log on. It's a good security precaution to take because it prevents someone from picking up a valid user name, which she can use in an attempt to break through your servers' security.

- **Shutdown: Allow system to be shut down without having to log on.**
Disabled by default, this policy (when enabled) allows the server to be shut
down simply by clicking a button on the logon screen. If enabled, this policy bypasses the "Shut down the system user" right. While it may seem
convenient to be able to shut down the server without having to log on, I
don't recommend enabling this policy because it creates an enormous security problem, enabling anyone who strolls by the server to shut it down
completely.

There are many other security options policies, and more can be installed when
you install additional server or networking software. You should review the available security policies and implement the ones that best fit your organization's
needs.

**Don't implement more than one or two policies at once, until
you've had a chance to verify and review their effect on your
operations. If you implement a bunch of policies and they cause
a problem, you'll have trouble tracking down the policy causing
the problem.**

World Metro Bank

World Metro Bank plans to use aggressive security policies to protect their
computers. They plan to apply policies regarding password length, account
lockout, and password age to all computers, ensuring that even local computer accounts will be more secure. World Metro Bank also plans to implement some common security best practices using their policies:

- Changing the Administrator account name
- Changing the Guest account name and disabling it
- Removing the Administrator account's ability to log on over the network,
  requiring anyone using the account to physically log on to the console or
  use Terminal Services
- Allowing users to log on using Terminal Services or over the network and
  removing their ability to log on at the server's console.

These security measures help make a network more secure and help prevent abuse by disgruntled or careless users.

Done!

REVIEW

In this session, you learned how Windows Server 2003 uses policies to manage local and domain security configurations. You learned how to manage local security policy, and you also learned how the local computer policy of a domain controller acts as the security policy for the entire domain.

QUIZ YOURSELF

1. How can you prevent members of a specific user group from logging on to a server? (See "User rights assignment policies.")

2. How can you keep network users from accessing the contents of a server's floppy drive, even if that drive has been shared? (See "Security options policies.")

3. What happens to the local security policies on your domain controllers when a change is made on only one of them? (See "Managing domain security policy.")

4. How can you change the local security policy of several member servers from a central location? (See, "Domain policy vs. local policy")

Using the Security Configuration Manager

Session Checklist

✔ How the Security Configuration Manager works, and what it's used for

✔ How to manage server and domain security with the Security Configuration Manager

✔ How to create and use security templates

**30 Min.
To Go**

I n Session 11, you learned how server and domain security can be configured using security policies and the Local Security Policy application. You learned how Windows replicates the "local" security policy of domain controllers to all other domain controllers, and how member and standalone servers' policies must be individually managed.

If your organization has a large number of servers, managing the local security policy of each can become very time-consuming. To help automate the task, Microsoft provides the Security Configuration Manager, or SCM. The SCM uses security templates to apply the same security policies to multiple servers, enabling you to quickly apply your preferred policies to a large number of servers without manually configuring the policies on each one.

In this session, you'll learn all about the SCM and how it works. You'll learn how to use the SCM to apply policies to computers, and you'll also learn how to create your own security templates by using the SCM.

About the SCM

The SCM is designed to analyze a computer and check its compliance with a given security template, apply a security template to a computer, or create a new security template based on a computer's policy settings. The SCM also includes a command-line utility, Secedit.exe, that enables you to create and apply security templates from the command line. Secedit.exe makes it easy to apply security templates in a semi-automated fashion, using batch files.

Opening the SCM

The SCM is a collection of tools, which are available as Microsoft Management Console (MMC) snap-ins. Windows Server 2003 may not create icons for these consoles on the Start menu; if you don't see them on your Start menu under the Administrative Tools folder, just follow these steps to create a new console and add the various SCM snap-ins:

1. Select Run from the Start menu.
2. Type mmc and click OK. Windows displays a blank MMC console.
3. Select Add/Remove Snap-Ins from the File menu.
4. Click the Add button.
5. Double-click the Security Configuration and Analysis and Security Templates items to add the snap-in to the console. You may also wish to add the Local Computer Policy snap-in, making your new console a convenient place to manage all of your computer's security settings.
6. Click OK to close the list of snap-ins.
7. Click OK to close the Add/Remove Snap-Ins dialog box.

 You can save your new console by using the File menu's Save Console As option. Saving the console enables you to load it more easily later.

When you open the SCM for the first time, you need to create a new security database and import a security template before you can use the Security Configuration and Analysis snap-in. To create a new database and import a template, just follow these steps:

1. Right-click the Security Configuration and Analysis item in the left-hand pane of the MMC.

2. Select Open Database from the pop-up menu.

3. Select a name and location for the new database and click OK. For example, you might use a name like `mysecurity.sdb`.

4. Select a template to import into the database. Microsoft provides several templates to get you started, and I'll describe them later in this session.

Working with the SCM

The SCM is comprised of several different tools, including the three main ones I'll discuss in this session:

- **Security Configuration and Analysis.** Used to analyze a computer's security policies and apply security templates

- **Security templates.** Used to create and manage security templates

- `Secedit.exe`. Command-line tool used to apply templates to a computer

Security Configuration and Analysis and `Secedit.exe` have overlapping functions. The purpose of `Secedit.exe` is to make it easier to automate security configuration by using batch files. Both Security Configuration and Analysis and Security Templates are MMC snap-ins; you work with them using a graphical user interface, or GUI, as shown in Figure 12-1.

The SCM also interacts with group policy, enabling you to apply a security template to a group policy object and apply that group policy to a collection of computers. However, a discussion of that procedure is beyond the scope of this book. You can learn more by reading Windows Server 2003's online help.

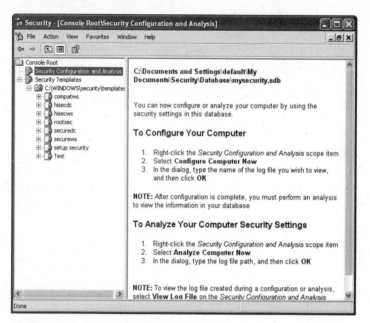

Figure 12-1 *The SCM's MMC snap-ins*

Security Templates

Security templates enable you to create standardized security policies for your computers, and then easily apply those settings to a group of computers, either using "Security Configuration and Analysis," Secedit.exe, or group policies. Microsoft provides several predefined security templates, and you can modify these or create your own.

Predefined templates

In order to get you started, Microsoft includes a number of predefined security templates with Windows Server 2003. You can use these templates as-is, or you can use the Security Templates tool to customize them. The predefined templates are

- **Default security** (Setup security.inf). This template applies the default security settings that Windows Server 2003 starts with after installation. This template effectively resets a computer's security policies to their post-installation values. You should not apply this template using group policy.

**20 Min.
To Go**

- **Compatible workstation or server** (Compatws.inf)**.** This template applies the default permissions to the Administrators, Power Users, and Users local user groups. This template is designed to make Windows Server 2003 behave like older versions of Windows, which granted additional privileges to these three local user groups.

- **Secure workstation or domain controller** (securews.inf or securedc.inf)**.** These two templates enhance a computer's security by defining stronger password policies, account lockout, and audit settings. These templates also limit backward compatibility with older versions of Windows. Take the following into consideration before you use this template:

  - If Securews.inf is applied to a member of a domain, all of the domain controllers in that domain must run Windows NT 4.0 Service Pack 4, or later.

  - Client computers running Windows for Workgroups 3.11, Windows 95, or Windows 98 may not be able to connect to servers that have Securews.inf or Securedc.inf applied, unless they have Microsoft's Directory Services Client Pack installed.

- **High security workstation or domain controller** (Hisecws.inf or Hisecdc.inf)**.** These templates build on the Secure templates by requiring additional levels of encryption for authentication and data.

  - Applying Hisecws.inf to a server or workstation requires that all domain controllers run Windows 2000 or later.

  - Applying Hisecdc.inf to a domain controller requires that all trusted and trusting domain controllers run Windows 2000 or later.

  - Clients running Windows 95 or Windows 98 must have the Directory Services Client Pack installed (which is included on the Windows Server 2003 CD-ROM).

  - Applying Hisecws.inf to a server requires that all clients attempting to connect to the server support and enable SMB packet signing. Windows 2000 and Windows XP enable SMB packet signing by default. To learn more about SMB packet signing and the security it provides, search for "SMB packet signing" in Windows Server 2003's online help system.

  - Hisecws.inf removes all members of the Power Users group.

  - Hisecws.inf removes all members of the local Administrators group except the local Administrator account and the Domain Admins user group.

Do not apply any security template until you have carefully reviewed how it will affect the operation of your network. More information on these templates and their effects can be found in Windows Server 2003's online help.

Editing and creating templates

The Security Templates snap-in enables you to edit the settings of existing templates or create new ones. To create a new template, right-click Security Templates in the MMC and select New Template from the pop-up menu. Windows prompts you to enter a name and description for the new template, and then Windows adds it to the list of templates.

To edit a template (either one you just created or an existing one), just expand the template in the left pane of the MMC. You can see all of the policy settings included in the template, as shown in Figure 12-2. You can edit the policies in the template just like you would edit the policies directly on a computer: Double-click any policy to change its value.

![Screenshot of the Security Templates snap-in in the Microsoft Management Console showing the Security Options policies for the hisecws template, with a list of policies and their computer settings.]

Figure 12-2   *Editing policies with the Security Template snap-in*

Policies in a template can be defined or undefined:

- When a policy is defined in the template, the policy's value overwrites a computer's local policy setting when the template is applied to that computer.

- When a policy is undefined in the template, a computer's local policy setting remains in effect when the template is applied to that computer.

As shown in Figure 12-3, you can select a check box within each policy to define that policy in the template. Clearing the check box makes the policy undefined in the template.

Figure 12-3   *Defining a policy in a template*

 Security templates can also define settings for the Registry, file system, services, and user groups on your computer. Never apply a template without investigating all of its settings with a tool such as Security Configuration and Analysis.

Security Configuration and Analysis

Security Configuration and Analysis enables you to work with the security settings on a single computer using an intuitive GUI. Security Configuration and Analysis enables you to work with security templates in a database, where you can analyze them before applying them to your computers. Security Configuration and Analysis enables you to perform the following tasks:

- **Import security templates.** You must import at least one security template into the analysis database. However, if you import more than one, the database merges the templates by default. This enables you to layer templates and review their combined result. To perform this task, right-click Security Configuration and Analysis and select Import Template from the pop-up menu.

- **Clear database prior to import.** When you import a template, you can tell Security Configuration and Analysis to clear its database prior to the import. Clearing the database enables you to start from scratch with the new template, rather than layering it over the templates already in the database.

- **Analyze your system.** Security Configuration and Analysis compares your computer's policy settings to the ones currently in the analysis database. To perform this task, right-click Security Configuration and Analysis and select Analyze Computer Now from the pop-up menu. The results of the analysis are displayed in the MMC, as shown in Figure 12-4.

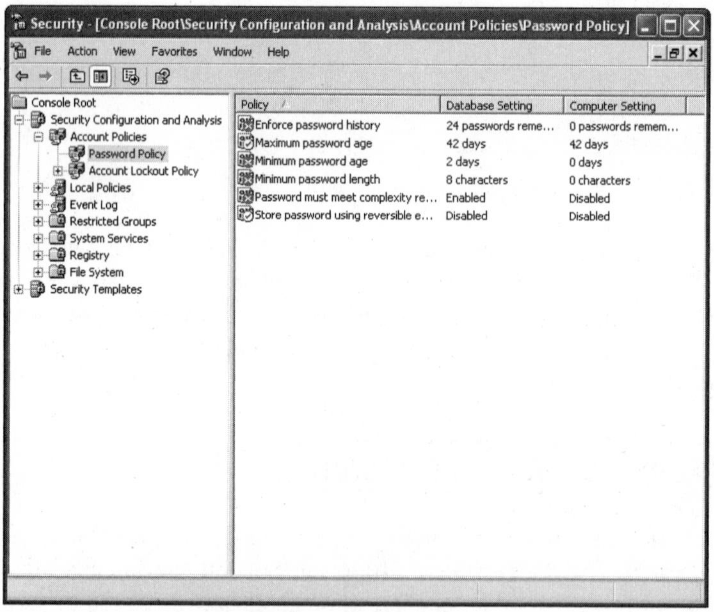

Figure 12-4　*Reviewing analysis results*

**10 Min.
To Go**

- **Note the icons next to each policy.** These icons indicate whether or not the policy, as defined in the database, is active on your computer. The icons are as follows:

  - A red "X" indicates that the policy values on your computer do not match those in the database.

  - A green checkmark indicates that the policy values on your computer match the ones in the database.

  - A question mark indicates that the policy is not defined in the database and was therefore not analyzed.

  - An exclamation point indicates that the policy exists in the database and does not exist on your computer.

- **Edit the database.** You can double-click any of the policy settings in the database to change their values. Your edits affect only the database, not the policies on your computer.

- **Configure your system.** This task applies the values in the analysis database to your computer's local policies. To perform this task, right-click Security Configuration and Analysis and select Configure Computer Now from the pop-up menu.

Secedit.exe

Secedit.exe is a command-line utility that enables you to perform most of the same tasks as the graphical Security Configuration and Analysis tool. Secedit.exe has four primary commands:

- Secedit /analyze performs an analysis. You must specify an existing security database file using the /db parameter — for example, Secedit /analyze /db mysecurity.sdb.

- Secedit /configure configures your computer with a security template. You must specify a security database using the /db parameter.

- Secedit /export exports the security settings on your computer into a template file. You must specify the output filename.

- Secedit /validate compares your computer to an existing template and reports on any differences.

More Than Just Policies

Security templates can define more than just policies, and Security Configuration and Analysis makes it easy to work with the additional settings a template can contain. Templates can define the following security settings:

- **Restricted groups.** Templates can define restricted groups, such as the local Power Users group, and define the membership of those groups. For example, a template might specify that the Power Users group contain no members. Security Configuration and Analysis then red-flags the group's name if analysis reveals that your computer's Power Users group contains members.

- **System services.** Templates can define the services that should be present on a computer and define their startup values. You can make servers more secure by stopping services that aren't used. You might disable the World Wide Web Publishing Service on servers that aren't used as Web servers, for example. Security Configuration and Analysis red-flags any services that don't match the template's definition.

- **Registry.** Templates can specify Registry settings and security, and Security Configuration and Analysis highlights any template-defined Registry settings that don't match your computer's Registry.

- **File System.** Templates can define file security settings for files and folders on your computer, and Security Configuration and Analysis highlights any security settings defined in the template that don't match the security settings on your computer.

Although you can perform these tasks with Security Configuration and Analysis, the graphical tool enables you to work only with a single computer at a time. Because Secedit.exe is a command-line utility, you can use it in batch files, which can be easily run on multiple computers, applying a security template to each.

World Metro Bank

World Metro Bank will create a number of standardized security templates for their member servers, domain controllers, and even their client computers. They'll use the Secedit.exe tool to apply the templates to the appropriate computers.

Because World Metro Bank is concerned about security, they'll select policies that enforce strict security, even on local user accounts. Policies that require long passwords, frequent password changes, and aggressive account lockout will help ensure that the Bank's network remains secure.

By applying these policies using Secedit.exe, the bank's network administrators save a great deal of time and effort. Once the templates are ready, they can be applied to an individual computer in a few seconds.

Done!

REVIEW

In this session, you learned how the Security Configuration Manager (SCM) consists of several tools that can help you manage computers' security policies and other security settings. The Security Templates snap-in enables you to modify and create security templates, which can be applied to computers. Security Configuration and Analysis enables you to view templates' settings and view the result of multiple overlapping templates. Security Configuration and Analysis also enables you to apply a set of templates to your computer. Secedit.exe duplicates most of Security Configuration and Analysis' key functionality but works from a command line, enabling you to perform analysis and configuration tasks from batch files.

QUIZ YOURSELF

1. How can you determine the effect of applying multiple different security templates to your computer? (See "Security Configuration and Analysis.")
2. What tool works from a batch file and makes it easier to automate the application of security templates? (See "Secedit.exe.")

3. How can you create your own security templates? (See "Security Templates.")

4. Which predefined security template resets a computer's security configuration to the post-installation default values? (See "Predefined templates.")

13

Networking with TCP/IP

Session Checklist

✔ How computers communicate by using TCP/IP

✔ How to configure Windows TCP/IP

✔ How to calculate subnet masks

30 Min.
To Go

Protocols are the languages computers use to communicate with one another. One of the most important protocols is TCP/IP, which is actually a protocol *suite,* or a collection of protocols that work together. *TCP* stands for Transport Control Protocol, and *IP* stands for Internet Protocol.

One of the reasons TCP/IP is so important is that just about every type of computer understands it. Whether you're using a UNIX computer, a Macintosh, a Windows server, or a mainframe computer, you can usually rest assured that your computer can talk to all of the others through TCP/IP protocols.

In this session, you'll learn how the various TCP/IP protocols work together, and how to configure Windows Server 2003 to work correctly on a TCP/IP network.

How TCP/IP Works

TCP/IP is a fairly complex protocol when you look at all the different things it can do, but it becomes pretty simple when you break it down. TCP/IP's operation is based on the configuration parameters that you program into your computers.

You program a computer with the following TCP/IP parameters:

- An IP address that is unique on your network
- A subnet mask
- The IP address of a default gateway
- The IP address of a name resolution server

Sending the data

When your computer needs to communicate with another computer, it usually knows only the other computer's name. That's all TCP/IP needs to jump into action. Here's how it works:

1. TCP/IP checks to see if it knows the IP address for the remote computer. If it doesn't, it contacts a name resolution server and asks that server to translate the computer name into an IP address. TCP/IP saves the IP address for several minutes, so that it doesn't have to ask the name resolution server for help as often.

2. TCP/IP uses its subnet mask to determine whether or not the remote computer is on the same *subnet*. A subnet is a single network that uses a single range of IP addresses. I'll show you how subnet masks work in the next section.

   If TCP/IP determines that the remote computer is on the same subnet, it follows these steps:

   1. TCP/IP sends out a special query using the Address Resolution Protocol (ARP). The query is read by all computers on the subnet, and it contains a simple question: "Which one of you is using this IP address?"

   2. The computer using the IP address in the ARP query responds: "I'm the one using it, and here is my physical address." The computer

includes its physical address in the reply. The physical address, also called a Media Access Control (MAC) address, is burned into the computer's network interface card (NIC) by the manufacturer.

3. TCP/IP receives the ARP reply. TCP/IP now knows the remote computer's MAC address and can send data directly to the remote computer.

If TCP/IP determines that the remote computer is not on the same subnet, it follows these steps:

1. TCP/IP sends the data destined for the remote computer to the default gateway you configured.

2. The default gateway is usually a network hardware device called a *router*, which is capable of connecting multiple subnets together. The router accepts data from computers and forwards the data to the appropriate subnet, based on the IP address of the data's destination.

Subnets and subnet masks

Clearly, one of the most complex tasks TCP/IP has to perform is determining whether or not a given IP address is on the same subnet. The task isn't really that complicated once you understand how TCP/IP uses its IP address and subnet mask.

An IP address looks something like this: 192.168.10.52. IP addresses always contain four numbers from 0–255, separated by periods. A portion of the IP address is called the *network ID* and acts as a unique identifier for a particular subnet. The rest of the IP address is called the *host ID* and uniquely identifies a particular computer or network device on that subnet. How can you tell which part of the IP address is which? By using the subnet mask. A subnet mask looks a lot like an IP address, with four groups of numbers: 255.255.255.0.

Remember, computers are binary devices that can think only in zeros and ones. For the subnet mask to make sense, you have to translate it and the IP address into binary.

You can switch the Windows Calculator into Scientific view, which enables you to convert numbers from decimal to binary.

Convert each of the four groups (called *octets*) of numbers into binary. For example, an IP address of 192.168.10.41 and a subnet mask of 255.255.255.0 look like this in binary:

Address or Mask	1st octet	2nd octet	3rd octet	4th octet
192.168.10.41	11000000	10101000	00001010	00101001
255.255.255.0	11111111	11111111	11111111	00000000

Everyplace you see a "1" in the subnet mask corresponds to the portion of the IP address that is the network ID. Everyplace you see a "0" in the subnet mask corresponds to the portion of the IP address that is the host ID. So, in this example, the network ID is 192.168.10, and the host ID is 41.

TCP/IP treats everything with an IP address that starts with 192.168.10 as if it were on the same subnet. Any IP address that starts with something other than 192.168.10 is treated as if it were on a different subnet.

Basic TCP/IP Services

A number of the protocols in the TCP/IP suite are considered core protocols, which means they are usually present on any network that uses TCP/IP. The core protocols provide basic services that no network can do without. These services include

- **Data transmission.** Handled by two protocols: the User Datagram Protocol (UDP) and the Transport Control Protocol (TCP). Computers use UDP when they need to send a small packet of data and don't care if the remote computer actually receives the data. Computers use TCP when a lot of data needs to be sent because TCP allows the remote compute to reply, confirming its receipt of the data.

- **Name resolution.** Provided by the Domain Name System, or DNS, protocol. DNS enables people to use easy-to-remember names like www.microsoft.com and allows computers to translate those names to numeric IP addresses. You'll learn more about DNS in Session 14.

- **Windows Internet Name System (WINS).** Older versions of Windows also use WINS to translate computer names into IP addresses. Windows Server 2003 is compatible with WINS, and you'll learn more about it in Session 15.

**20 Min.
To Go**

- **Address Resolution Protocol (ARP).** Provides address resolution. As you learned in the previous section, ARP allows computers on a subnet to determine the physical address of a computer that is using a specific IP address.

- **IP configuration.** Provided by the Dynamic Host Configuration Protocol, or DHCP. DHCP usually runs on a server and is responsible for issuing IP addresses and other configuration information to client computers on the same network. You'll learn about DHCP in Session 16.

- **Application services.** Such as Web servers and file transfer servers. Each application uses a different TCP/IP protocol to accomplish its task. For example, the HyperText Transport Protocol, or HTTP, is responsible for carrying Web pages across a TCP/IP network, while the File Transfer Protocol, or FTP, is responsible for carrying file transfer traffic across the network. You'll learn more about these and other application protocols in Session 17.

Designing services into a network

The basic TCP/IP services (WINS, DNS, and DHCP) aren't automatically included in a network because you usually install them on only one or two servers. That means you have to decide which servers will run the various services, and you have to make sure the services remain available to your network users.

Most organizations include two DNS servers on their network, so that if one stops working, the other can continue servicing name resolution requests. Most organizations also include two WINS servers for the same reason.

Most organizations also include two DHCP servers on their network, although you have to be careful with that scenario. After all, you don't want the two servers issuing the same IP addresses to different client computers, because that behavior would cause your network to stop working correctly. Organizations usually configure the two DHCP servers to each issue separate ranges of valid IP addresses.

If you're starting to add up the number of servers required, don't worry! Most of the basic TCP/IP services can all be installed on a single pair of servers, so that each server runs DNS, WINS, DHCP, and perhaps a Web or FTP server. Especially large organizations may need more than one pair of servers to handle the workload imposed by their users. Other organizations use multiple servers because their network is spread across multiple geographic locations, and using separate servers for each location can sometimes improve performance.

You'll learn more about configuring DNS, WINS, DHCP, and Web
and FTP servers in Sessions 14 through 17.

TCP/IP services and Windows Server 2003

Some companies run their DNS and DHCP servers on UNIX-based computers.
However, Windows Server 2003 includes the software necessary to provide all of the
basic TCP/IP services to your network, so you don't need to purchase any other
operating systems. All of the basic TCP/IP services are included as separate installation options, enabling you to choose which Windows Server 2003 computers on
your network run those services.

To install any of the basic TCP/IP services, just run the Add/Remove Programs
utility from the Control Panel. Select the Add/Remove Windows Components
option, and then select the service you want to install:

- To install a Web server or FTP server, select Internet Information Services
  (IIS). Modify the IIS installation option to include a Web server, FTP server,
  or both, as appropriate.

- To install a DHCP server, select DHCP Service from the Networking options.

- To install a WINS server, select WINS Service from the Networking options.

- To install a DNS server, select DNS Service from the Networking options.

After installing a TCP/IP service on Windows Server 2003, you have to configure the service. As you'll learn in Sessions 14–17, some services require more
configuration than others. Once the services are configured properly, you have to
configure your client computers to take advantage of the services. For example,
Windows client computers, including Windows 95, Windows 98, Windows Me,
Windows NT Workstation, Windows 2000 Professional, and Windows XP Professional
all enable you to configure the IP address of a DNS server and a WINS server, and
they all enable you to configure the operating system to use a DHCP server if one
is available.

Set up a DHCP server and configure your client computers to use
DHCP. You can then configure most other network options,
including the addresses of WINS and DNS servers, through the
central DHCP server, rather than configuring each client individually. Read Session 16 for more information.

To DHCP or Not: The Argument

As you will learn in Session 16, the DHCP protocol, as its name implies, is completely dynamic. That means a computer that uses DHCP might receive a new IP address each time it restarts. That behavior doesn't present a problem for client computers because very few other users are attempting to access resources like files and printers on a client computer.

Users are always trying to access the resources on a server, though — that's the whole point of a server. Using DHCP to issue IP addresses to servers can cause network problems because the server's IP address can change, making it difficult or impossible for client computers to connect to the server. For that reason, many administrators prefer to manually configure their servers' IP address and other IP options.

Manual configuration, however, means having to manually *reconfigure* all of your servers anytime something on your network changes, such as the IP address of a DNS server or WINS server. In recent years, Microsoft has taken major steps that make DHCP a completely viable option for servers:

- As you'll learn in Session 16, DHCP can be configured to always issue the same IP address to a given computer through a reservation. This technique allows a server to always receive the same IP address but still receive its other IP configuration information from the DHCP server's centralized configuration database.

- On a network that uses only Windows 2000 or later computers, servers whose IP addresses change are accommodated by Dynamic DNS. When a server receives an IP address, it updates its name resolution records in the DNS server automatically. Since Windows 2000 and later operating systems all use DNS to translate computer names into IP addresses, the server's dynamic IP address doesn't cause a problem.

I recommend using DHCP to configure your servers' IP address information unless your servers are running an application that requires a static IP address. For example, the DHCP Service itself can run only on a server with a manually configured IP address (otherwise, it would have to somehow issue an address to itself).

Configuring TCP/IP

Windows Server 2003 requires you to configure its TCP/IP settings, just as you would with any client computer on your network. You can manually configure all of the TCP/IP settings, or you can have the server configure itself by using a DHCP server on your network.

To configure the TCP/IP settings in Windows Server 2003, follow these steps:

1. Select Connect To from the Start menu, and then select All Connections. Windows displays the Network Connections window, as shown in Figure 13-1. The window includes icons for all of your network connections.

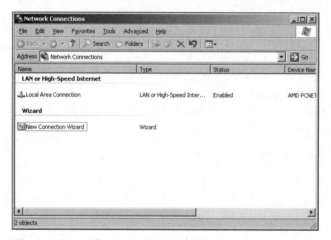

Figure 13-1   *The Network Connections window*

2. Locate the icon for your local area network (LAN) connection, right-click it, and select Properties from the pop-up menu. Windows displays the connection's properties, as shown in Figure 13-2.

**10 Min.
To Go**

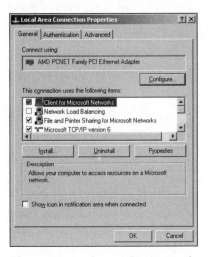

Figure 13-2   *Connection properties*

3. Select the TCP/IP protocol from the list, and click the Properties button. Windows displays the TCP/IP Properties dialog, as shown in Figure 13-3.

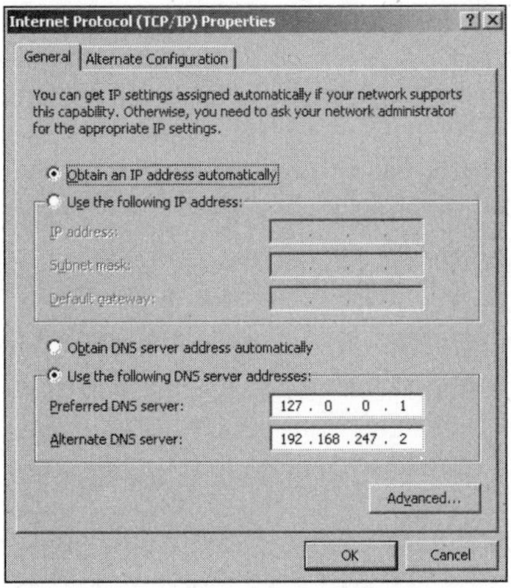

Figure 13-3   *TCP/IP Properties*

The TCP/IP Properties window gives you several options:

- Select the "Obtain an IP address automatically" button to have the server use DHCP to obtain an IP address. If you select this option, you can also select the "Obtain DNS server address automatically" button, and the server obtains DNS server information from the DHCP server.

- Select the "Use the following IP address" option and manually configure an IP address, subnet mask, and default gateway. If you select this option, you must also provide the IP addresses of your network's DNS servers.

4. Click the Advanced button to display the Advanced TCP/IP properties dialog box, and select the WINS tab, as shown in Figure 13-4. You can configure the IP addresses of one or two WINS servers that the server should use for name resolution.

Figure 13-4   *WINS properties*

 If your network contains older Windows clients, then you should configure Windows Server 2003 with the address of a WINS server. Otherwise, those older clients may be unable to locate the server by name.

Done!

REVIEW

In this session, you learned how computers use TCP/IP to communicate over a network. You also learned how TCP/IP works, and how the basic TCP/IP services provide the necessary features for TCP/IP to function on a network. You learned how Windows Server 2003 provides the necessary software to implement the basic TCP/IP services, and you learned how to configure the TCP/IP settings on a Windows Server 2003.

QUIZ YOURSELF

1. What are the four TCP/IP settings you have to configure on a Windows Server 2003? (See "How TCP/IP Works.")

2. What TCP/IP protocol translates IP addresses into MAC addresses? (See "How TCP/IP Works.")

3. Which TCP/IP protocols translate computer names into IP addresses? (See "Basic TCP/IP Services.")

4. How can you configure Windows Server 2003 to obtain IP address and configuration information from a DHCP server? (See "Configuring TCP/IP.")

5. How can you configure a Windows Server 2003 to use DHCP, and still ensure that it always receives the same IP address? (See the sidebar "To DHCP or Not: The Argument.")

Managing the Domain Name System Service

Session Checklist

✔ How DNS works

✔ How to install the DNS Service

✔ How to configure the DNS Service

✔ How to create and manage DNS records

**30 Min.
To Go**

A s you learned in Session 13, the Domain Name System (DNS) is one of the key TCP/IP network services required by all TCP/IP-based networks. DNS provides name resolution services, allowing computers to translate human-friendly names like www.microsoft.com into TCP/IP addresses like 192.168.34.214. In this session, you'll learn how DNS works, and how to install and configure Microsoft's DNS Server software, which is provided with Windows Server 2003.

How DNS Works

DNS is a database that is designed to cross-reference names and IP addresses. Like any database, DNS is built on a set of records. Each record cross-references a single name to an IP address. Most DNS servers require an administrator to manually

5. The google.com DNS server looks up www in its database and finds an A record that lists the IP address for www. The DNS server returns that IP address to your ISP's DNS server.

6. Your ISP's DNS server saves the IP address for www.google.com in its cache for future use and sends the IP address to your computer in a DNS reply.

7. Your computer uses the HTTP protocol to contact the IP address returned by your ISP's DNS server and begins downloading the Web page you requested.

This process happens millions of times every minute on the Internet. Most computers cache DNS replies for a short period, so that, for example, your computer doesn't have to contact your ISP's DNS server every time it needs to contact www.google.com. Your computer retains the DNS reply for several minutes, which speeds up Internet access.

Dynamic DNS

The DNS Service included with Windows Server 2003 supports Dynamic DNS, which helps alleviate the need to manually configure host records. Client computers that are Dynamic DNS compatible (including Windows 2000, Windows XP, and Windows Server 2003) register their own host records when they start up.

Dynamic DNS allows your DNS server to maintain accurate host records even when hosts are receiving dynamic IP addresses through Dynamic Host Configuration Protocol (DHCP). When a computer receives a new IP address, it contacts the Dynamic DNS server and updates its own host record.

You can use non-Microsoft DNS servers to support Windows Server 2003, provided they support Dynamic DNS. Dynamic DNS is a key requirement for Windows Server 2003–based networks to function properly.

Setting Up DNS

Windows Server 2003 does not automatically install its DNS Server. You need to install the DNS Service and then configure it before you can begin using it on your network.

Installing DNS

To install the DNS Service on Windows Server 2003, follow these steps:

1. Open the Control Panel from the Start menu.
2. Double-click Add/Remove Programs.
3. Click Add/Remove Windows Components.
4. Place a checkmark next to Network Services, and click the Details button.
5. As shown in Figure 14-1, place a checkmark next to the network services you want to install, such as the DNS Service.

Networking Services

To add or remove a component, click the check box. A shaded box means that only part of the component will be installed. To see what's included in a component, click Details.

Subcomponents of Networking Services:

☑ 🖳 COM Internet Services Proxy	0.0 MB
☑ 🖳 Domain Name System (DNS)	1.5 MB
☑ 🖳 Dynamic Host Configuration Protocol (DHCP)	0.0 MB
☑ 🖳 Internet Authentication Service	0.0 MB
☑ 🖳 QoS Admission Control Service	0.0 MB
☑ 🖳 Simple TCP/IP Services	0.0 MB
☑ 🖳 Windows Internet Name Service (WINS)	0.9 MB

Description: Enables DCOM (Distributed Component Object Model) to travel over HTTP via the Internet Information Server (IIS).

Total disk space required: 2.6 MB
Space available on disk: 15162.8 MB

Details...

OK   Cancel

Figure 14-1　*Installing the DNS Server software*

Once you are finished installing the DNS Service software, you can begin configuring it for use on your network.

Make sure your Windows Server 2003 computer has a static IP address before you start using the DNS Service. Client computers cannot use DNS reliably if the server has a dynamic IP address.

Configuring DNS

You manage the DNS Service using a Microsoft Management Console (MMC) snap-in. When you install the DNS Service, Windows automatically adds an icon for the DNS Server Manager to the Start menu, under the `Administrative Tools` folder. Launch the DNS Manager, and then follow these steps to configure the DNS Server:

1. Right-click the server's name in the left pane of the MMC. Select Configure a DNS Server from the pop-up menu.

2. Select the appropriate scenario for your DNS server. Most organizations need the "Medium office/large office" option, which allows the server to be authoritative for a domain.

3. Select Yes to allow the Wizard to create a new forward lookup zone.

   Zones contain DNS records and represent a single domain. Forward lookup zones allow client computers to translate names to IP addresses; a reverse lookup zone translates IP addresses to computer names.

4. Create a *primary zone* if this is your first DNS server. A *secondary zone* depends on an already existing primary zone. Secondary zones allow more than one DNS server to be authoritative for a single domain, since the secondary zones are just copies of a master primary zone.

5. Type your domain name.

6. Accept the default for the new zone file, unless you want the DNS server to use a zone file from another DNS server.

7. Select the appropriate option to allow or not allow dynamic DNS updates.

Types of Zones

Windows Server 2003 stores DNS records in one of two places: a *zone file* or Active Directory. When the DNS Server is running on an Active Directory domain controller, you can choose either type of storage; when DNS isn't running on a domain controller, you have only the option to use zone files.

Zone files are simply text files that store the DNS records for the zone. Most non-Windows DNS servers use zone files. Active Directory–integrated zones store DNS records right in Active Directory (AD). AD-integrated zones can take advantage of AD's fault tolerance and replication. For example, if a zone file becomes corrupted, the DNS server is useless. AD-integrated zones, however, are copied to every domain controller in a domain. That means no single server is responsible for protecting the zone data, and that any domain controller can become a DNS server if you install the DNS Service software.

I recommend using AD-integrated zones whenever possible. Use zone files only if you can't run the DNS Service software on a domain controller.

8. Select the option to skip creation of a reverse lookup zone. Reverse lookup zones allow DNS clients to look up a computer's IP address by using its name; you can create a reverse lookup zone later if you need that functionality on your network.

9. Select the appropriate option to forward DNS requests. Generally, you should configure your DNS server to forward requests to your ISP's DNS server. That way, your server can use request forwarding to provide name resolution for servers outside your organization.

The Wizard finishes setting up the DNS Service. Once it's done, you can begin adding DNS records or allowing Dynamic DNS clients to create their own records.

Managing DNS

The DNS Manager snap-in enables you to create, delete, and modify the DNS records in your zones. You can also view the dynamic records that client computers create in your zone, although you won't need to manually manage those records. DNS Manager also enables you to manage multiple Microsoft DNS servers by connecting to them. To connect to a new DNS server, just right-click on DNS in the left pane of the MMC and select Connect to Computer. Type the computer name, and DNS Manager adds that DNS server to the list.

DNS Manager displays all of the records in an individual zone, as shown in Figure 14-2.

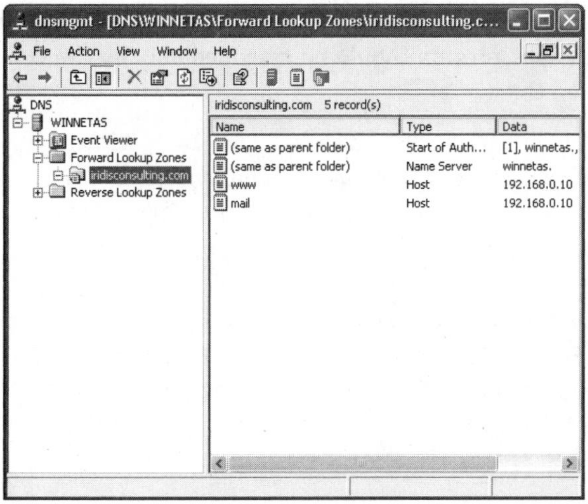

Figure 14-2 Managing a DNS zone

10 Min. To Go

Part III — Saturday Afternoon
Session 14

DNS Manager enables you to perform several management tasks:

- To create a new record, right-click the zone folder and select the type of record you want to create. If the record type you need isn't listed on the pop-up menu, select Other New Records. As shown in Figure 14-3, you can then select from any of the supported DNS record types.

Figure 14-3   *Creating new DNS records*

- To delete a record, right-click it and select Delete from the pop-up menu.

Don't delete dynamically created records unless you're sure the client that registered the record won't try to modify it in the future. Dynamic records should be managed only by the computer that created them.

- To modify a record, double-click it. As shown in Figure 14-4, Windows displays a dialog box that enables you to edit the record's properties. The appearance of the dialog box changes depending on the type of record you're editing.

If your network primarily consists of Windows 2000 Server and Windows Server 2003 computers, you won't need to spend much time managing your DNS records. Those computers are capable of managing their own DNS records through Dynamic DNS.

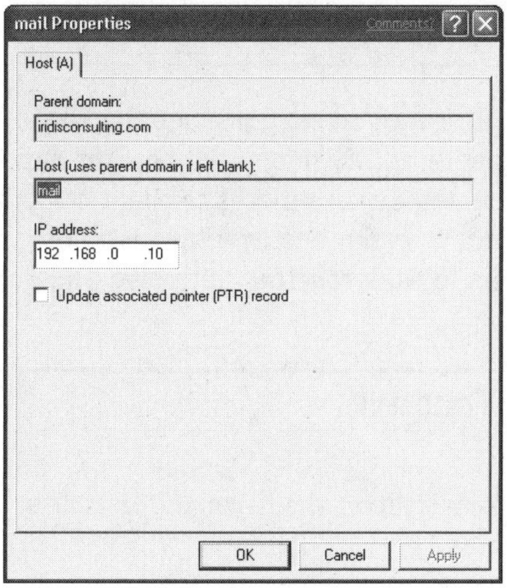

Figure 14-4 *Editing DNS records*

Placing DNS Servers

Deciding where to place DNS servers on your network can be tricky. If you're not using AD-integrated zones, you have to place a single primary DNS server and one or more secondary servers as appropriate to handle your user traffic. Figuring out how many DNS servers to use can be challenging.

Using AD-integrated zones makes it easier to decide where to place DNS servers. Remember that only domain controllers can be DNS servers in an AD-integrated zone. You don't want to make *every* domain controller a DNS server, though, because the DNS software does lower a server's performance somewhat. Also keep in mind that each domain requires its own DNS server.

Large organizations like World Metro Bank generally install DNS on a domain controller in their headquarters. In the bank's case, they would install one in their American and European headquarters. Because the bank is using a delegated domain structure, they'll also install DNS on a single domain controller in each domain.

Part III — Saturday Afternoon
Session 14

Done!

REVIEW

In this session, you learned how to install, configure, and manage the Windows Server 2003 DNS software. You also learned how DNS works, and how the various types of DNS record work to provide name resolution services to client computers. You also learned how DNS request forwarding works, and how the distributed nature of DNS allows multiple DNS servers to work together to resolve DNS queries.

QUIZ YOURSELF

1. What type of DNS record tells an e-mail server the name and IP address of your e-mail server? (See "DNS records.")

2. What tool do you use to administer Windows Server 2003's DNS software? (See "Managing DNS.")

3. How can you reduce the amount of manual DNS configuration in your organization? (See "Dynamic DNS.")

4. How does your ISP's DNS server resolve DNS queries for Internet addresses? (See "The DNS process.")

Managing the Windows Internet Name System Service

Session Checklist

✔ How the WINS Service works

✔ How to install and configure the WINS Service

✔ How to manage the WINS Service

**30 Min.
To Go**

As you learned in Session 14, the Domain Name System (DNS) translates (or *resolves*) Internet names into IP addresses. Windows 2000 and Windows Server 2003 use DNS as their primary means of name resolution. Older versions of Windows, however, use the Windows Internet Name System, or WINS, as their primary means of name resolution. Windows Server 2003 includes the WINS Service to support those older operating systems.

How WINS Works

Beginning with Windows 2000, computers running a Windows operating system primarily used Internet-style computer names, which is why they use DNS as their primary means of name resolution. Prior to Windows 2000, however, Windows operating systems used a *NetBIOS* computer name. DNS servers don't work with NetBIOS names, and so Microsoft provided the WINS Service to resolve NetBIOS names to IP addresses.

WINS, DNS, NetBIOS, and Internet Names

Ever since the first computer networks were created, users have needed to locate computers and network resources by using names. When the Internet became ubiquitous in the early 1990s, the Internet's technique for name-to-address resolution — DNS — became popular, and operating system manufacturers like Microsoft started building DNS (and other Internet protocols) into their products.

Before the Internet became common, however, users still needed a way to address computers and resources by name. One of the earliest network protocols included with the Windows operating systems was NetBIOS, which allowed computers to be configured with names of up to 15 characters. When the TCP/IP protocol was added to the Windows operating systems, WINS was introduced to resolve NetBIOS names to IP addresses.

As the Internet became more and more popular, Microsoft decided to use Internet-style host names as the primary computer name for Windows operating systems, starting with Windows 2000. To provide backward compatibility with older versions of Windows, Windows 2000 (and Windows Server 2003) computers still have a NetBIOS name.

Windows 2000 and Windows Server 2003 work fine with WINS. However, they always try to resolve names using DNS first, so they rarely actually use WINS to resolve names on a properly configured network.

Name registration

When you configure a Windows-based computer with the IP address of a WINS server, the computer starts using the WINS server on its next reboot. The first interaction between a WINS server and a client computer is *name registration*. Here's how it works:

1. The client computer contacts the WINS server and sends the client computer's NetBIOS name and IP address.

   Note that the client computer sends this information *after* using the Dynamic Host Configuration Protocol, or DHCP, to receive an IP address, if necessary. You'll learn more about DHCP in Session 16.

2. The WINS server checks its database to see if another computer has already registered the client's NetBIOS name. If no other computer has done so, then the WINS server adds the client's computer name and IP address to the database, along with a *lease time* (more on that later).

   If the client's NetBIOS name has already been registered, then the WINS server sends an error message to the client computer. The client computer then warns the user of the conflict by displaying an error message.

3. All WINS servers are configured with a lease time, which is the length of time a computer can use a NetBIOS name without re-registering it. Once a computer successfully registers a name, WINS responds with the length of the lease.

4. After half of the lease time has passed, the client computer contacts the WINS server to renew the lease. This process continues until the client computer is shut down.

 WINS registration occurs even if the client computer has a static IP address.

WINS ensures that every computer's NetBIOS name and IP address is listed in its database. If a name registration lease expires, WINS removes the entry from its database, helping ensure that the database remains up-to-date at all times.

 WINS name registration works a lot like Dynamic DNS name registration, which you learned about in Session 14.

Name resolution

When a client computer needs to resolve a NetBIOS name to an IP address, it sends a name resolution request to a WINS server. The WINS server checks its database and returns any name-to-IP address mappings that it finds.

Part III — Saturday Afternoon
Session 15

WINS: Not Just for Computer Names

Computer names aren't the only thing a WINS server keeps track of. User names, Windows NT domain names (including the *downlevel* NetBIOS domain names supported by Active Directory domains), and workgroup names are all registered with WINS servers.

All of these NetBIOS names are limited to 15 characters, although WINS actually keeps track of *16* characters. The sixteenth character indicates the type of the name: user, domain, workgroup, or computer. When a computer sends a WINS name registration, it includes its own name, the name of any user logged on to the computer, and the name of its domain or workgroup.

Those extra name registrations help NetBIOS-based services (like the Messenger service, which allows computers to send pop-up messages to users or other computers) to find the IP address associated with a user, a domain, or a computer.

Configuring WINS

You can install the WINS Service on any Windows Server 2003 computer. After installing the WINS Service, you need to configure your client computers and other services to use it.

**20 Min.
To Go**

Installing WINS

To install the WINS Service on Windows Server 2003, follow these steps:

1. Open the Control Panel from the Start menu.
2. Double-click Add/Remove Programs.
3. Click Add/Remove Windows Components.
4. Place a checkmark next to Network Services, and click the Details button.

You cannot install WINS on a server unless that server is configured with a static IP address. If you try to do so, Windows displays an error message warning you that a client computer will be unable to use the WINS server until you configure it with a static IP address.

5. As shown in Figure 15-1, place a checkmark next to the network services you want to install, such as the WINS Service.

Figure 15-1   *Installing the WINS Service software*

Once you are finished installing the WINS Service software, you can begin configuring your client computers to use it.

Configuring computers to use WINS

You have to configure your client computers to use WINS, by configuring them with the IP address of a WINS server.

You can configure client computers with two WINS server addresses. If the first server is unavailable, the client automatically tries the second one.

How you configure client computers depends on what version of Windows they're running; follow these steps to configure a Windows XP Professional computer:

1. Open All Connections from the Settings folder on the Start menu.

2. Right-click the Local Area Network icon and select Properties from the pop-up menu.

3. Double-click TCP/IP Protocol.

4. Click the Advanced button and then the WINS tab, as shown in Figure 15-2.

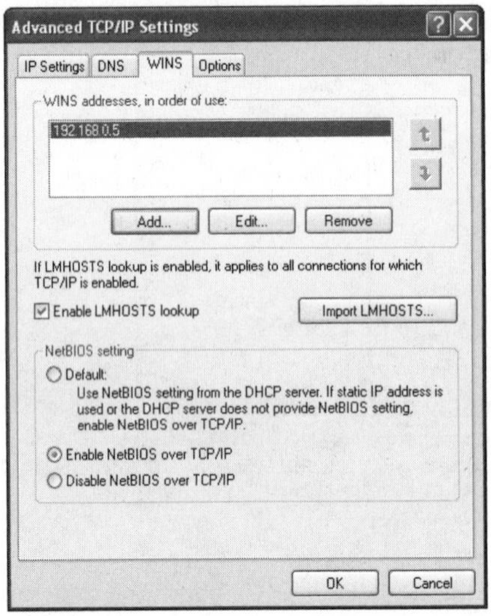

Figure 15-2   *Configuring client computers to use WINS*

Managing WINS

You manage WINS by using the WINS snap-in to the Microsoft Management Console (MMC). The snap-in enables you to view the WINS database of name-to-IP address mappings, create static WINS entries, and manage WINS replication. The snap-in is shown in Figure 15-3.

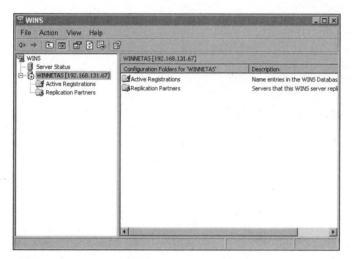

Figure 15-3   *The WINS management snap-in*

The WINS database

The WINS database contains all of the name-to-IP address mappings in a WINS server. To display mappings in the database, right-click the Active Registrations folder and select Display Records from the pop-up menu. Windows displays the Display Records dialog box, shown in Figure 15-4, which enables you to specify search criteria for the records you want to display. For example, you might want to display records containing a certain name or IP address.

Figure 15-4   *Displaying WINS records*

Static WINS entries

Some environments may require you to create static WINS entries. For example, if your network contains servers that are not WINS compatible, as well as older versions of Windows that rely on WINS for name resolution, then you may need to manually create WINS entries for those servers so that the clients can find them.

 Do not create static entries for any computer capable of dynamically registering itself with WINS. If you do, you'll create a name conflict that may prevent other computers from properly resolving the first computer's name.

You should use static WINS entries only when absolutely necessary because it's very easy to forget that they're in the database. If you change the IP address for a computer that has a static WINS entry, you need to remember to update the WINS entry yourself, or that computer may be inaccessible to the rest of the network.

To create a static WINS entry, follow these steps:

1. Right-click Active Registrations and select New Static Mapping from the pop-up menu.

2. Enter the computer name and IP address for the static mapping. Select the appropriate mapping type (use Unique if the static entry represents a computer).

3. Click OK.

WINS replication

**10 Min.
To Go**

Replication enables you to have multiple WINS servers on your network. For example, if your network spans two different offices, you might want to include a WINS server in each office to provide faster WINS services to the users in each office.

Normally, the problem with having multiple WINS servers is that they don't share name-to-IP address mappings. Consider World Metro Bank, which plans to include WINS servers in several of their offices. The users in each office will be configured to use their local WINS server. Users in the Houston office, however, wouldn't be able to resolve the IP addresses of computers in the Dallas office, because the Houston WINS server wouldn't contain entries for Dallas computers. WINS replication is designed to solve that problem, by copying the WINS records from one WINS server to one or more other WINS servers, ensuring that all of the servers contain the same records.

To enable replication between WINS servers, follow these steps:

1. Right-click Replication Partners and select New Replication Partner from the pop-up menu.

2. Enter the name of the WINS server you want to replicate with, and click OK.

WINS adds new replication partners as push/pull partners, which means both WINS servers will send records to one another and request new records from one another. You should normally leave replication partners configured for push/pull operation, unless you are upgrading from Windows NT 4.0 and you need to duplicate a different replication configuration.

REVIEW

Done!

In this session, you learned about NetBIOS computer names and how WINS resolves those names to IP addresses. You learned how to install WINS on a server, and how to configure servers and client computers to use WINS. You also learned how to manage WINS, including examining the WINS database and creating static WINS entries in the WINS database.

QUIZ YOURSELF

1. How can you allow WINS client computers to look up the IP addresses of non-WINS computers? (See "Static WINS entries.")

2. What should you configure if you have more than one WINS server on your network? (See "WINS replication.")

3. How do you configure client computers to use a WINS server? (See "Configuring computers to use WINS.")

4. What name-to-IP address mappings, aside from computer names, does WINS provide? (See "WINS: Not Just for Computer Names.")

16

Managing the Dynamic Host Configuration Protocol

Session Checklist

✔ How the Dynamic Host Configuration Protocol works

✔ How to install and configure the Dynamic Host Configuration Protocol

✔ How to manage the Dynamic Host Configuration Protocol

**30 Min.
To Go**

O n a network with thousands of computers, manually configuring the TCP/IP settings of each computer can be very time-consuming. Very large companies could easily employ several people full-time just to keep up with TCP/IP configurations — an expensive proposition! Fortunately, the Dynamic Host Configuration Protocol, or DHCP, exists to help automate TCP/IP configuration.

How DHCP Works

DHCP is a client-server process, which means that client computers must communicate with a central DHCP server in order to obtain their TCP/IP configuration information. Client computers running Windows operating systems can be set to use DHCP or to use manually-configured TCP/IP information.

When discussing DHCP, the term "client" refers to any computer that uses DHCP to obtain TCP/IP configuration information. DHCP clients may include server operating systems like Windows Server 2003, as well as clients like Windows XP Professional.

When a client computer is configured to use DHCP, here's how it obtains its TCP/IP configuration:

1. When the client computer starts, it realizes that it doesn't have an IP address or other IP settings but is instead configured to use DHCP.

2. The client computer broadcasts a DHCP request packet. All computers on the local subnet receive the broadcast, but only a DHCP server recognizes the request and processes it.

For subnets without a DHCP server, you can configure your routers to pick up the DHCP request packet and forward it to a subnet that does have a DHCP server. This technique enables you to use a single DHCP server for multiple subnets.

3. The DHCP server selects an available IP address from its database. The address matches the subnet that the DHCP request came from, ensuring that the client will be able to use the address.

4. The DHCP server sends a DHCP offer packet to the client's physical address. The offer includes the IP address the DHCP server selected, as well as other configuration information, like the IP addresses of the DNS server that the client should use.

5. The DHCP client acknowledges receipt of the IP configuration information and begins using the new settings. The IP address the client received is *leased* from the DHCP server for a specific period of time.

6. When 50 percent of the lease time has expired, the DHCP client sends a DHCP renew packet to the DHCP server. The server renews the DHCP lease, allowing the client to continue using the IP configuration it already has, without performing another DHCP request.

DHCP servers can issue many different IP settings to DHCP clients. An administrator must configure those settings on the DHCP server. The settings can include:

- The IP address of one or more DNS servers
- The IP address of one of more WINS servers
- The IP address of the default gateway
- The domain name that client computers should use

If a DHCP server receives a DHCP request but doesn't have any IP addresses available to issue to the DHCP client, then the DHCP server sends the client a DHCP non-acknowledgment, or DHCP nack. The DHCP nack tells the client that no IP configuration is available, and the client computer has to take other steps to obtain IP address information.

Most client computers temporarily disable their TCP/IP protocol when they receive a DHCP nack, preventing the computer from communicating with the TCP/IP protocol.

DHCP in the World Metro Bank

While a single DHCP server can serve an almost unlimited number of sub-nets, especially large organizations will want to have more than one DHCP server. World Metro Bank wants to have more than one DHCP server in case one should fail.

Having more than one DHCP server is no problem provided you follow some basic guidelines:

- No two DHCP servers should issue the same IP addresses. If they did, they might issue the same address to two different clients, causing con-flicts on the network.

- When a client sends a DHCP request, multiple DHCP servers may respond, since DHCP servers don't communicate with one another to coordinate DHCP information.

- DHCP servers should be configured with the same IP settings, so that clients receive the correct settings no matter which DHCP server responds to their DHCP request.

World Metro Bank plans to include two DHCP servers in all of its major offices. While they could use a single pair of servers, they want to avoid placing too much workload on a single pair. The bank will configure its routers so that DHCP requests aren't forwarded over wide area network (WAN) connections in offices that have their own DHCP servers. That router configuration will ensure that DHCP clients use only their local DHCP servers, rather than contacting DHCP servers in another office across the WAN.

Configuring DHCP

Although DHCP centralizes and automates the configuration of your DHCP client computers, the DHCP server itself isn't automatically configured. You have to manually configure the server with information about your network, so it can issue that information to DHCP clients.

Installing DHCP

To install the DHCP Service on a Windows Server 2003, follow these steps:

1. Ensure that the server is using a manually configured TCP/IP address. A DHCP server cannot use DHCP to obtain IP addressing information; that information must be configured by an administrator.

2. Launch Add/Remove Programs from the Control Panel.

3. Click on Add/Remove Windows Components.

4. Select the Network Services item, and then click Details. Windows displays the network services that you can install. Place a checkmark next to the Dynamic Host Configuration Protocol, as shown in Figure 16-1.

Networking Services

To add or remove a component, click the check box. A shaded box means that only part of the component will be installed. To see what's included in a component, click Details.

Subcomponents of Networking Services:

☑ 📡 COM Internet Services Proxy	0.0 MB
☑ 📡 Domain Name System (DNS)	1.5 MB
☑ 📡 Dynamic Host Configuration Protocol (DHCP)	0.0 MB
☑ 📡 Internet Authentication Service	0.0 MB
☑ 📡 QoS Admission Control Service	0.0 MB
☑ 📡 Simple TCP/IP Services	0.0 MB
☑ 📡 Windows Internet Name Service (WINS)	0.9 MB

Description: Enables DCOM (Distributed Component Object Model) to travel over HTTP via the Internet Information Server (IIS).

Total disk space required: 2.6 MB
Space available on disk: 15162.8 MB   Details...

OK   Cancel

Figure 16-1   *Installing the DHCP service*

5. Click OK, and then click OK again. Windows may prompt you to insert the product CD while it installs the DHCP service.

**20 Min.
To Go**

After you install the DHCP service, you can create an initial DHCP configuration.

Authorizing DHCP Servers

As you might expect, unauthorized (or *rogue*) DHCP servers can cause problems on your network. Unauthorized servers might respond to DHCP requests and issue inaccurate IP configuration settings, causing the client computers on your network to stop functioning correctly.

Windows 2000 and Windows Server 2003 include features to help stop unauthorized DHCP servers. Whenever the DHCP service starts on a Windows 2000 or Windows Server 2003 computer *that belongs to a domain*, the DHCP service checks the domain's Active Directory to see if that server is on a list of authorized DHCP servers. If the server isn't on the list, the DHCP service shuts itself down.

Unfortunately, this feature doesn't work when the DHCP service starts on a standalone server that isn't a member of a domain, nor does the feature stop Windows NT computers or non-Windows computers from starting an unauthorized DHCP server.

To authorize a server in your domain to run the DHCP service:

1. Launch Active Directory Users and Computers.

2. Locate the server in your Active Directory tree.

3. Right-click the server and select Authorize DHCP Server from the pop-up menu.

Setting an initial DHCP configuration

Your DHCP server's initial configuration should include the following:

- **One or more *scopes*.** Each scope represents a single subnet on your network and includes a range of IP addresses that are valid on that subnet. DHCP draws from that range of addresses when it responds to client requests from that subnet.

- **One or more *server options*.** Each option configures a specific TCP/IP setting, such as the IP address of your DNS server. Global options are issued to all clients, no matter what scope their IP address is drawn from.

- **One or more *scope options*.** Each option configures a specific TCP/IP setting, such as the IP address of a subnet's default gateway. Scope options
  are tied to a specific scope and are issued only to clients who receive an IP
  address from that scope. If a scope and global option conflict, DHCP issues
  the scope option.

**Use server options for networkwide settings, such as DNS and
WINS server addresses. Use scope options for subnet-specific
options, such as the default gateway address.**

You configure DHCP by using the DHCP console, shown in Figure 16-2.

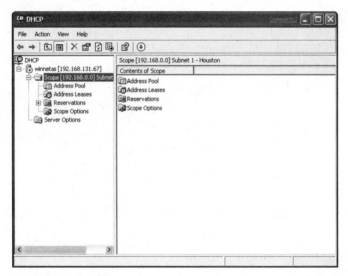

Figure 16-2   *The DHCP console*

**The DHCP console can connect to multiple DHCP servers, enabling
you to manage all of your organization's DHCP servers from a single window.**

To create a new scope:

1. Right-click the DHCP server name, and select New Scope from the pop-up
    menu.

2. Provide a name and description for the scope.

3. Specify the starting and ending IP address that the scope will use, and specify the subnet mask the scope will use.

4. You may also specify the most common scope options at this point, including DNS servers, domain name, WINS servers, and default gateways.

When specifying scope options, skip any options that you have defined as server options, unless you need to override the server options for the scope you just created.

You can also use the DHCP server to activate and deactivate scopes. DHCP stops issuing addresses from a scope when you deactivate it, although clients who already have addresses from the scope can continue to use them. Deactivating enables you to change a scope and ensure that no additional clients will receive addresses from it until you activate it again.

Configuring clients to use DHCP

You have to configure your client computers to use DHCP. Different client operating systems require different configuration steps, although most Windows operating systems require very similar steps. To configure Windows XP Professional to use DHCP, follow these steps:

1. Select "Show all connections" from the Connect to menu on the Start menu.

2. Right-click your Local Area Network connection, and select Properties from the pop-up menu.

3. Select the TCP/IP protocol from the list of protocols, and click Properties.

4. As shown in Figure 16-3, select "Obtain IP address automatically" and "Obtain DNS server address automatically". Selecting those options disables the other options on the dialog box, since the computer will obtain the IP configuration information automatically by using DHCP.

5. Click OK to close the TCP/IP properties, and click OK to close the connection properties.

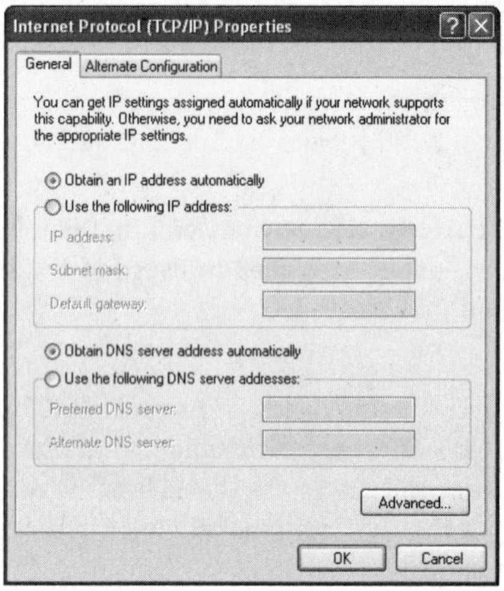

Figure 16-3   *Configuring Windows XP Professional to use DHCP*

Managing DHCP

DHCP servers don't require much in the way of day-to-day management. You can use the DHCP console to create new scopes when necessary or to modify server and scope options to reflect changes to your network's configuration. The two main administrative tasks you must perform, however, are creating reservations and viewing the DHCP database.

Creating reservations

Reservations ensure that some computers always receive the same IP address. Reservations enable you to combine the stability of static IP addresses with the convenience of DHCP's centralized IP configuration. Many companies use reservations to issue addresses to their servers, since client computers have an easier time connecting to servers when the servers' IP addresses never change. You could just manually configure your servers with static IP addresses, but then you'd have to reconfigure the servers anytime your network's DNS servers, WINS servers, or other configuration settings changed.

To create a reservation, follow these steps in the DHCP console:

1. Right-click Reservations, and select New Reservation from the pop-up menu.

**10 Min.
To Go**

2. Provide a name and description for the reservation, as well as the IP address the reservation should use and the physical (MAC) address of the computer that the reservation applies to.

3. Click OK.

Reservations should use IP addresses that are valid within the scope that contains the reservations, to ensure that the client computers receiving the reservations will work properly.

Viewing DHCP database information

As shown in Figure 16-2, you can use the DHCP console to view the addresses that the server has leased from each of its scopes. Viewing lease information enables you to see when an IP address was issued, what computer is using the address, and how long the lease has before it expires.

If you find that your scopes are running out of IP addresses, use the DHCP console to view the lease information for the scopes. If you find that the same computer has leased multiple IP addresses, then the computer may not be releasing its older leases properly. One solution to that problem is to decrease the lease time of the scope. If lease times are shorter, the DHCP server can try to reuse old addresses even though the original lessee hasn't released them.

> **Decreasing the lease time to less than about three days can generate an unnecessary amount of network traffic. Remember that a client computer renews its lease after 50 percent of the lease time expires.**

Troubleshooting DHCP

DHCP usually works without a snag, but sometimes client computers don't receive an address through DHCP, or they receive incorrect address information. When trouble occurs, use this checklist to help solve the problem:

- Make sure your network doesn't contain any unauthorized DHCP servers. The Windows Server 2003 CD includes a utility named DHCPLoc.exe. When you run DHCPLoc.exe, it sends out a DHCP request and lists the servers that respond with a DHCP offer. Make sure no unauthorized servers are included on the list.

- Make sure your DHCP scopes have sufficient available IP addresses by using the DHCP console.

- Have clients try to release their DHCP address and obtain a new one. On Windows NT 4.0 and higher clients computers, you can run `ipconfig /release` and then `ipconfig /renew` from a command line to release the client's address and obtain a new one.

- If your network contains a large number of notebook computers that users take in and out of the office, you may need to decrease the DHCP lease time on your DHCP servers. Decreasing the lease time helps ensure that the DHCP server reuses an IP address when the computer that the address was issued to is no longer connected to the network. Setting the lease option to three days (the default is eight) usually is sufficient.

- Make sure your client computers' DHCP requests can reach a DHCP server that contains a scope for their subnet. You need to check your routers' configuration to ensure the routers are forwarding DHCP requests properly.

Done!

REVIEW

In this session, you learned about DHCP, the Dynamic Host Configuration Protocol. You learned how DHCP clients work with a DHCP server to obtain IP addresses and configuration settings, and how to manage a DHCP server using the DHCP console. You learned how to configure a DHCP server and DHCP clients, and you learned how to create DHCP reservations for computers that always need to have the same IP address. You also learned basic troubleshooting steps to help resolve DHCP problems.

QUIZ YOURSELF

1. How do DHCP clients locate a DHCP server? (See "How DHCP Works.")
2. What happens when a network contains two DHCP servers? (See "How DHCP Works.")
3. What tool can help you locate unauthorized DHCP servers on your network? (See "Troubleshooting DHCP.")
4. How can you ensure that a DHCP client will always receive the same IP address? (See "Creating reservations.")
5. What do you have to do to a DHCP server that belongs to a domain to ensure that it will start up? (See "Authorizing DHCP Servers.")

PART

III

Saturday Afternoon Part Review

1. What are some of the common configuration options that DHCP can configure on a client computer?

2. How can you use DHCP and still ensure that a computer always uses the same IP address?

3. How can you use DHCP to configure client computers to use a WINS or DNS server?

4. How do you configure two WINS servers to exchange name-to-IP address mappings with each other?

5. How can you use the WINS snap-in to manage more than one WINS server at once?

6. How do you ensure that WINS clients can look up the IP addresses of servers that aren't compatible with WINS?

7. What type of DNS record allows another computer to determine the IP address of your company's e-mail server?

8. How can your DNS server help resolve Internet host names that are not contained within its database?

9. What type of DNS record allows a computer to have a nickname?

10. How does a computer decide whether or not data should be sent to the computer's default gateway?

11. What protocol does a computer use to determine the physical address of another computer?

12. What TCP/IP protocol does a computer use when it wants to ensure that data transmissions are received by the destination computer?

13. What piece of information allows a computer to determine which portion of an IP address identifies a network and which identifies a computer?

14. What tool enables you to apply a security template to a computer by using a batch file?

15. Why are security templates better than configuring security on individual computers?

16. How does the Security Configuration Manager enable you to analyze the result of applying several security templates?

17. How do you configure domain security policies?

18. What are three major classes of security policies?

19. What effect does a policy have when it is undefined?

20. How can you create your own security templates?

PART

IV

Saturday
Evening

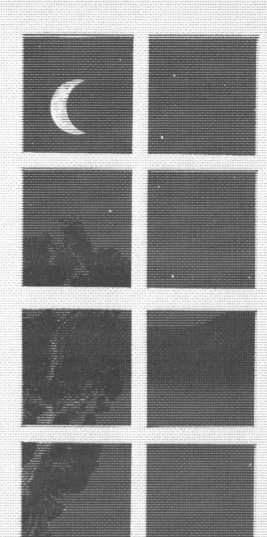

Managing Internet Information Services

Session Checklist

✔ How IIS works

✔ How to add Web sites

✔ How to add File Transfer Protocol sites

✔ How IIS manages e-mail and network news protocols

**30 Min.
To Go**

Internet Information Services (IIS) is included with every copy of Windows Server 2003. IIS provides a complete solution for delivering information to users across the Internet or an intranet. IIS is much more than a Web server, as you'll learn in this session. I'll also show you how to install and manage IIS.

The next session focuses exclusively on managing Web sites with IIS, since Web sites are the most popular way to deliver information across the Internet or on an intranet.

How IIS Works

Windows Server 2003 includes version 6.0 of IIS, the most powerful version to date. IIS acts as a one-stop solution for Internet information, allowing your servers to provide information in the four most popular protocols. IIS also includes Active Server Pages (ASP), a powerful software development technology that enables programmers to quickly create interactive Web applications.

Since ASP is primarily important to software developers, I won't talk about it in this book. If you want to learn about ASP, visit Microsoft's Web site at `msdn.microsoft.com`**.**

Installing IIS

You can install IIS by using the Add/Remove Programs Control Panel utility. Open the utility and select Add/Remove Windows Components, and then select Internet Information Services from the list. Click the Details button to install specific IIS subcomponents, as shown in Figure 17-1.

Figure 17-1   *Installing IIS subcomponents*

You can save space on your servers by installing only the IIS subcomponents that you plan to use. The subcomponents are:

- **Common Files.** This subcomponent is required for all IIS installations because it contains files that are used by all of the IIS subcomponents.

- **Documentation.** This subcomponent includes HTML-based documentation for IIS. If you're not familiar with IIS, you should install the documentation so that it is readily available.

- **File Transfer Protocol (FTP) Service.** This subcomponent allows IIS to be an FTP server, enabling users to upload and download files to and from the server.

- **FrontPage 2000 Server Extensions.** Microsoft FrontPage 2000 has special capabilities that are available only when this subcomponent is installed on your server, such as the ability to publish Web sites directly to the Web server.

- **Internet Information Services Snap-In.** This subcomponent enables you to manage IIS using the Microsoft Management Console.

- **Internet Services Manager (HTML).** This subcomponent enables you to manage IIS using your Web browser.

- **NNTP Service.** This subcomponent allows IIS to host Internet newsgroups, which act as public discussion forums, using the Network News Transport Protocol, or NNTP.

- **SMTP Service.** This subcomponent allows IIS to work with e-mail using the Simple Mail Transport Protocol, or SMTP. Specifically, this subcomponent allows software developers to create Web sites capable of sending e-mail and allows a limited amount of functionality for the server to process e-mail that it receives. This service does not provide a complete e-mail solution like Microsoft Exchange Server.

- **Visual InterDev RAD Remote Deployment.** This subcomponent is required if your software developers use Microsoft Visual InterDev to develop and deploy Web sites.

- **World Wide Web Service.** This subcomponent allows IIS to be a Web server, providing users with access to files and Web pages by using the HyperText Transport Protocol, or HTTP.

Managing IIS

You manage IIS using a Microsoft Management Console snap-in named Internet Services Manager, as shown in Figure 17-2. Windows provides a console preconfigured with the correct snap-in; you can find the preconfigured console under the Administrative Tools folder on the Start menu.

Figure 17-2 *Managing IIS with the MMC snap-in*

You can also manage some IIS functions by using a Web-based administrative interface, if you selected that subcomponent when you installed IIS. The Web-based administrative interface provides a convenient way to manage IIS without having to install special software. You just have to launch your Web browser and point it to the IIS server.

No matter which way you choose to administer IIS, you can create new Web sites, File Transfer Protocol (FTP) sites, Simple Mail Transport Protocol (SMTP) sites, and Network News Transport Protocol (NNTP) sites.

Web Sites

**20 Min.
To Go**

Configuring an IIS Web site enables IIS to act as a Web server. Web sites are the most common use for IIS. IIS can actually act as several Web servers at once because each Web site you create acts as a *virtual server*.

Let's take World Metro Bank as an example. The bank wants to maintain a public Web site, www.worldmetrobank.com, where new customers can learn about the products and services the bank offers. The bank also wants to maintain a Web site, named customers.worldmetrobank.com, just for existing customers. Both Web sites can be hosted on a single Windows Server 2003 running IIS — with each site implemented as a separate virtual Web server.

Make sure your server can handle the number of users who will try to access your Web sites. You may actually need several servers to handle a single Web site if a large number of users (say, a thousand at once) will be regularly trying to access that site.

Once you create a new Web site, you can modify a number of its properties to customize the site's behavior. Figure 17-3 shows the Properties dialog box for a Web site.

Figure 17-3 Web site properties

When you install IIS, it automatically creates a Web site named Default Web Site. You can use that Web site as a starting point, renaming it if you wish to meet your needs. You can also create additional Web sites, and you can even delete the Default Web Site if you don't need it.

Session 18 goes into more detail on managing Web sites with IIS.

File Transfer Protocol Sites

The Internet's File Transfer Protocol, or FTP, was the primary way Internet users sent files to one another when the Internet was young. Today, users are more

Part IV — Saturday Evening
Session 17

likely to attach files to an e-mail or access them through a Web server. Many organizations still use FTP for backward compatibility, though, and IIS provides the ability to act as an FTP server.

Just as IIS can act as several Web servers using virtual servers, it can also act as several different FTP servers using virtual FTP servers, or FTP sites. IIS also creates an FTP site when you install IIS (if you selected the FTP subcomponent). That FTP site is named Default FTP Site, and you can modify it or delete it to suit your needs.

FTP sites are managed using the IIS MMC snap-in or using the Web-based administrative interface. FTP sites have a much simpler Properties dialog box, as shown in Figure 17-4 because FTP sites provide less overall functionality than Web sites.

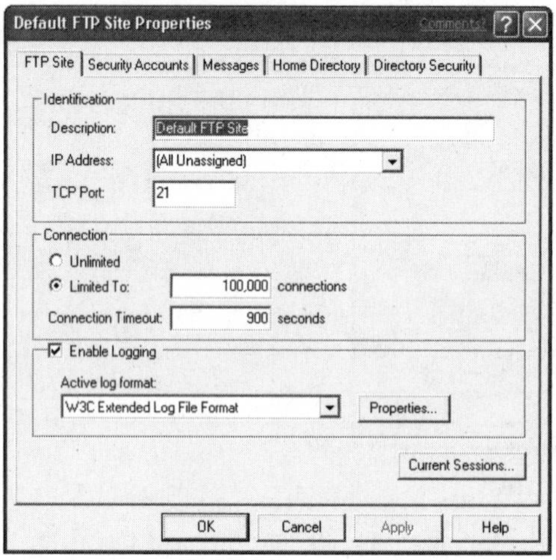

Figure 17-4 FTP site properties

The main thing you need to configure on an FTP site is its home directory. When users log on to the FTP server, they have access to the files and folders in the home directory. The Default FTP Site's home directory is c:\inetpub\ftproot, and you can change that configuration if you want to.

Another configuration item is the FTP site's directory security. By default, IIS allows anonymous access to the FTP server, which means users don't have to provide a user name or password. You can modify the directory security to require that users provide a valid user name and password in order to upload or download files. You can also modify the file permissions on the files in the FTP site's home directory. By modifying the file permissions, you can designate files as read-only or restrict access to specific users.

Securing Web Access

Many companies, including the fictional World Metro Bank, are concerned about security. Web pages are being used to transmit very sensitive information, especially in the case of a bank's Web site. IIS provides the technology necessary to secure your Web pages, protecting them from electronic eavesdropping. The technology is called Secure Sockets Layer (SSL) encryption, which works with the HTTP protocol to provide secure, encrypted transmission of Web pages.

Secure Web pages are referred to by the HTTPS protocol in their address. For example, https://secure.worldmetrobank.com. Before IIS can serve up secure Web pages, though, the server needs a digital encryption certificate. You can use the IIS MMC snap-in to create a new certificate request. Just display a Web site's properties, select the Directory Security tab, and click the Certificates button.

The Create New Certificate Wizard, shown in the figure, collects the information necessary to create a certificate request. The request must then be sent to a certificate authority like VeriSign (www.verisign.com), who is responsible for issuing the actual digital certificate.

The Create New Certificate Wizard

Your company can also set up its own certificate authority. I'll show you how in Session 28, where I'll also give you more information on how digital certificates work.

Part IV — Saturday Evening

Session 17

Simple Mail Transport Protocol Sites

When you install the SMTP Service subcomponent of IIS, IIS gains limited e-mail capabilities. IIS' e-mail capabilities are primarily intended to allow software developers to create Web sites that send e-mail. For example, World Metro Bank's Web site might send a confirmation e-mail whenever a customer submits a request for product information. IIS' SMTP Service also provides limited capabilities for processing incoming e-mail, although a software developer must still write program code to tell IIS how to handle the incoming e-mail.

When you install the SMTP Service subcomponent, IIS creates a Default SMTP virtual server. Like FTP and Web sites, IIS can run multiple SMTP virtual servers, although one is usually sufficient to handle the e-mail needs of a single server. You use the IIS MMC snap-in to modify the properties of an SMTP site, as shown in Figure 17-5.

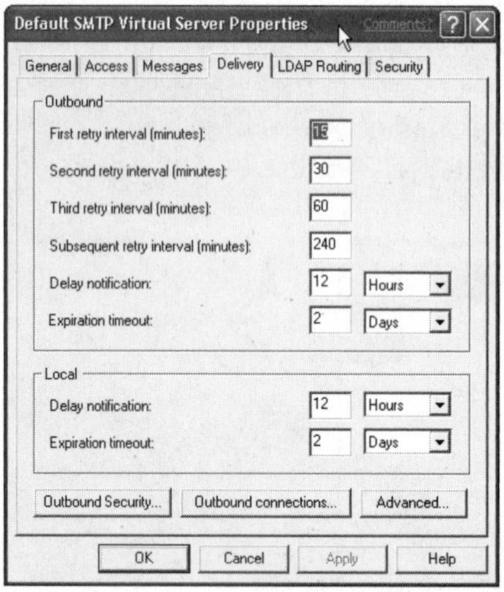

Figure 17-5   *SMTP site properties*

You need to modify the Default SMTP virtual server properties to fit your environment. Specifically, you need to configure security on the virtual server so that only authorized users can send e-mail with it.

Never use the default security settings on an SMTP virtual server. They allow anyone to send e-mail through the server, turning your server into a means for unauthorized users to send unsolicited bulk e-mail (called *spam*).

Configuring an SMTP virtual server usually requires a software developer because the configuration has to match the way the developer intends to use the virtual server to send e-mail or process received e-mail.

Network News Transport Protocol Sites

**10 Min.
To Go**

In the early days of the Internet, USENET newsgroups were an easy way for multiple users to take part in discussions. Today, newsgroups are simply called "newsgroups" or "Internet newsgroups," but they serve the same function: providing a way for users to share ideas and information with one another.

Newsgroups are like electronic bulletin boards. Users post a message to the newsgroup, and other users can retrieve that message, read it, and reply to it. Users must have a news reader application that uses the Network News Transport Protocol (NNTP) to send and retrieve messages to and from a news server. The news server provides a central repository for the newsgroup messages, giving users a single place where they can access messages.

IIS can run one or more virtual NNTP servers, each of which allows the server to become a news server. IIS can retrieve newsgroup messages from other news servers, too, providing your users with a local news server for nationally or internationally available newsgroups.

IIS newsgroups can be managed with the IIS MMC snap-in. When you install the NNTP Service subcomponent, IIS creates a Default NNTP virtual server, which you can reconfigure to meet your needs. The Properties dialog box for an NNTP virtual server is shown in Figure 17-6.

A discussion of configuring and managing NNTP virtual servers is beyond the scope of this book. News servers often require large amounts of hard disk space and memory to do their jobs; you should review the IIS documentation for tips on using NNTP virtual servers.

Default NNTP Virtual Server Properties

General | Access | Settings | Security |

☑ Allow client posting
  ☑ Limit post size (KB):   1000
  ☑ Limit connection size (MB):   20
☑ Allow feed posting
  ☑ Limit post size (KB):   1500
  ☑ Limit connection size (MB):   40
☑ Allow servers to pull news articles from this server
☑ Allow control messages

SMTP server for moderated groups:

Default moderator domain:

Administrator e-mail account:
Admin@Corp.com

        OK   Cancel   Apply   Help

Figure 17-6 *NNTP virtual server properties*

Done!

REVIEW

In this session, you learned how IIS works with Web sites, FTP sites, SMTP sites, and NNTP sites. You learned how to create new sites, and what capabilities are available with each type of site. You also learned how IIS can ensure the confidentiality of the information it transmits by using SSL encryption technologies.

QUIZ YOURSELF

1. What type of site enables users to retrieve HTML pages from a server? (See "Web Sites.")

2. What protocol ensures that Web pages remain secure while they are transmitted to a user? (See "Web Sites.")

3. What types of sites enable users to download software from a server? (See "Web Sites" and "File Transfer Protocol Sites.")

4. What e-mail capabilities does IIS include? (See "Simple Mail Transport Protocol Sites.")

5. What kinds of public discussions can IIS handle? (See "Network News Transport Protocol Sites.")

SESSION

18

Managing Web Sites

Session Checklist

✔ How to create new Web sites

✔ How to configure Web site properties

✔ How to manage Web site security

**30 Min.
To Go**

A s you learned in the previous session, Windows Server 2003 includes Internet Information Services (IIS), a fully functional platform for publishing information by using the Internet. While IIS supports a number of Internet protocols, its most common use is to create and manage Web sites. Web sites provide information by using the HyperText Transport Protocol, or HTTP, which users can access by using a Web browser such as Internet Explorer.

In this session, you'll learn how to configure multiple Web sites on IIS, and how to manage the properties and security settings of those Web sites.

Creating a Web Site

As you learned in the previous session, you can use the Internet Services Manager console to create new Web sites in IIS. IIS includes the ability to host multiple Web sites on a single server, and the console enables you to manage each of those virtual Web sites independently.

The challenge of multiple sites

Take a moment to think about what it means to host multiple Web sites on a single server. When users on the Internet try to reach a Web server, their Web browser uses the Domain Name Service (DNS) protocol to translate the Web server's name into an IP address. For example, the Web site `www.braincore.net` uses the IP address 205.217.9.61.

You learned about DNS in Session 14.

Once the Web browser knows the IP address, it attempts to contact the Web server on TCP port 80, which is the default port used by the HTTP protocol. IIS receives the request and responds with the appropriate Web page.

When a server hosts multiple Web sites, though, it's as if the server is running multiple copies of IIS at the same time. So when the server receives an HTTP request from a browser, which copy of IIS will respond to the request? After all, each copy is monitoring the same IP address and TCP port!

The solution for multiple sites

Actually, the different virtual Web sites *don't* monitor the same IP address and port. When you create multiple Web sites on IIS, IIS has to be able to distinguish between them, so it can tell which Web site should receive incoming HTTP requests. IIS uses three properties to distinguish between Web sites, and each Web site must have a unique combination of those three properties. They are

- **IP address.** If your Windows Server 2003 computer is configured with multiple IP addresses, then those addresses can be split up among your virtual Web sites.

- **Port.** While 80 is the default HTTP port, you can tell any virtual Web site to listen to a different port number.

- **Host header.** A feature of the HTTP 1.1 protocol, a host header tells the Web server which Web site the browser is trying to access. The Web server can use that information to direct the incoming request to the proper virtual Web site.

Your virtual Web sites can use any combination of these three properties to be unique. For example, all of your sites might use the same IP address and port number, so long as they each define a different host header. Or they might all use the same IP address and host header, but a different port number. In the next three sections, I show you how to configure each of these three properties.

IP address

Normally, your Windows Server 2003 computers are configured with only a single IP address. For most uses, that's all they need. But you can configure them to respond to multiple IP addresses, which enables you to assign different IP addresses to your IIS Web sites. To configure your server with multiple IP addresses, follow these steps:

1. Open the properties for your server's local area network (LAN) connection.

2. Double-click the TCP/IP protocol to display the protocol's properties.

3. Click the Advanced button to display the Advanced TCP/IP Settings dialog box, shown in Figure 18-1.

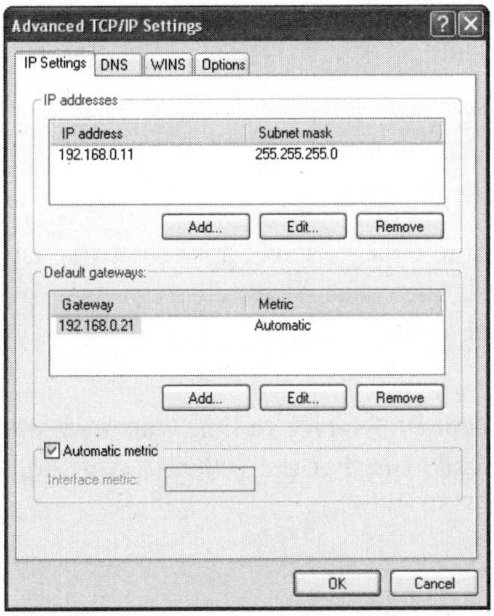

Figure 18-1 *Advanced TCP/IP properties*

4. The IP Addresses list is shown at the top of the dialog box. Click the Add button to add a new address, or highlight an address and click the Remove button to remove an address.

5. Click OK to close each dialog box and save your changes.

**20 Min.
To Go**

Once you configure your server with multiple IP addresses, you can modify the properties of a Web site so that the Web site uses a different IP address. Simply right-click a Web site in the Internet Information Services console to display its properties. As shown in Figure 18-2, you can select the IP address that the Web site will use, or you can select All Unassigned.

Figure 18-2 *Modifying a Web site's IP address*

Only the IP addresses that you configure on your server appear on the list. If you select All Unassigned from the list, then that Web site listens to all IP addresses that you've configured on your server and haven't specifically assigned to another Web site.

Make sure you modify your DNS server so that your Web site's name resolves to the IP address that the Web site is using.

Port number

Port numbers are easier to configure than IP addresses. You just have to configure the properties of a Web site, as shown in Figure 18-3, and modify the port number.

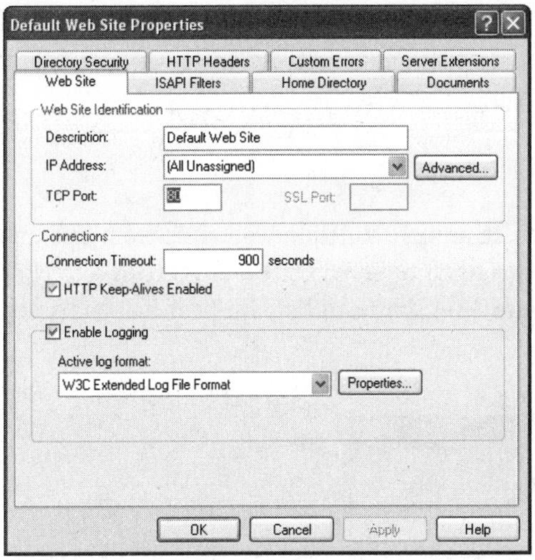

Figure 18-3 *Modifying a Web site's TCP port number*

Port numbers might seem like the easiest way to identify Web sites, since you can just assign a different port number to each site. From a configuration standpoint, that's true, but port numbers definitely make it harder for users to find your Web sites.

When a user types a Uniform Resource Locator (URL) into her Web browser, she doesn't have to specify a port number — the browser assumes that she wants to use port 80, which is the default HTTP port. For example, if you type `http://www.braincore.net` into your Web browser, the browser uses port 80 to contact the Web server.

If you configure your Web sites to use a different port, your users have to specify the port number in the URL. For example, if you created a second Web site at `www.braincore.net` and used port 81, your users would have to type `http://www.braincore.net:81` into their browsers.

Typing a port number isn't intuitive, and not many users know about port numbers or how to include them in a URL. Also, if a user doesn't know the correct port number to type, there's no way for him to look it up except to call you or send you an e-mail. That's because TCP/IP doesn't provide any automated resolution service for port numbers, as it does with DNS for IP addresses.

The best time to use a different port number is for internal, administrative Web sites. For example, Microsoft Application Center 2000 software sets up an administrative Web site when you install it. The Web site is intended only for system administrators, and it uses a port number like 4225. Since the site is intended to be used only by experienced administrators, Microsoft can safely assume that they'll know how to type the port number into the URL.

Host header

Host headers are the third way to distinguish multiple Web sites from one another. To modify the host header a Web site uses, open the site's properties and click the Advanced button. As shown in Figure 18-4, you can list the host headers associated with the site.

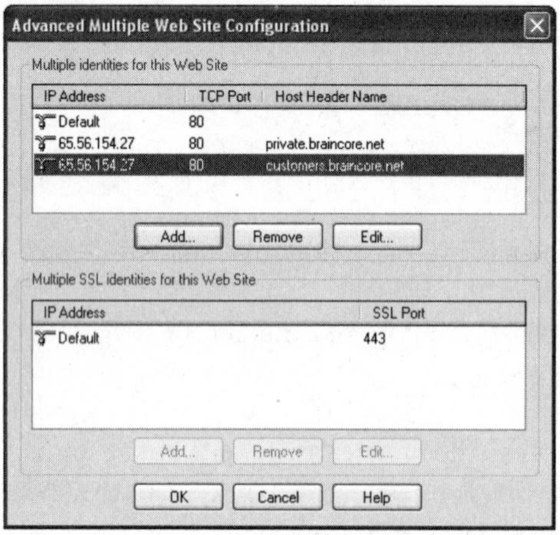

Figure 18-4   *Modifying a Web site's host headers*

Host headers allow multiple Web sites on the same computer to use the same IP address and port number and still direct users to the correct site. Those are important benefits, because unique IP addresses can be difficult to obtain, and I've already discussed the disadvantages of using port numbers other than 80. Host headers seem to offer a great solution. Here's how they work:

1. Bob types a URL into his Web browser — for example, `http://private.braincore.net`. Jane types a different URL into her Web browser — say, `http://www.braincore.net`.

2. Both Web browsers use DNS to translate the names into IP addresses. In this case, both browsers resolve the URLs to the same IP address.

3. Because neither Bob nor Jane typed a port number in the URL, both of their browsers attempt to contact the server's IP address on port 80. Both

browsers include the original URL in the HTTP request headers that they send to the server.

4. The server receives the two HTTP requests and examines their headers. By reading the original URL from the headers, IIS can determine that the requests are for two different virtual Web sites and send the appropriate Web pages to Bob and Jane.

Host headers have a couple of disadvantages that can prevent you from using them effectively:

- Host headers are defined in version 1.1 of the HTTP protocol. Most newer browsers support HTTP 1.1, but older browsers do not. If your Web server receives a request from a non-1.1 browser, that request won't contain host headers, and so IIS will direct the user to the `Default Web Site`.

- Many users access the Internet through a corporate proxy server. If the proxy server does not support HTTP 1.1, it removes the host headers, even if the user's browser sent them. Most newer proxy servers support HTTP 1.1, although many enable an administrator to turn that support on or off.

- If you use reporting software to analyze your Web site's performance and utilization, host headers may confuse the reports and make them meaningless. Check with your reporting software vendor to make sure they support the use of host headers.

Managing Web Site Operations

Once you've set up a Web site, you can configure different operating parameters to customize the way the site behaves. For example, you might want to change the folder that the Web site pulls Web pages from — known as the Web site's *home directory*. The Web site's properties dialog box contains several tabs to enable you to customize this and other properties, as shown in Figure 18-5.

Some of the properties you can configure include:

- The Web site's home directory.
- Whether or not the Web site logs its activities to a log file.
- Custom error messages, so that errors fit the "look and feel" of your Web site.
- The default page for each folder in your Web site. Normally, IIS looks for `default.htm` or `default.asp`, but you can add additional filenames if you want.

Figure 18-5   *Default Web Site Properties dialog*

When you make changes to a Web sites' properties, the changes take place immediately. If your changes will significantly affect the way the Web site works, you might want to stop the Web site, to prevent users from accessing it while you make your changes.

To stop a Web site, simply right-click its name in the console and select Stop from the pop-up menu. When you stop a Web site, it immediately stops responding to user requests, even ones that it's in the middle of processing.

A more polite way to take a Web site offline is to first pause the site. You pause a Web site by right-clicking it and selecting Pause from the pop-up menu. Once paused, the Web site does not accept any new requests, but it continues processing the ones it has already accepted. Wait several minutes for those requests to finish, and then stop the Web site.

Avoid cutting users off in the middle of a request by pausing Web sites whenever possible, enabling them to finish what they're doing, and then stopping the Web site.

When you're done making changes to a Web site, you can place it back in service by right-clicking it and selecting Start from the pop-up menu.

**10 Min.
To Go**

Web Site Security

One of the most important concerns any administrator should have is for security, especially for Web servers that are accessed across the Internet. Hackers delight in crashing Web servers, often just to show that they *can*. Larger companies with popular Web sites are the most popular targets, but no Web site is completely safe unless you take steps to secure it.

IIS offers a number of features to protect your Web sites:

- You can modify a Web site's properties to allow only certain IP addresses to access the site. That's useful if you need only a small group of computers to use the Web site. You can also deny access to specific IP addresses, such as those you know to be used by hackers.

- You can configure IIS to require a user name and password for anyone attempting to access the site.

- You can protect specific files and folders within a Web site by applying file permissions to them. You can do so only if your files are stored on a hard drive that uses the NTFS file system. For more information about file and folder permissions, read Session 6.

- You can configure IIS to use digital certificates to encrypt data, which prevents electronic eavesdroppers from intercepting information sent between your Web site and your users' Web browsers.

Configuring IIS security is an advanced topic. For more information or for specific step-by-step procedures, consult the Windows Server 2003 documentation.

**Part IV — Saturday Evening
Session 18**

REVIEW

In this session, you learned how to create and manage Web sites by using Internet Information Services (IIS). You learned how IIS distinguishes multiple Web sites from one another, and how IIS integrates with Windows Server 2003's security features to protect the content of your Web sites.

Done!

Keeping IIS Up To Date

Like any software application, IIS and Windows Server 2003 may contain bugs. Unfortunately, those bugs sometimes enable hackers to gain unauthorized access to your server through IIS. For that reason, it's very important that you keep IIS up to date with all of the latest bug fixes released by Microsoft.

You can easily update your IIS server by using the Windows Update Web site. Just log on to your server and browse to windowsupdate. microsoft.com. The site can scan your server and install any fixes that your server is missing.

To provide even better protection for your servers, don't install IIS at all unless you really need it. Windows Server 2003 installs IIS by default, but if you don't plan on using a server as a Web server (or one of IIS' other functions), remove IIS. That way your server won't be made vulnerable by any bugs in the IIS software.

QUIZ YOURSELF

1. What three pieces of information distinguish Web sites from one another on the same server? (See "Creating a Web Site.")

2. How do you prevent anonymous users from accessing a Web site? (See "Web Site Security.")

3. How can you ensure that IIS is not vulnerable to attacks from hackers on the Internet? (See "Keeping IIS Up To Date.")

4. How can you change the folder that a Web site uses as its home directory? (See "Managing Web Site Operations.")

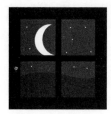

Managing Routing and Remote Access Services

Session Checklist

✔ How Routing and Remote Access Services works

✔ How to configure a server to accept incoming connections

✔ How to manage remote access security and profiles

✔ How to manage remote access connections

**30 Min.
To Go**

I n today's business world, more and more employees do business remotely. Whether it's a salesperson who needs to check in with the main office while he's on the road, or a telecommuter who's working from her home office, remote business is a part of almost every company's technological needs.

Windows Server 2003 enables you to meet those needs by providing Routing and Remote Access Services (RRAS). RRAS provides a variety of technologies that allow a Windows Server 2003 to act as the gateway to your corporate network for remote users. In this session, you'll learn how RRAS works, and how to configure it to accept incoming connections. You'll also learn about RRAS' security features, which help protect your network from remote intruders.

How RRAS Works

On a network, a *router* works like a traffic cop, directing network traffic to its destination. Networks can also contain *bridges,* which translate one type of network traffic to another. Figure 19-1 shows a router moving traffic between several network segments, and a bridge connecting a segment that uses a different networking protocol.

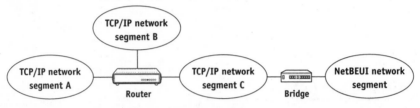

Figure 19-1 *Routers and bridges on a network*

RRAS is capable of acting as both a router and a bridge. Because RRAS can bridge between completely dissimilar types of networks — for example, between a local area network and a dial-up connection — it is also referred to as a *gateway*.

 You'll learn how RRAS can act as a standard network router in Session 22.

The most common use for RRAS is as a gateway, enabling remote users to connect to your corporate network. That's where the "Remote Access" part of RRAS' name comes from. RRAS provides two primary ways for remote users to connect:

- Users can dial in to a modem that is connected directly to the RRAS server. This is a traditional dial-up connection. Users can utilize regular phone lines (referred to as POTS, or Plain Old Telephone Service), or they can use higher-bandwidth phone lines such as ISDN (Integrated Services Digital Network).

- Users can connect over a local (or wide) area network using a virtual private network, or VPN. VPNs enable users to use public networks like the Internet to connect to RRAS, while encrypting the data transmitted between the user and RRAS to ensure privacy.

RRAS for dial-up connections

Figure 19-2 shows how RRAS can be used to accept dial-up connections from remote users.

Figure 19-2   *Accepting dial-up connections with RRAS*

Windows Server 2003 gives you the ability to connect several modems to a single server. Using products from companies like Digi (www.digi.com), you can connect up to 128 modems to a single server. Such a large number of modems is often referred to as a *modem bank*. The ability to use modem banks is important because each modem provides a connection for a single user. If you want to enable multiple users to connect, you need multiple modems.

Dial-up connections have disadvantages and advantages:

- Dial-up connections are relatively inexpensive because modems and POTS phone lines are inexpensive. However, you pay for POTS lines even when they aren't in use, so make sure you don't purchase more than you'll need.

- POTS lines are considered fairly secure. Because data travels through the phone company's private network, data isn't subject to electronic eavesdropping. However, serious hackers can physically tap into phone lines to eavesdrop on the data the line is carrying.

- POTS lines provide a maximum connection speed of 53 kilobytes per second (Kbps), and you can achieve that maximum only if your company and your remote users have top-quality, noise-free phone lines. Typical connection speeds range from 33 Kbps to 50 Kbps. Compare that to the speed of a slow local area network — 10 *mega*bits per second (Mbps) — and you'll realize that connections made over POTS lines are pretty slow.

What about that 56K modem you have? Government regulations and the capabilities of America's telephone system limit actual speeds to 53 Kbps for downloaded data, and 33 Kbps for uploaded data.

- ISDN lines provide connections of up to 128 Kbps, which is still pretty slow compared to a local area network. ISDN is also expensive and difficult to configure.

- POTS lines are available almost everywhere. ISDN phone lines are available in most cities, although you usually have to special order them from the local phone company. The ready availability of POTS lines make them the choice for business travelers because hotel rooms can almost always provide a POTS connection.

RRAS for VPN connections

VPNs have been gaining in popularity as the Internet has become more popular and easy to access. The Internet originally provided a great way for users to connect to remote networks. All users needed to do was connect to an Internet Service Provider (ISP), and they could access the resources of any network that was connected to the Internet. However, companies quickly realized that the Internet was unregulated and unprotected, and allowing anyone on the Internet to access the company network was foolish.

VPNs provide a way to use the public Internet as a private network. Figure 19-3 shows an RRAS server accepting a VPN connection over the Internet.

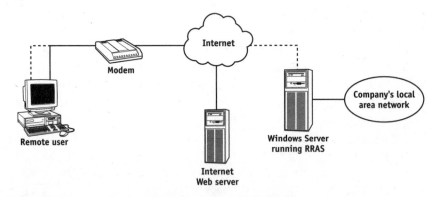

Figure 19-3 *Accepting VPN connections with RRAS*

In Figure 19-3, the remote user is using a modem to connect to an ISP, which provides a connection to the public Internet. The user's computer is connecting to two Internet-based resources, shown by the two lines coming from the user's laptop computer. Both connections are passed by the modem to the Internet, where the data travels to its destination.

The solid lines represent unencrypted data, which is being used to access a public Web server on the Internet. The dashed lines represent traffic that is encrypted with a VPN. That connection is used to connect to the company's VPN server. The VPN server accepts the connection, decrypts the traffic, and passes the now-unencrypted traffic to the company network.

VPNs provide a number of advantages to the remote user:

- High-speed Internet connectivity is becoming more readily available. Hotels are offering high-speed access in business-class hotel rooms, and technologies like Digital Subscriber Lines (DSL) are providing home users with connection speeds in excess of 640 Kbps. VPNs allow these high-speed Internet connections to act as high-speed private connections to the company network, while still permitting users to access Internet-based resources like Web servers.

- VPNs encrypt the data that passes through them. The encryption ensures that only the two endpoints of the VPN — the remote user and the company's network — can read the data in the VPN.

- VPNs work equally well over phone lines or high-speed connections, providing the highest possible security for remote users' connections.

VPNs can be complicated to set up and manage. I'll show you more about VPNs in Session 21.

Configuring RRAS

**20 Min.
To Go**

RRAS is an optional component that must be installed from the Windows Server 2003 CD-ROM. To install RRAS, open the Add/Remove Programs application from the Control Panel, and click Add/Remove Windows Components. Locate Routing and Remote Access on the list, place a checkmark next to it, and click OK.

When you install RRAS, Windows adds a Routing and Remote Access console icon to your Administrative Tools folder on the Start menu. The first time you open the console, you need to configure RRAS. To do so, right-click the Routing and Remote Access item in the console's left pane, and select Configure and Enable Routing and Remote Access from the pop-up menu.

The Routing and Remote Access Setup Wizard helps you configure your server for the appropriate RRAS tasks. For example, you can configure the server as a

Remote Access Server, which allows the server to accept incoming dial-up connections from remote users. You can also configure the server as a Virtual Private Network Server, which allows it to accept connections from remote users via a VPN.

If you want your server to accept both dial-up and VPN connections, select Manual Configuration in the Wizard. Doing so enables you to configure both types of connections on the server.

Configuring dial-up connections

Before you configure new dial-up connections, you need to attach and configure the modems that RRAS will use for the connections. The modems must be compatible with Windows Server 2003, and you should install them according to the modem manufacturer's instructions.

Once the modems are attached, follow these steps to create new dial-up connections in RRAS:

1. Open the RRAS console.

2. Locate your server's name in the left pane of the console.

3. Expand your server's configuration hierarchy.

4. Right-click Ports and select Properties from the pop-up menu. RRAS displays the available ports, which should include the modems you installed.

5. Select an available port and click Configure.

6. Place a check next to "Remote access connections only (inbound)". Clear the other check boxes on the dialog box.

7. Click OK to close the dialog boxes.

You can now click on the Remote Access Clients item in the console to view clients that have connected to your RRAS server. You can view the ports that you configured by clicking on the Ports item. Double-click any port (in the right pane) to view the port's status or to reset the port.

If a modem is "hung" and won't respond, you can double-click it in the Ports list and reset it by clicking the Reset button on the Port Status dialog box.

Selecting a VPN Protocol

RRAS sets up five L2TP ports and five PPTP ports so that you don't have to select which protocol to use — you can use both. But you'll still need to decide which protocol to configure on your user's client computers.

Both L2TP and PPTP offer *tunneling* capabilities. In other words, both are capable of creating a virtual network connection across the Internet. PPTP also includes built-in encryption capabilities, making it a complete virtual *private* network solution. PPTP also requires very little configuration on the client or server, making it easy to set up.

L2TP tunnels can be encrypted using the IP Security, or IPSec, protocol. IPSec encryption generally requires the use of digital certificates, which makes an L2TP/IPSec VPN much more difficult to configure. However, IPSec provides stronger encryption capabilities than those built into PPTP, so the additional configuration effort results in a somewhat more secure VPN connection.

Generally, the type of VPN client you use determines which protocol you use the most. Microsoft client operating systems have included PPTP support since Windows 95 but have supported L2TP only since Windows 2000. Most non-Microsoft VPN clients, such as those from Cisco, only support L2TP.

Configuring VPN connections

You can configure new VPN connections in much the same way as dial-up connections. In fact, when you choose to manually configure RRAS in the RRAS Setup Wizard, RRAS automatically creates ten VPN ports for you. Five ports are configured to accept L2TP connections, and five are configured to accept PPTP connections. All are configured to accept incoming connections from remote clients.

L2TP and PPTP are VPN protocols. L2TP, the Layer 2 Tunneling Protocol, is a newer VPN protocol that is supported by many non-Microsoft VPN clients. PPTP, the Point-to-Point Tunneling Protocol, is a Microsoft VPN protocol that is supported by Windows 95 and later versions of Windows.

When you right-click the Ports item in the RRAS console and select Properties, you'll notice that only one L2TP port and one PPTP port are listed. Select either one and click Configure, and the configuration dialog box shows you that each port is configured for five instances. That's why each port type appears five times on the port list. If you want to accept more than five incoming PPTP connections, simply configure that port type to include more instances.

A powerful server with no other responsibilities can generally handle several dozen VPN connections at once. I've used a dual-processor Pentium III server to successfully handle over sixty simultaneous PPTP connections.

RRAS Security and Policies

RRAS includes a complete security system that enables you to specify who can and cannot connect to an RRAS server. RRAS also includes powerful security protocols that allow it to identify the users who attempt to connect to it.

**10 Min.
To Go**

RRAS security

RRAS enables users to log on to dial-up or VPN connections by using their Windows usernames and passwords, smart cards, or a variety of other techniques. You choose which methods RRAS allows by right-clicking your RRAS server in the RRAS console and selecting Properties from the pop-up menu. On the Security tab, you can select the authentication provider and authentication methods that you want to use in your organization.

RRAS policies

If RRAS isn't configured to use a RADIUS server, it uses Remote Access Policies to determine whether or not users can connect to remote access ports. You configure these policies in the RRAS console. By default, all users are permitted to connect to the remote access ports because RRAS starts with a policy that permits it.

RRAS policies can examine several different criteria to determine if a user is allowed to connect:

- You can grant or deny dial-up permission to specific users or user groups.
- You can grant or deny permission during specific hours of the day.
- You can specify that a specific authentication protocol be used.
- You can specify that a specific level of data encryption be used.
- You can apply the policy to specific remote access ports.
- You can also create custom policies for unusual situations.

Using RADIUS

RRAS enables you to use a RADIUS server for authentication. When using a RADIUS (Remote Authentication Dial-In User Service) server, RRAS temporarily accepts all incoming connections and asks for logon credentials, such as a username and password. RRAS passes that information to a RADIUS server, which verifies the individual's right to log on. The RADIUS server tells RRAS whether or not to permit the connection, and RRAS complies.

If you have several RRAS servers, a single RADIUS server can work with all of them, enabling you to centralize your remote access security on the RADIUS server, rather than individually configuring each RRAS server.

Windows Server 2003 includes a RADIUS server, called the Internet Authentication Service, or IAS. You'll learn more about IAS in Session 20.

For example, you might specify a policy that grants dial-up permission to all users between the hours of 5 p.m. and 6 a.m.

Remote Access Policies are listed in the RRAS console in the order that RRAS considers them. You can change the order by dragging policies to the desired order within the list. When a user attempts to connect, RRAS starts examining its policies. If a user does not match the conditions of the policy, then RRAS ignores the policy. If the user matches the conditions of the policy — for example, the policy specifies a user group that the user belongs to — then RRAS allows or denies the connection based on the policy. If RRAS examines all of its policies without finding one that applies to the user, the user is denied access.

Done!

REVIEW

In this session, you learned about Windows Server 2003's Routing and Remote Access Services, or RRAS. You learned how RRAS can be used to accept dial-up or VPN connections, and you learned about the different types of connections, including POTS, ISDN, L2TP, and PPTP. You learned how to install and configure RRAS, and you learned how to configure RRAS security and profiles.

Part IV — Saturday Evening
Session 19

Quiz Yourself

1. How can you prevent users from connecting to dial-up connections during business hours? (See "RRAS Security and Policies.")

2. What VPN protocol does Windows 95 support? (See "Selecting a VPN Protocol.")

3. What are the advantages of POTS over ISDN? (See "RRAS for dial-up connections.")

4. What are the advantages of using VPN connections over dial-up connections? ("See "RRAS for VPN connections.")

5. How can you prevent specific users from accessing dial-up connections on an RRAS server? (See "RRAS Security and Policies.")

Managing the Internet Authentication Service

Session Checklist

✔ How the Internet Authentication Service works

✔ How to configure the Internet Authentication Service

✔ How to use the Internet Authentication Service as a proxy

✔ How to use the Internet Authentication Service to account for remote access utilization

30 Min. To Go

In a large organization, you may be required to set up several Windows Server 2003 computers that use the Routing and Remote Access Service (RRAS) to enable remote users to connect to your network. While RRAS enables you to configure Remote Access Policies on each RRAS server, doing so for a large number of servers can be time-consuming. When changes to your Remote Access Policies occur, as they inevitably will, you'll have to spend even more time reconfiguring each individual server.

As you learned in the previous session, RRAS enables you to use a RADIUS (Remote Authentication Dial-In User Service) server to centralize your remote policies and other RRAS management information. RRAS simply asks the RADIUS server if users are allowed to connect, and the RADIUS server examines its policies and lets the RRAS server know what to do.

Windows Server 2003 includes a RADIUS-compatible server called the Internet Authentication Service (IAS). In this session, you'll learn how IAS works, how to configure it on a Windows Server 2003, and how to manage it in your organization. You'll also learn about some of IAS' advanced features, which can make it an even more valuable component of your network.

How IAS Works

IAS is designed to be installed on a Windows Server 2003 that already has RRAS installed. IAS receives requests from network access servers (NASs), such as RRAS or third-party dial-up products, and uses its local Remote Access Policies to determine whether or not the user is allowed to connect. Here's how the process works in detail:

1. A user attempt to connect to a NAS like RRAS.
2. The user types in his logon credentials, such as his username and password.
3. The NAS transmits the logon credentials to IAS. The NAS includes other details about the connection, such as the phone number the user is calling from (assuming the NAS has the capability of receiving Caller ID information from the phone company), the protocol the user is trying to use, and so forth.

> **RRAS is capable of receiving Caller ID information only when connected to Caller ID-compatible modems. Most third-party dial-up hardware, such as dial-up products from Cisco, is capable of receiving Caller ID information.**

4. IAS validates the username and password against Active Directory. If the username and password aren't valid, IAS instructs the NAS to reject the connection.
5. IAS examines the local Remote Access Policies to determine whether or not the user is allowed to connect. If the policies permit the connection, IAS instructs the NAS to accept it. Otherwise, IAS instructs the NAS to reject the connection.

IAS' strength is that it enables you to use a single IAS server to provide consistent authentication and access policies for any number of remote access servers.

What's a NAS?

The term *network access server*, or NAS, is a generic term used to refer to devices that permit remote users to connect to your network. RRAS, which you learned about in the previous session, allows a Windows Server 2003 computer to be a NAS. Other manufacturers, including 3Com, Cisco, Nortel, and Shiva, sell standalone NAS devices as well.

Because IAS is a standard RADIUS server, it is capable of working with third-party NAS devices as well as with RRAS. That capability enables you to add a variety of remote access devices to your network to meet your organization's specific needs, and continue using IAS to centrally control who is allowed to access your network through those devices.

If you only have one, or maybe two, RRAS servers, you probably don't need an IAS server. If you have more than two RRAS servers, or if you have non-Microsoft NAS devices, use IAS to centralize your remote access authentication and access.

Configuring IAS

IAS doesn't require a lot of complex configuration tasks. Basically, you install the IAS server on a Windows Server 2003 that already has RRAS installed. Then you configure IAS with a list of NAS devices or RRAS servers that will use IAS. IAS automatically uses the Remote Access Policies you configured on the local RRAS server and starts working immediately.

Installing IAS

**20 Min.
To Go**

To install IAS, open the Add/Remove Programs application on the Control Panel. Click Add/Remove Windows Components, and select the Network Services option. Place a checkmark next to Internet Authentication Service (and any other services you want to install), as shown in Figure 20-1.

Networking Services

To add or remove a component, click the check box. A shaded box means that only part of the component will be installed. To see what's included in a component, click Details.

Subcomponents of Networking Services:

☑ 🖳 COM Internet Services Proxy	0.0 MB
☑ 🖳 Domain Name System (DNS)	1.5 MB
☑ 🖳 Dynamic Host Configuration Protocol (DHCP)	0.0 MB
☑ 🖳 Internet Authentication Service	0.0 MB
☑ 🖳 QoS Admission Control Service	0.0 MB
☑ 🖳 Simple TCP/IP Services	0.0 MB
☑ 🖳 Windows Internet Name Service (WINS)	0.9 MB

Description: Enables DCOM (Distributed Component Object Model) to travel over HTTP via the Internet Information Server (IIS).

Total disk space required: 2.6 MB

Space available on disk: 15162.8 MB

Details...

OK   Cancel

Figure 20-1   *Installing IAS*

Click OK, and Windows Server 2003 installs IAS for you. Windows also creates an icon for the Internet Authentication Service console, which you use to manage IAS. The icon can be found under the Administrative Tools folder on the Start menu.

Configuring IAS clients

IAS provides a sensitive service on your network because it enables users to access your network. For that reason, IAS permits only designated NAS devices to utilize IAS services. You determine which NAS devices (including RRAS servers) can use IAS by configuring IAS with a list of RADIUS clients.

The IAS console includes a list of authorized RADIUS clients. To add a client to the list, right-click RADIUS clients and select New Client from the pop-up menu. IAS displays the Add Client dialog box as shown in Figure 20-2.

You need to specify the client's name, the IP address it will use to connect to IAS, and a *shared secret*. The shared secret is just a password that the client uses when it sends authentication requests to IAS. After adding the client to IAS, you also need to configure the NAS with the address of the IAS server and the shared secret.

Follow the instructions provided by your NAS device manufacturer to configure your devices. For information on configuring RRAS to use IAS, see Session 19.

Figure 20-2 *Adding a new RADIUS client to IAS*

When clients send requests to IAS, IAS will check to make sure the shared secret matches, and that the request was sent from the IP address you configured.

Don't allow your RADIUS clients to contact IAS from a different IP address. IAS ignores requests sent from any IP address that isn't on its list of RADIUS clients. And if you change the IP address of your NAS devices, be sure to update the client list in IAS to reflect the change.

Managing IAS

You use the IAS console to manage IAS on a day-to-day basis. Generally, the main thing you need to regularly reconfigure are the Remote Access Policies, which have to change to meet your organization's needs as they grow and evolve.

As shown in Figure 20-3, you can use the IAS console to modify the Remote Access Policies of the IAS server.

The Remote Access Policies IAS uses are the *same ones* that RRAS uses. If you modify the policies in the IAS console, they are modified in the RRAS console and vice versa.

Part IV — Saturday Evening
Session 20

Internet Authentication Service

File   Action   View   Help

Internet Authentication Service (Local)
  Clients
  Remote Access Logging
  Remote Access Policies
  Connection Request Processing

Name	Order
Don't allow users during business hours	1
Allow access if dial-in permission is enabled	2

Figure 20-3   *Remote Access Policies in IAS*

IAS provides a great deal of flexibility in creating Remote Access Policies. Remember, IAS evaluates the policies in the order they are listed in the console. As soon as it finds a policy that matches an incoming connection request, it applies that policy to the request, granting or denying access as appropriate.

For more information on how Remote Access Policies work, see Session 19.

To create a new policy, right-click Remote Access Policies and select New Policy from the pop-up menu. You can also double-click an existing policy to edit it, as shown in Figure 20-4.

Policies can contain a number of parameters, such as the time of day, the user's name, the phone number the user is calling from, and so forth. In the policy shown in Figure 20-4, users are granted access if they call during certain hours on certain days and if the number they are calling from is in the 702 area code.

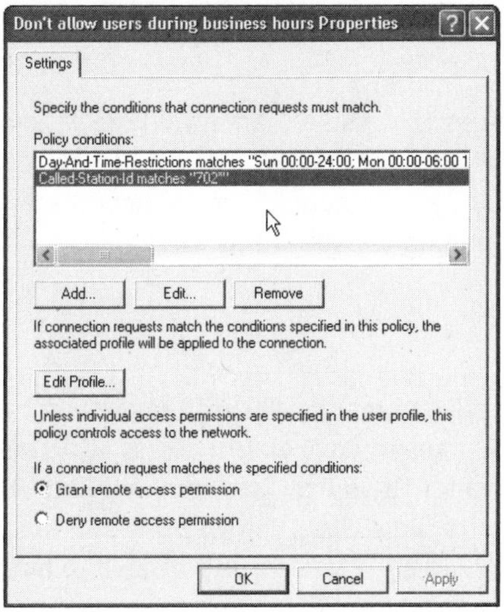

Figure 20-4   *Editing a remote access policy*

Remote Access Policy Conditions

You might not be able to use every policy condition in your environment. For example, the ability to restrict users based on the phone number they are calling from requires that your modems have Caller ID capability, and that your phone lines have the Caller ID service. Different NAS devices also provide different information, which affects the conditions that IAS can examine in a policy.

Consult the documentation that came with your NAS devices to determine what RADIUS information the devices provide to IAS. Then you will know which IAS policy conditions are appropriate for your environment.

Don't use policy conditions that aren't supported by your devices. For example, if you create a policy that enables users only in a certain area code to dial in, and your NAS devices don't send a phone number to IAS, then IAS will deny all requests simply because it can't determine whether or not they're coming from the correct area code.

Advanced IAS Features

IAS includes a number of advanced features that make it an even more valuable component on your network. In Windows Server 2003, IAS introduces new features for RADIUS forwarding, wireless access, and much more. The most important advanced IAS features are RADIUS proxying, and RADIUS accounting.

Using IAS as a RADIUS proxy

In a very large organization, you may have a number of RADIUS servers on the network. For example, World Metro Bank plans to have dial-in access at its larger regional offices, with separate IAS servers for the North American and European divisions. When a European employee visits the U.S.A., however, she will dial into an office that uses a North American IAS server — which won't be able to authenticate the European user.

By using RADIUS proxying, or forwarding, the North American IAS server can forward requests to the European IAS server when necessary.

You configure RADIUS forwarding by creating connection request policies in the IAS console, as shown in Figure 20-5.

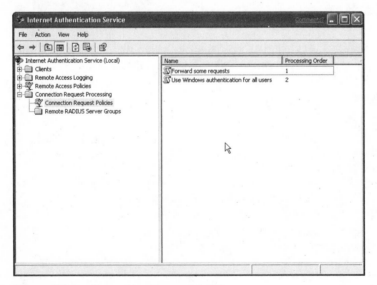

Figure 20-5   *Connection Request Policies*

A connection request policy is similar to a remote access policy because it specifies characteristics of a user, including the number he is calling from, the IP address he is using, his username, and so forth. Unlike a remote access policy, connection request policies specify whether the local IAS server authenticates the connection, or whether the connection is forwarded to another RADIUS server.

When new connections come in, IAS examines its connection request policies. If it finds a policy that matches a new connection, IAS forwards the request or handles the request itself, depending on how the policy is configured.

Using IAS for remote access accounting

10 Min. To Go

By default, IAS creates a log file that contains information about IAS activities. If your NAS devices or RRAS servers are configured to send RADIUS accounting information to IAS, then IAS can include that accounting information in its log.

RADIUS accounting information falls into three categories:

- **Periodic information.** Sent on a regular basis when users remain connected to the NAS device.

- **Logon information.** Sent whenever a user connects or disconnects from a NAS device.

- **Accounting requests.** Sent whenever a NAS device needs to start or stop an accounting session.

By including accounting information in the IAS log file, you can use third-party utilities to process the log files and generate remote access activity reports.

To configure IAS to include accounting information in its log, use the IAS console to view the list of IAS log files. Right-click a log file to edit its properties, as shown in Figure 20-6.

When you include accounting information in the IAS log files, they can grow quickly, especially if you have a lot of remote access activity. The Local File tab of the log file's properties dialog box enables you to configure properties that help keep the log file manageable in size. As shown in Figure 20-7, you can configure IAS to create new log files on a periodic basis, and you can configure a maximum size for each log file.

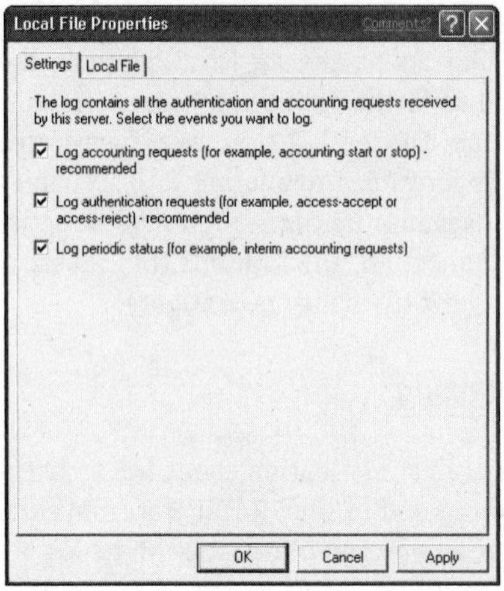

Figure 20-6 *Configuring the log to include accounting information*

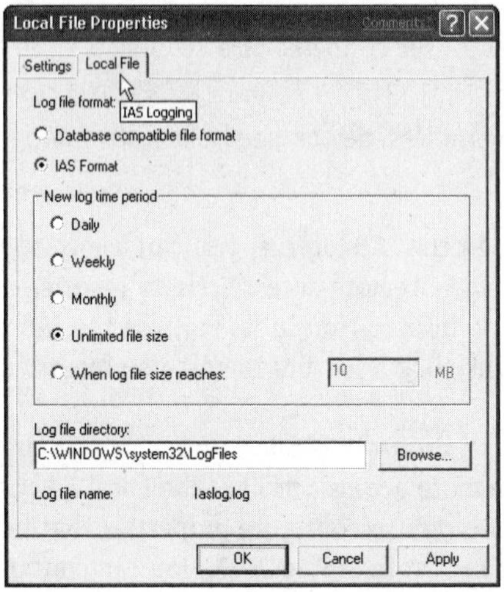

Figure 20-7 *Configuring log file properties*

Done!

REVIEW

In this session, you learned about the Internet Authentication Service (IAS) and how it can be used to provide centralized remote access administration and accounting for a large organization. You learned how to install and configure IAS, and you learned about advanced IAS features like RADIUS proxy and remote access accounting.

QUIZ YOURSELF

1. What kind of information is included in RADIUS accounting? (See "Using IAS for remote access accounting.")
2. How does IAS determine whether to handle a new connection request or forward it to another RADIUS server? (See "Using IAS as a RADIUS proxy.")
3. What types of NASs can IAS support? (See "What's a NAS?")
4. What do you have to do in order for IAS to permit an RRAS server to use IAS for authentication? (See "Configuring IAS.")

Saturday Evening
Part Review

1. What three properties can IIS use to distinguish between multiple virtual Web sites on a single server?

2. What four types of sites can you set up in IIS?

3. What is the primary use for an IIS SMTP site?

4. How can you prevent anonymous users from accessing a particular file on an IIS Web site?

5. What is the default TCP port for an IIS Web site?

6. Why are FTP sites used when HTTP offers similar file download capabilities?

7. What client software enables users to interact with an NNTP site?

8. What client software enables users to interact with an FTP site?

9. How can you configure a Web site to save information about user activity to a log file?

10. What happens if a user tries to access a Web site that is uniquely identified by a host header, but the user's proxy server removes the HTTP 1.1 headers from the request?

11. What two types of remote connections are most commonly used with RRAS?

12. What two VPN protocols does RRAS support?

13. What two protocols are necessary to create an encrypted VPN with clients who are not PPTP-compatible?

14. How can you monitor the users who are currently dialed in to an RRAS server?

15. How can you centralize the Remote Access Policies for several RRAS servers?

16. What standard protocol does IAS use?

17. How does RRAS authenticate users through IAS?

18. What service must already be present in order for IAS to operate?

19. How can IAS be used to forward RADIUS requests to another RADIUS server?

20. How can IAS help monitor your remote access utilization?

☑ Friday

☑ Saturday

 Sunday

PART

V

Sunday Morning

21

Managing Virtual Private Networks

Session Checklist

✔ How virtual private networks work

✔ How to set up a virtual private network

✔ How to troubleshoot virtual private networks

30 Min.
To Go

As you learned in Session 19, Windows Server 2003's Routing and Remote Access Services (RRAS) is capable of accepting connections through a virtual private network (VPN). VPNs enable users to securely connect to your company network over a public, unsecured network like the Internet.

You can also use VPNs to connect multiple computers at one location to the computers at another location. For example, World Metro Bank has smaller branch offices throughout the United States. They can use VPNs to connect those small offices to larger offices, or to their main office, over the Internet.

In this session, you'll learn how VPNs work from the inside out. You'll also learn how to set up a Windows Server 2003 to act as an interoffice router, using a VPN to connect two corporate offices. Finally, you'll learn some of the most common troubleshooting techniques to use when a VPN stops working.

How VPNs Work

Imagine that the data transmitted by computers across networks are tiny envelopes containing information. The envelope contains addressing information, and the contents are the data the computer is sending. Network devices like routers read the envelope to determine where the "mail" is supposed to go.

The problem with the envelopes is that anybody with access to the network can open them and read them without the sender or recipient being aware of it. It's as if you had a master key to the local post office, could open everyone's letters, read them, and reseal them without anyone knowing.

VPNs *encapsulate* network data, thereby placing the envelopes in the equivalent of locked boxes. Only the sender and the intended recipient have keys to the locks, and so only they can open the boxes and retrieve the envelopes within. Figure 21-1 shows how the encapsulation process works.

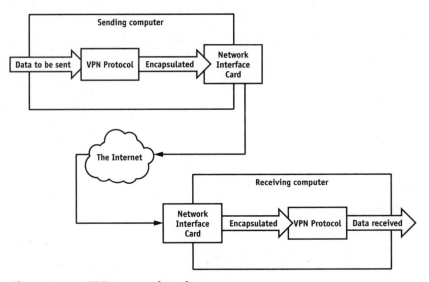

Figure 21-1   *VPNs encapsulate data*

VPNs are normally set up to grab all of the traffic leaving one computer and encapsulate it. The encapsulated data travels directly to the receiving end of the VPN, where the data is unencapsulated. Because all of the data between the sender and receiver is encapsulated by the VPN protocol, VPNs are often referred to as *tunnels*. In fact, both of the major VPN protocols have "tunneling" in their names.

Encapsulation Details

VPNs make use of a network protocol called General Routing Encapsulation, or GRE. GRE is a very low-level protocol, just like the IP protocol. The biggest problem most administrators encounter is getting the GRE protocol to successfully make it through their network's routers and, most especially, firewalls.

Most firewall administrators are accustomed to configuring their firewalls to permit different types of IP-based traffic. The HyperText Transport Protocol (HTTP), for example, usually uses TCP port 80 under the IP protocol.

HTTP is a high-level protocol, however. There are no ports that a firewall administrator can open to pass GRE, because GRE doesn't run under the IP protocol. In networking terms, GRE is a *peer* of the IP protocol.

Firewall administrators have to configure their firewalls to pass *protocol ID* 40, which is the ID that GRE uses. IP has its own protocol ID, which your firewall administrator is probably already familiar with.

Types of VPNs

Two common protocols are used to create VPNs. The Point-to-Point Tunneling Protocol, or PPTP, is most commonly found in Microsoft products. It was the first VPN protocol to gain widespread acceptance. PPTP includes built-in encryption capabilities, which means that the data sent through the tunnel is encrypted before it is encapsulated.

The Layer 2 Tunneling Protocol (L2TP) is a newer VPN protocol. Most non-Microsoft VPN software supports L2TP. L2TP is responsible only for the tunneling portion of the VPN; it does not provide any built-in capabilities for encryption. That means data in an L2TP tunnel is still subject to eavesdropping and tampering. However, L2TP works in conjunction with the IP Security (IPSec) protocol to provide powerful encryption. The two protocols together actually provide somewhat stronger security than PPTP. While PPTP encrypts the data before encapsulating it, L2TP/IPSec encrypts the data *after* encapsulating it. That means any eavesdroppers won't even know that the data they're looking at is part of a VPN, whereas with PPTP they can examine the encapsulation headers and determine that the data is part of a PPTP-based VPN.

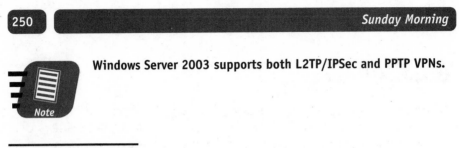

Windows Server 2003 supports both L2TP/IPSec and PPTP VPNs.

Setting Up a VPN

I already described how one common use for VPNs is to connect branch offices to a main office, as shown in Figure 21-2. That's how the World Metro Bank plans to use RRAS because it's cheaper to obtain Internet connections for their offices and then use those connections to link the various offices.

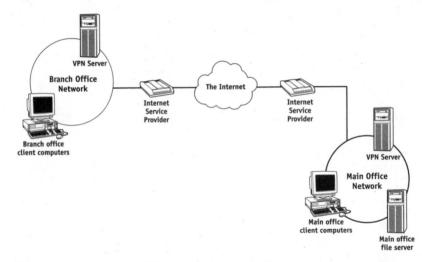

Figure 21-2 *Using a VPN server to connect offices*

In Figure 21-2, the client computers at both offices can connect to one another securely. That's because they are configured to send their data to the VPN server, which acts as a router. The VPN server encapsulates and encrypts the data, and then sends it across the Internet to the other VPN server. The other server decrypts and unencapsulates the data, and then routes it to its recipient on that office's network.

The configuration shown in Figure 21-2 uses two RRAS servers as routers. If you want to configure RRAS to accept VPN connections from individual users, refer to Session 19.

Configuring RRAS

After installing RRAS (see Session 19 for installation instructions), follow these instructions to configure RRAS as a VPN router:

1. Open the RRAS console.

2. Right-click on your server's name and select Configure Routing and Remote Access from the pop-up menu.

If you already configured RRAS, you may need to disable it first in order to follow these directions. Note that disabling RRAS deletes your current RRAS configuration and then enables you to reconfigure the server according to these directions.

3. Select Virtual Private Network (VPN) Server in the Configure RRAS Wizard.

4. Confirm that the correct protocols are already installed on the server. RRAS displays a list of protocols; make sure that all of the network protocols used on your network are listed. If some are missing, exit the wizard and install the necessary protocols. Then start over with Step 1.

5. Decide whether or not you want RRAS to create VPN-only filters by selecting the appropriate option, as shown in Figure 21-3.

**20 Min.
To Go**

Figure 21-3 *Decide if you want to apply VPN filters to your RRAS server*

If you apply the filters, then your RRAS server will accept only VPN communications. That's useful if the server will be directly connected to the Internet because the filters make the server ignore any potentially harmful Internet traffic. However, if you want your server to be able to accept other types of traffic, do not apply the filters.

6. Tell the Wizard how remote clients will receive IP addresses. RRAS dynamically assigns addresses to incoming VPNs; it can do so using a DHCP server on your network (if one exists) or by using a range of IP addresses you specify. If you have a DHCP server, select the DHCP option.

7. Tell the Wizard whether or not you want to use a RADIUS server to authenticate incoming VPN connections.

Session 20 covers Microsoft's Internet Authentication Server, a RADIUS-compatible server included with Windows Server 2003.

Creating a routing interface

Once RRAS is configured to act as a VPN server, you can create a VPN routing interface. If both offices will use RRAS servers as their VPN routers, you have to perform the following steps on both servers:

1. Open the RRAS console.

2. Right-click Routing Interfaces and select New Interface from the pop-up menu. RRAS launches the New Routing Interface Wizard.

3. Enter a name for the new interface. The name should help remind you what the interface will be used for. For example, you might type the name of the office that the interface will connect to.

4. Enter the IP address of the VPN server in the other office.

5. Indicate which network protocols will be carried through the VPN by selecting the appropriate protocols, as shown in Figure 21-4. Also select the option to create a user account.

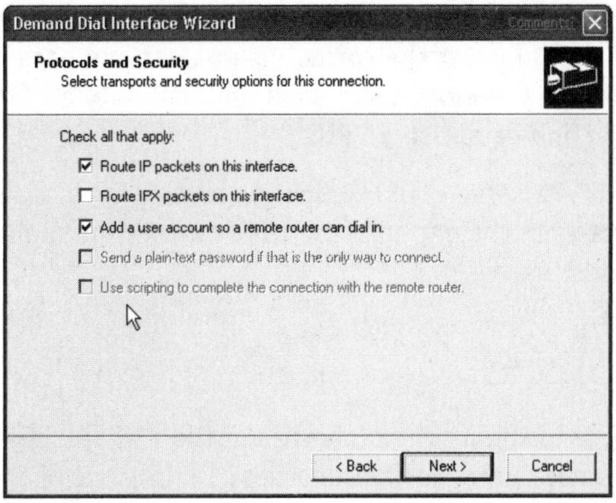

Figure 21-4 *Selecting the protocols that the VPN will carry*

6. Select a password for the user account that RRAS will create, as shown in Figure 21-5. This user account will be used by the other office's VPN server, so be sure to document the username and password.

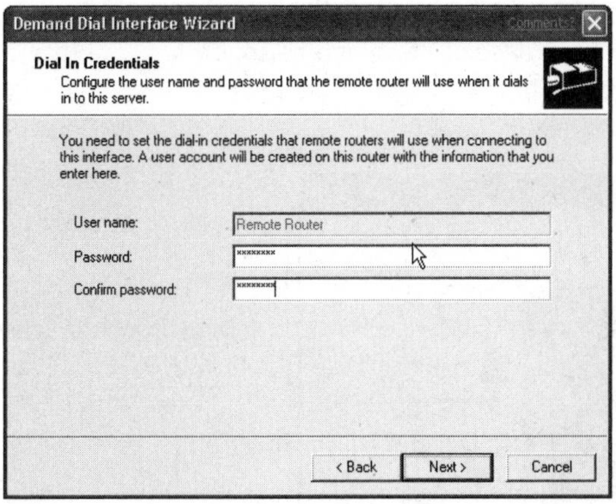

Figure 21-5 *Selecting a password for the remote router account*

7. Enter the username, domain, and password that RRAS should use when logging into the other office's VPN server.

Remember to configure both offices' VPN routers using the same steps. Make sure you enter the correct usernames and passwords into the Wizard, or the RRAS servers will be unable to authenticate each other and establish a VPN.

Once you've configured both VPN servers, right-click the routing interface on one of them and select Connect from the pop-up menu. The two servers should connect to one another and establish a VPN.

Fine-tuning the routing interface

You can use the RRAS console to configure the properties of the VPN routing interfaces. Just right-click the interface's entry in the console and select one of these options:

- **Set Logon Credentials.** Changes the username and password the interface sends to the remote VPN server. Use this option if the logon credentials change, or if you entered them incorrectly when you set up the interface.

- **Set Dial-out Hours.** Changes the hours during which the interface can be used, as shown in Figure 21-6. If your Internet access is billed by the amount of time it is in use, you can configure RRAS to disable the interface during hours when it isn't needed or during periods when the Internet connection is most expensive.

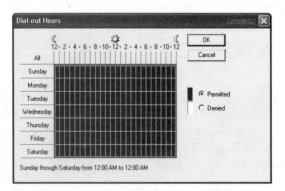

Figure 21-6 Setting interface dial hours

- **Properties.** Configures interface options. For example, as shown in Figure 21-7, you can set the interface as Demand-dial or Persistent. Demand-dial interfaces connect automatically when someone on your network needs to access the other office; Persistent interfaces are always connected. Again, if your company pays for Internet access as it uses the connection, a Demand-dial interface may help save money.

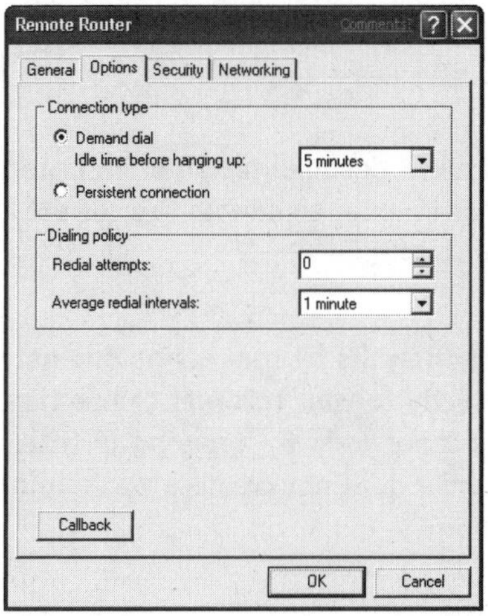

Figure 21-7　*Configuring interface options*

Troubleshooting VPNs

10 Min. To Go

VPNs can be pretty picky, and it's often difficult to get them working initially. In this section, I'll cover the most common VPN problems and give you some tips for troubleshooting them in your environment.

Firewall issues

Firewalls cause the most problems for VPNs. Even if your network doesn't contain a firewall, your ISP probably does use a firewall. Here are some tips for configuring firewalls to work with VPNs:

- If the firewall performs Network Address Translation (NAT), it can support the PPTP protocol only if it contains a special feature called a *GRE editor* that allows it to also perform NAT for GRE call IDs. The L2TP protocol is not compatible with firewalls that use NAT.

- The firewall must allow protocol ID 40, the GRE protocol, to pass through in both directions.

- The firewall must also open the correct TCP port for the VPN protocol you are using. For example, the PPTP protocol uses TCP port 1723.

- Proxying firewalls are not generally compatible with VPNs. If you have a firewall that proxies all traffic, consult the documentation to determine whether or not the firewall works with VPNs.

You should consult your firewall documentation or an experienced firewall administrator in order to enable the correct firewall features to support a VPN.

You can avoid the hassle of firewalls by connecting one network card of your VPN server directly to your Internet connection and another network card to your network. By applying IP filters, you can ensure that the VPN server does not create a weak point in your network's security.

Miscellaneous issues

VPNs are susceptible to a number of other issues that can be hard to troubleshoot. If the two VPN servers just won't connect, check the interface logon credentials on both ends, and make sure that a firewall isn't causing any problems (see the previous section for information on troubleshooting firewalls).

If the two VPN servers are connecting but client computers in one office can't access resources in the other office, follow these troubleshooting steps:

1. From one VPN server, use the ping command to try to reach the other VPN server's address. Use the address that is connected to the remote office's network. If the ping command fails, check the routing interface configuration and make sure the two servers are connecting properly.

2. Use the tracert command from a client computer to try to access a computer on the remote network. The tracert command shows you where the VPN isn't working. For example, if packets of data are making it to the remote office, but the replies aren't making it back, then the remote VPN server isn't routing packets back. Check its routing configuration.

You'll learn more about how to use RRAS as a router in the next session.

3. Make sure your client computers are configured to use the VPN server on their network as their default gateway. Otherwise, outgoing packets won't be routed to the VPN server, and the traffic won't make it through the tunnel to the remote office.

REVIEW

In this session, you learned how VPNs work, and you learned about the two major VPN protocols, PPTP and L2TP. You also learned how to configure RRAS as an office-to-office VPN router, and how to create and configure VPN routing interfaces. You also learned how to troubleshoot the most common VPN problems that you might encounter.

Done!

QUIZ YOURSELF

1. What TCP port is required by the PPTP protocol? (See "Firewall issues.")
2. What are two methods you can use to save money when running a VPN over an Internet connection that charges you by the amount the connection is used? (See "Fine-tuning the routing interface.")
3. What protocol do VPNs use to encapsulate data? (See "How VPNs Work.")
4. What VPN protocol is compatible with firewalls that perform NAT? (See "Firewall issues.")

Managing Advanced Network Services

Session Checklist

✔ How to configure routing

✔ How to share Internet connections

✔ How to use Windows Server 2003 as a firewall

✔ How to integrate advanced network services

**30 Min.
To Go**

I
n sessions 19, 20, and 21, you learned about some of the capabilities of
Windows Server 2003's Routing and Remote Access Services (RRAS), including
accepting remote connections, creating Virtual Private Networks (VPNs), and
authenticating users with Internet Authentication Services (IAS). Windows Server
2003 and RRAS still have a few useful tricks up their sleeves, though, and you'll
learn about them in this session.

Specifically, I'll show you how to manage static routing on RRAS. I'll also show
you how you can use RRAS and Internet Connection Sharing (ICS) to use a
Windows Server 2003 as an Internet gateway. Finally, I'll show you how Windows
Server 2003 can help protect your network with the Internet Connection Firewall
(ICF) and RRAS IP filters.

Unfortunately, these technologies are laden with TLAs (three-letter acronyms). Don't forget to refer back to these introductory paragraphs whenever the acronyms get too confusing!

Routing with RRAS

RRAS is capable of acting as a fully functional network router whenever it is installed on a Windows Server 2003 that has more than one network interface card (NIC) and the server is connected to multiple network segments. For example, in Figure 22-1, a Windows Server 2003 running RRAS is connected to two different network segments. Client computers on either segment can use the server as their default gateway, and the server routes packets between the two segments.

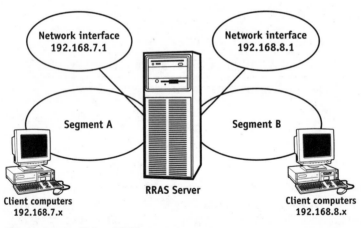

Figure 22-1 *Using RRAS as a router*

While RRAS can perform many of the same functions as a dedicated hardware router, it often can't perform them as quickly. Whenever possible, you should always use a dedicated hardware router for your network's routing needs.

RRAS makes a great router when you're first setting up a network or when you're setting up a test lab network and don't need the performance of a dedicated router. One feature that makes RRAS so easy to use is that it usually configures itself. For example, in Figure 22-1, no additional configuration should be needed for RRAS to work properly. It automatically sets up routes between its two network interfaces, which means it will route data correctly between the two segments.

The need for static routes

You sometimes may need to configure static routes in RRAS. You usually have to do this when you want RRAS to route to a network that it isn't directly connected to. For example, in Figure 22-2, RRAS is connected to two network segments, and a third segment is connected via a hardware router. RRAS doesn't know about segment C, and so it won't be able to route data from segments A or B to C.

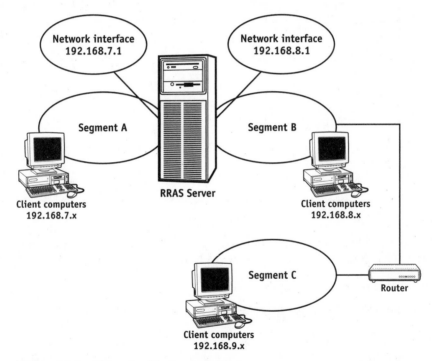

Figure 22-2   *Network with three segments*

In a situation like the one depicted in Figure 22-2, you have to add a static route, so that RRAS knows how to reach addresses in the 192.168.9.x range.

Adding static routes

Adding static routes is easy with the RRAS console. Open the IP Routing item in the console, and then click on Static routes. You'll see the static routes that are already configured, if any exist, as shown in Figure 22-3.

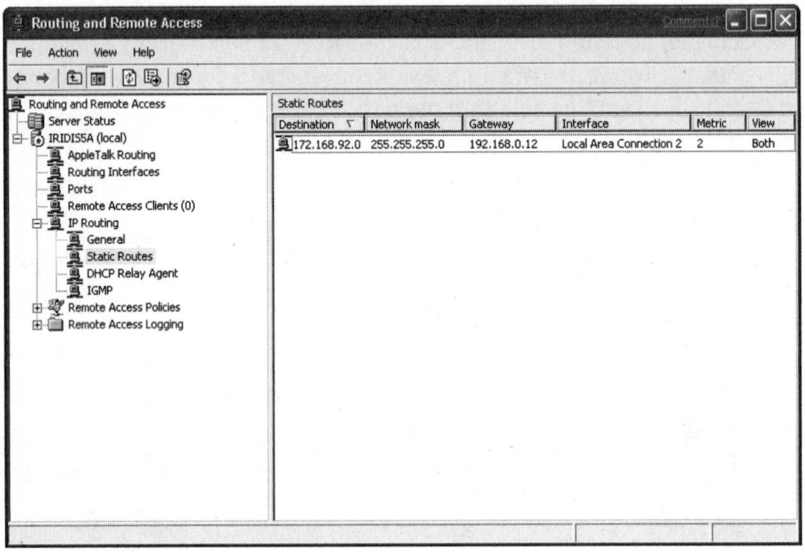

Figure 22-3 *Viewing static routes*

You can add a new route by right-clicking Static routes and selecting New Route from the pop-up menu. RRAS displays the New Static Route dialog box, as shown in Figure 22-4.

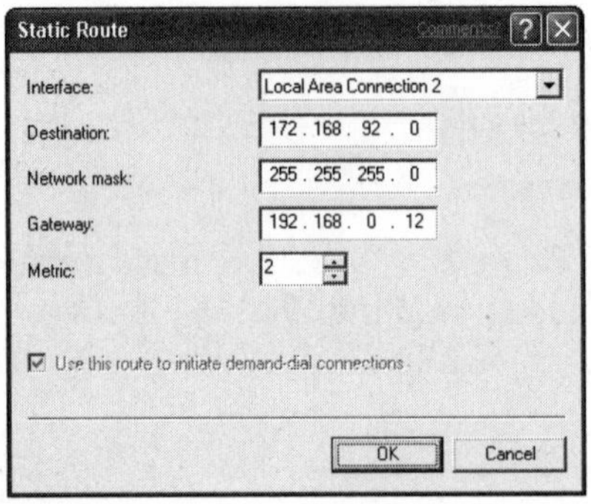

Figure 22-4 *Adding a new static route*

When you add a new route, you need to provide the following information:

- The interface that the route applies to. Select the interface that RRAS will receive packets on.

- The destination that the route applies to. This is the destination that the packet will contain. You can enter part of a network address if you want the route to apply to a range. For example, to have the route apply to 172.192.68.x, just enter 172.192.68.0 in the dialog box.

- The network mask that the route applies to.

- The gateway for the route. This is the IP address that RRAS will send packets to. This might be the address of a router that is directly connected to the destination segment.

- The metric. This is the cost of the route. You can configure RRAS with multiple routes for the same destination. RRAS always uses the "least expensive" route or the route with the lowest metric, if it is available. If that route isn't available, RRAS tries other routes. This design enables you to configure backup routes that might use more expensive or slower network connections, for example.

RRAS can also use *routing protocols* such as Open Shortest Path First (OSPF) or Routing Interface Protocol (RIP). These protocols allow RRAS to communicate with other routers on your network to automatically determine the correct routes for your entire network. You should select the routing protocol that your other network devices support, and you should consult the RRAS documentation for details on configuring the routing protocols.

Internet Connection Sharing

20 Min. To Go

Most businesses today connect their networks to the Internet. Large networks use high-powered, dedicated firewalls and other devices to maintain this connection, but smaller networks, or home networks, might not have the money for those expensive, dedicated devices. Windows Server 2003 is capable of acting as an Internet gateway for these networks, allowing all of the computers on the network to share a single Internet connection. Figure 22-5 shows how the network might look with Windows Server 2003 acting as an Internet gateway.

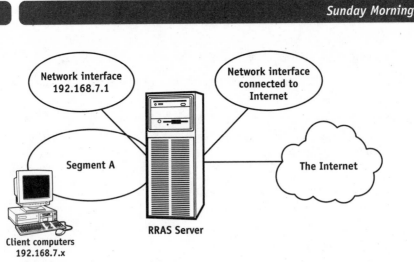

Figure 22-5 *Using Windows Server 2003 as an Internet gateway*

When acting as an Internet gateway, Windows Server 2003 can share any type of Internet connection, including dial-up connections or broadband connections like frame relay or Digital Subscriber Lines (DSL). Windows Server 2003 provides two distinct methods for acting as an Internet gateway: Internet Connection Sharing, or ICS, and RRAS.

Enabling ICS

ICS is a feature included only in Windows Server 2003. It is not included in Windows Enterprise Server or Datacenter Server. ICS provides an easy-to-configure Internet gateway for small office or home networks.

To enable ICS, open your server's list of network connections. Right-click the Internet connection that you want to share, and select Properties from the pop-up list. On the Advanced tab, enable Internet Connection Sharing as shown in Figure 22-6.

You can also select the check box that makes Windows activate the Internet connection (in the case of dial-up connections) when someone on the network needs to use it. If you do so, the Internet gateway will function automatically.

Figure 22-6 *Enabling ICS*

When you enable ICS, Windows makes several configuration changes, and you need to make a few of your own for ICS to work:

- Windows sets the IP address of the server's NIC to 192.168.0.1.
- Windows sets up a special service, similar to DHCP, that issues addresses to the client computers on your network.
- You need to configure your client computers to obtain their IP addresses automatically, and you need to disable any DHCP server that is already on your network.

Once you're done, ICS is completely automatic.

RRAS as an Internet gateway

If you're using Enterprise Server, Web Server, or Datacenter Server, ICS is not available to you. However, you can configure RRAS to perform the same tasks. Perform the following steps on an unconfigured RRAS server:

If your RRAS server is already configured, disable it by right-clicking the server name in the RRAS console and selecting Disable from the pop-up menu. Disabling RRAS erases the server's RRAS configuration.

1. In the RRAS console, right-click your server's name and select Configure Routing and Remote Access Service.

2. When the Wizard prompts you to select a configuration option, select Internet Connection Server.

3. Select ICS or Network Address Translation (NAT) Router. On Web Server, Enterprise Server or Datacenter Server, the ICS option is grayed out, so select the NAT Router option.

4. Select the network interface that is connected to the Internet, as shown in Figure 22-7.

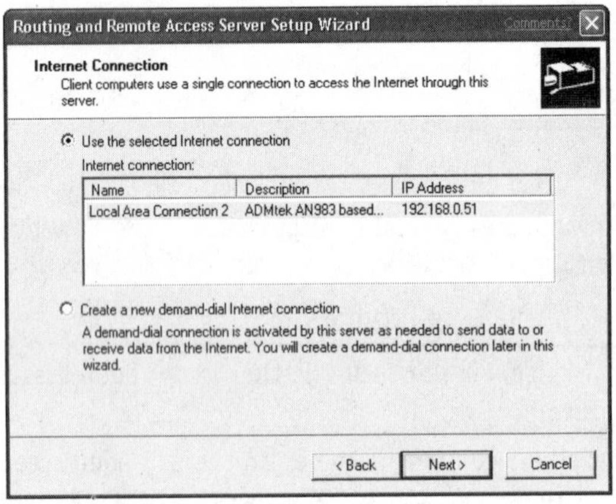

Figure 22-7   *Selecting your Internet connection*

5. Complete the Wizard, and RRAS will be configured to act as an Internet gateway. You also need to configure your client computers to use the RRAS server as their default gateway.

Internet Connection Firewall

When you use RRAS as your Internet gateway, you need that server to also protect your network against intruders and hackers on the Internet. Windows offers the Internet Connection Firewall (ICF) and RRAS IP filters to help make a Windows Server 2003 into a basic firewall.

If your security requirements are more complex than simple port filtering, you should investigate a third-party firewall product or Microsoft's Internet Security and Acceleration Server, which is a full-fledged firewall.

As with ICS, ICF is not available on Web Server, Enterprise Server or Datacenter Server. On those platforms, you need to configure RRAS IP filters to perform the same tasks as ICF.

Enabling ICF

You enable ICF from the same dialog box that you used to enable ICS, shown in Figure 22-6. You can click the Settings button on that dialog box to configure advanced ICF features, as shown in Figure 22-8.

Figure 22-8 *Advanced ICF settings*

By default, ICF allows traffic to leave your network and go to the Internet and allows replies to come back from the Internet. No new connections are allowed from the Internet to your internal network. By selecting the appropriate check boxes in the advanced ICF settings, you can instruct ICF to allow certain IP protocols in from the Internet. Those connections are routed to the computer that will handle them. For example, when you enable the File Transfer Protocol (FTP) in ICF, you need to specify the name or IP address of the server on your network that will handle FTP traffic. ICF will route all incoming FTP traffic to that server.

RRAS as a basic firewall

**10 Min.
To Go**

If you can't use ICF, or if you want to maintain a finer degree of control over your firewall services, you can configure input and output IP filters in RRAS. These filters tell RRAS what traffic to accept and what traffic to ignore.

To view or create filters, follow these steps:

1. In the RRAS console, open the IP Routing item.

2. Click on the General item to view a list of network interfaces on the server.

3. Right-click the interface that you want to apply filters to, and select Properties from the pop-up menu.

4. Click the Input filters button to view input filters, or click the Output filters button to view output filters. Input filters restrict the traffic that the server receives and are the logical choice when you're trying to protect the server from hackers.

5. Click the Add button to add a new filter, as shown in Figure 22-9.

```
┌─────────────────────────────────────────┐
│ Edit IP Filter            Comments ? X   │
├─────────────────────────────────────────┤
│  ☐ Source network                        │
│      IP address:      [            ]      │
│      Subnet mask:     [            ]      │
│  ☐ Destination network                   │
│      IP address:      [            ]      │
│      Subnet mask:     [            ]      │
│                                          │
│  Protocol:            [TCP        ▼]      │
│  Source port:         [0          ]      │
│  Destination port:    [80         ]      │
│                                          │
│                    [  OK  ]  [ Cancel ]   │
└─────────────────────────────────────────┘
```

Figure 22-9   Adding a new IP filter

1. If you want the filter to apply to traffic from a specific source IP address or network, select the Source network check box and provide the IP address and subnet mask that the filter will look for.

2. If you want the filter to apply to traffic sent to a specific destination, select the Destination network check box and provide the IP address and subnet mask the filter will look for.

3. If you want the filter to apply to a specific protocol, select that protocol from the Protocol list. Also provide the source and destination ports for the protocol. Enter a zero to have the filter match any port.

When configuring a filter, you can specify as much or as little information as necessary for your needs. In Figure 22-9, the filter shown will match on all traffic using destination port 80 of the TCP protocol — Web traffic.

6. Click OK to view the updated list of filters, as shown in Figure 22-10. Notice that you can instruct the server to ignore all traffic *unless* it meets the filter conditions, or accept *all* traffic unless it meets the filter conditions. Thus, your filters can be turned into a list of traffic to specifically accept or a list of traffic to specifically reject. In Figure 22-10, the filters are configured to reject all traffic not matching a filter, which means the server will accept only incoming Web traffic. All other traffic will be rejected.

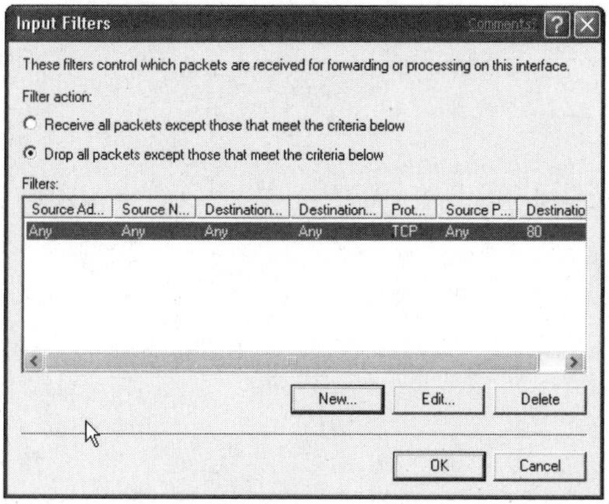

Figure 22-10   *Viewing IP filters*

7. Click OK to close the dialog boxes. New filters take effect immediately.

**Part V — Sunday Morning
Session 22**

Done!

REVIEW

In this session you learned how RRAS and Windows Server 2003 can provide routing services for your network. You also learned how they can enable a server to act as an Internet gateway and a basic firewall, either by using Internet Connection Sharing and the Internet Connection Firewall, or by using features of RRAS. You learned how to configure these features and apply them to your network.

QUIZ YOURSELF

1. How can you use Windows Enterprise Server to protect your network from Internet-based hackers? (See "Internet Connection Firewall.")

2. How can you use Windows Server 2003 to act as an Internet gateway? (See "Internet Connection Sharing.")

3. How can you use Windows Server 2003 as a router and avoid having to configure manual routes? (See "Adding static routes.")

4. When is it appropriate to use RRAS as a network router? (See "Routing with RRAS.")

Using Network Monitor

Session Checklist

✔ How Network Monitor works

✔ How to capture data with Network Monitor

✔ How to analyze data with Network Monitor

✔ How to automate Network Monitor

**30 Min.
To Go**

Windows Server 2003 includes a powerful network analysis tool called Network Monitor, or NetMon. NetMon is a network packet analyzer, similar to third-party products such as Network General's Sniffer. NetMon enables you to look at the raw data transmitted on your network and can be useful when you're troubleshooting problems with WINS, DNS, DHCP, or other services that require network communications.

In this session, you'll learn how NetMon works, and how to use it to capture and analyze data from your network. You'll also learn how to automate NetMon, enabling you to perform more advanced troubleshooting tasks.

You can install Network Monitor on almost any version of Windows, including Windows XP Professional. In this session, however, I focus on how to use NetMon directly on a Windows Server 2003 computer.

How NetMon Works

Normally, network interface cards (NICs) see all of the traffic transmitted on their network segment, but they pay attention only to traffic sent to their own physical address or traffic that is broadcasted to all computers. NetMon works by placing your server's NIC into *promiscuous mode,* where the NIC pays attention to *all* traffic on the network.

Your server's NIC and NIC device driver must support promiscuous mode. Consult your NIC documentation for more information on whether or not the NIC supports this feature.

Once the NIC is looking at all of the traffic on the network, NetMon starts *capturing* the traffic into a special area of memory called a *buffer.* Capturing the data simply means storing it in the buffer, where you can look at it later. Capturing data requires NetMon to devote its complete attention to the server's NIC, so you can't do anything else with NetMon while it's capturing. Once the capture is complete, you can analyze the data in the buffer. NetMon does *not* enable you to view the traffic on your network in real time.

The Two Versions of NetMon

The version of NetMon included with the Windows operating system is limited in functionality. For security reasons, it captures only traffic transmitted to or from the computer on which NetMon is running, including broadcast traffic.

Microsoft does make a full version of NetMon that can capture all network traffic, whether or not it was sent to or from the server. That version is bundled with Microsoft Systems Management Server. You can also obtain the full version of NetMon with certain Microsoft Official Curriculum courses.

Other than the restriction on what traffic can be captured, the two versions are identical. The full version of NetMon is more useful as a troubleshooting tool because it enables you to capture all network traffic.

The NetMon Agent

Windows operating systems based upon NT, including Windows 2000, Windows XP, and Windows .NET, can also run a special service called the Network Monitor Agent. The NetMon Agent's job is to capture traffic on whatever network segment the computer is attached to, and to transmit that traffic back to a computer running NetMon. This design enables you to capture traffic on network segments that you aren't physically connected to.

To use a NetMon Agent to capture data, tell the NetMon console to connect to the computer running the NetMon Agent. The NetMon Agent service must be installed and started in order for NetMon to connect to it.

NetMon obstacles

Modern network design creates many obstacles for using NetMon. For example, many companies use switches, rather than hubs, to connect their networked computers to one another.

When a hub receives data on one port, it retransmits that data out all of its other ports. That basic functionality allows networks to function — after all, if computers couldn't "see" the data transmitted by other computers, there wouldn't be a network. NetMon works great with hubs, because the hub makes sure that all the traffic on the network makes it to the NIC of the computer NetMon is running on. Figure 23-1 shows how hubs retransmit data.

The problem with hubs is that they create a lot of extra traffic. For example, if Computer A needs to transmit something to Computer B, there's no reason for every other computer on the network to have to see that transmission. Remember that only one computer on a network can "talk" at a single time, so when the hub transmits Computer A's request on all of its hub ports, Computer A is effectively stopping any other communications for a brief time.

Companies solve this problem by using switches. A switch looks a lot like a hub, but when it receives data on one port, it retransmits the data only to the port that contains the destination. So when Computer A transmits, only the port that Computer B is connected to is tied up. Computers on other ports can carry on their own conversations. Figure 23-2 shows how switches work.

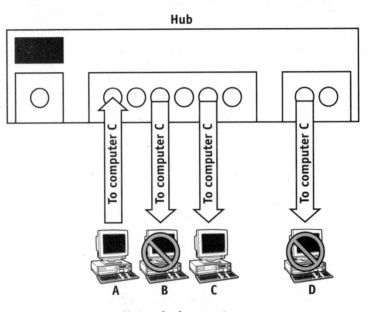

Hub

Networked computers

Figure 23-1   How hubs retransmit data

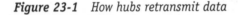

20 Min. To Go

Switches are great for networks because they effectively increase the amount of traffic the entire network can carry at any given time. Switches are horrible for NetMon, though, because they prevent the computer that NetMon is running on from "seeing" all of the traffic on the network.

Higher-end switches enable you to configure certain switch ports in promiscuous mode, which makes the switch transmit all network traffic that it receives on that port, in addition to whatever other ports the traffic needs to go through. By connecting your NetMon computer to a promiscuous switch port, you can ensure that NetMon will "see" all of the traffic on your network. Using promiscuous mode may decrease overall performance on your switch because the switch has to work harder to transmit the extra traffic. Consult your switch documentation, and consider using promiscuous mode only when you need to capture data with NetMon. Figure 23-3 shows a switch with one port in promiscuous mode.

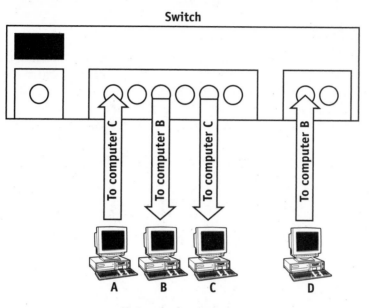

Figure 23-2 *How switches retransmit data*

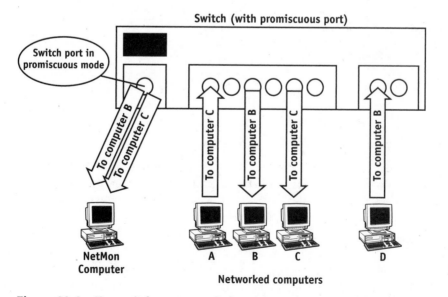

Figure 23-3 *How switches retransmit data in promiscuous mode*

Capturing Data

When you first launch NetMon, it asks you to select the NIC that you want to use to capture data. If your computer has more than one NIC, be sure to select the one that is connected to the network segment that you want to capture data from. After you select the NIC that NetMon will use, click the Capture button in the toolbar to begin a capture. NetMon displays its capture statistics screen, as shown in Figure 23-4.

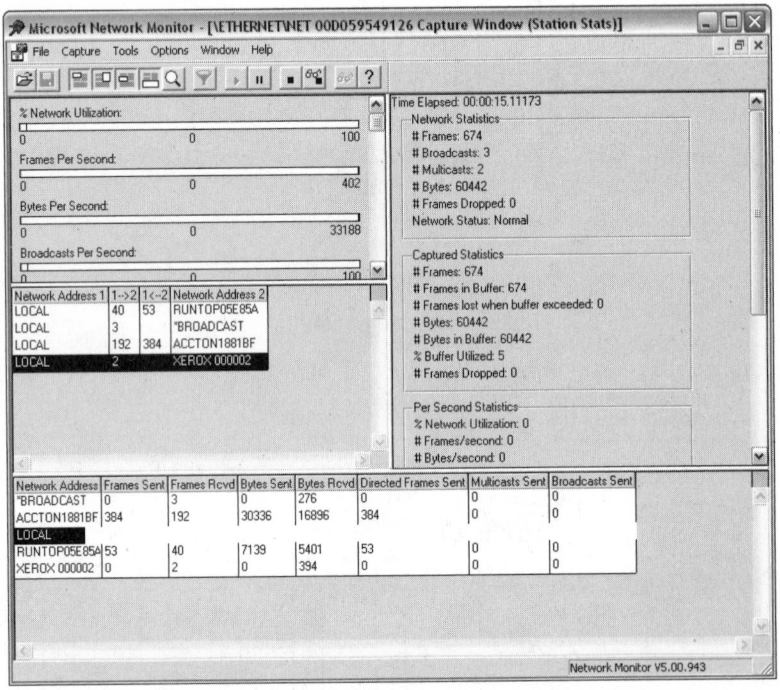

Figure 23-4 *NetMon's capture screen*

To stop the capture at any time, click the Stop button. To stop the capture and immediately view the captured data, click the Stop and View button. Once your capture is complete, you can also save the captured data to disk for later analysis.

Using capture filters

Most networks carry an incredible amount of data, and you won't usually want to look at all of it. NetMon enables you to create capture filters, which restrict the traffic NetMon captures. Capture filters provide a couple of important benefits:

- Filters cut down the traffic you have to analyze, making it easier to examine the traffic you capture.

- Filters help prevent NetMon's capture buffer from filling up. When the buffer fills, NetMon discards older packets to make room for newer ones. By using filters, you reduce the amount of traffic that goes into the buffer, saving space for the packets you want to analyze.

To create a capture filter, click the Filter button on the toolbar in NetMon's capture window. NetMon displays the Capture Filter dialog, which is shown in Figure 23-5.

Figure 23-5 *Viewing capture filters*

You can use the Capture Filter dialog to add new filter conditions. Only traffic matching the conditions you specify will be captured into the buffer. The conditions you can use include

- Traffic sent from a specific address
- Traffic sent to a specific address
- Traffic that contains a data pattern that you specify
- Traffic sent on specific protocols, such as TCP/IP or IPX/SPX

 You must specify capture filters while capturing is stopped. You cannot change filters once NetMon begins capturing unless you first stop the capture.

Your capture filters can't include conditions for high-level protocols like HTTP or FTP, because NetMon doesn't have enough time during the capture process to examine packets that closely.

Using triggers

You'll often want to use NetMon to capture a small amount of traffic and then analyze it immediately. Other times, you'll want NetMon to capture traffic over a long period of time. For example, you may create a capture filter that captures only specific traffic sent by one computer on your network. You might want to let the capture run overnight, to get as much data as possible for analysis the next day.

Letting NetMon run unattended is no problem, although it can cause undesired results. For example:

- NetMon's buffer may fill up, causing NetMon to discard some of the data it captured.

- NetMon can't normally respond to certain types of traffic with alarms or other actions.

- You may want to use NetMon as a troubleshooting tool and have it run a batch file or an administrative script when it detects specific data patterns in the traffic it captures.

NetMon's capture triggers are ideal for solving these problems. You can create a new trigger by selecting Trigger from the Capture menu in NetMon's capture screen. As shown in Figure 23-6, capture triggers can look for a variety of situations, such as data patterns or a full buffer, and automatically take action, such as stopping the capture, sounding an alarm, or executing another program.

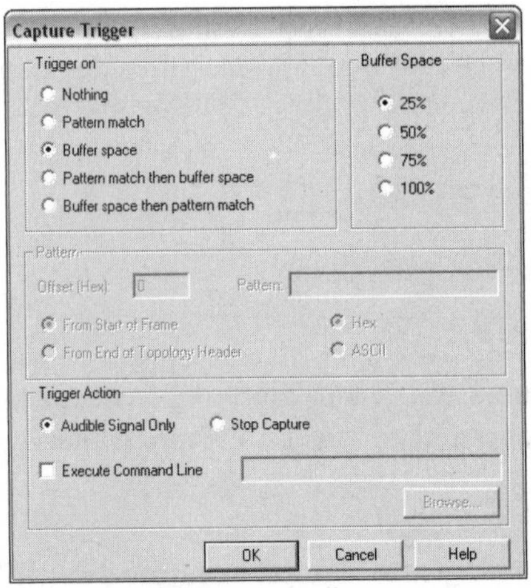

Figure 23-6 Creating a capture trigger

Analyzing Data

Once you've captured the data you want, you can use NetMon's View window to analyze the data, as shown in Figure 23-7.

Window title: Microsoft Network Monitor - [Capture: 2 (Summary)]
Menu: File   Edit   Display   Tools   Options   Window   Help

Frame	Time	Src MAC Addr	Dst MAC Addr	Protocol	Description
1	0.590850	LOCAL	XEROX 000002	Bone	Security Check (0x03)
2	5.357704	LOCAL	ACCTON1881BF	DNS	0x4E:Std Qry for iridis5a.braincorenevada.c...
3	5.357704	ACCTON1881BF	LOCAL	ICMP	Redirect: Use Gateway 192.168.00.11 to reac...
4	5.357704	ACCTON1881BF	LOCAL	DNS	0x4E:Std Qry for iridis5a.braincorenevada.c...
5	5.357704	LOCAL	ACCTON1881BF	DNS	0x4E:Std Qry for iridis5a.braincorenevada.c...
6	5.357704	ACCTON1881BF	LOCAL	ICMP	Redirect: Use Gateway 192.168.00.11 to reac...
7	5.357704	ACCTON1881BF	LOCAL	DNS	0x4E:Std Qry for iridis5a.braincorenevada.c...
8	5.357704	LOCAL	ACCTON1881BF	DNS	0x4E:Std Qry for iridis5a.braincorenevada.c...
9	5.357704	ACCTON1881BF	LOCAL	ICMP	Redirect: Use Gateway 192.168.00.11 to reac...
10	5.357704	ACCTON1881BF	LOCAL	DNS	0x4E:Std Qry for iridis5a.braincorenevada.c...
11	5.357704	LOCAL	ACCTON1881BF	DNS	0x4E:Std Qry for iridis5a.braincorenevada.c...
12	5.357704	LOCAL	RUNTOPOSE85A	TCP	....S., len: 0, seq:2268048839-226804883...
13	5.357704	ACCTON1881BF	LOCAL	ICMP	Redirect: Use Gateway 192.168.00.11 to reac...
14	5.357704	ACCTON1881BF	LOCAL	DNS	0x4E:Std Qry for iridis5a.braincorenevada.c...
15	5.357704	LOCAL	ACCTON1881BF	DNS	0x4E:Std Qry for iridis5a.braincorenevada.c...
16	5.357704	RUNTOPOSE85A	LOCAL	TCP	.A.S., len: 0, seq: 692137963-692137963...
17	5.357704	LOCAL	IRIDIS5A	NBT	SS: Session Request, Dest: IRIDIS5A ...
18	5.357704	ACCTON1881BF	LOCAL	ICMP	Redirect: Use Gateway 192.168.00.11 to reac...
19	5.357704	ACCTON1881BF	LOCAL	DNS	0x4E:Std Qry for iridis5a.braincorenevada.c...
20	5.357704	LOCAL	ACCTON1881BF	DNS	0x4E:Std Qry for iridis5a.braincorenevada.c...
21	5.357704	IRIDIS5A	LOCAL	NBT	SS: Positive Session Response, Len: 0
22	5.357704	ACCTON1881BF	LOCAL	ICMP	Redirect: Use Gateway 192.168.00.11 to reac...
23	5.357704	ACCTON1881BF	LOCAL	DNS	0x4E:Std Qry for iridis5a.braincorenevada.c...
24	5.357704	LOCAL	ACCTON1881BF	DNS	0x4E:Std Qry for iridis5a.braincorenevada.c...
25	5.357704	ACCTON1881BF	LOCAL	ICMP	Redirect: Use Gateway 192.168.00.11 to reac...
26	5.357704	ACCTON1881BF	LOCAL	DNS	0x4E:Std Qry for iridis5a.braincorenevada.c...
27	5.357704	LOCAL	ACCTON1881BF	DNS	0x4E:Std Qry for iridis5a.braincorenevada.c...
28	5.357704	ACCTON1881BF	LOCAL	ICMP	Redirect: Use Gateway 192.168.00.11 to reac...
29	5.357704	ACCTON1881BF	LOCAL	DNS	0x4E:Std Qry for iridis5a.braincorenevada.c...
30	5.357704	LOCAL	ACCTON1881BF	DNS	0x4E:Std Qry for iridis5a.braincorenevada.c...
31	5.357704	ACCTON1881BF	LOCAL	ICMP	Redirect: Use Gateway 192.168.00.11 to reac...
32	5.357704	ACCTON1881BF	LOCAL	DNS	0x4E:Std Qry for iridis5a.braincorenevada.c...

Network Monitor V5.00.943   F#: 1/688   Off: 0(x0)   L:

Figure 23-7   *Viewing captured data*

For the captured data to make any sense, you need to be familiar with how the various protocols work. You can learn the basics of how Windows' core protocols work in sessions 13 through 22.

Each line in the View window represents a single packet of network data. If you double-click one of these lines, NetMon displays the packet's details in a hierarchical format. For example, Figure 23-8 shows the details of a DNS packet.

10 Min.
To Go

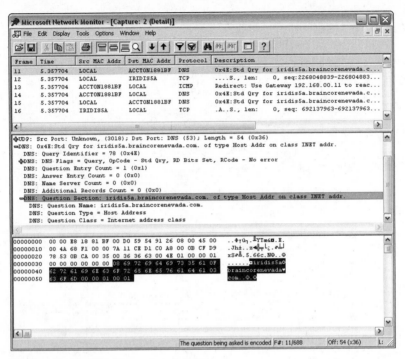

Figure 23-8 *Viewing packet details*

Filtering captured data

While NetMon doesn't enable you to create highly detailed capture filters, it does enable you to create very complex filters in the View window. The filters don't delete any captured data, but they do limit the amount of data you see. For example, you might want to view only captured DNS or DHCP data. To modify the current filter, just click the Filter button on the View window's toolbar. NetMon displays the Display Filter dialog box, as shown in Figure 23-9.

You can create filters that include the following conditions:

- Traffic sent from a specific address
- Traffic sent to a specific address
- Traffic that contains a data pattern that you specify
- Traffic sent on specific protocols, such as TCP/IP or IPX/SPX
- Traffic sent using specific subprotocols, such as HTTP, DNS, or DHCP

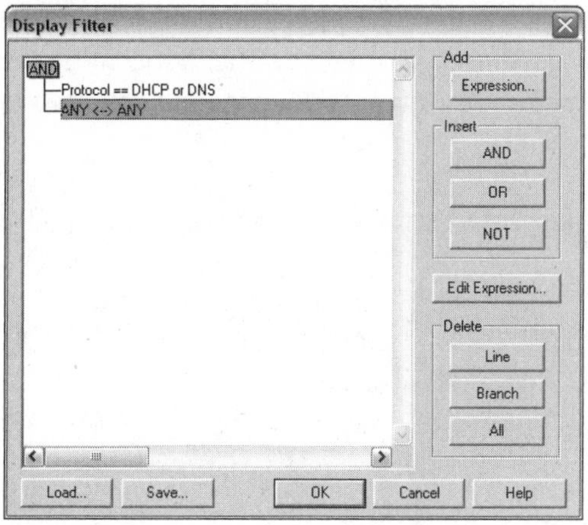

Figure 23-9   *Filtering captured data*

Running analysis experts

NetMon also includes analysis experts, which are preconfigured modules that help you determine specific information about your network, based on the data you captured from the network.

To see the list of experts and select one or more to run, select Experts from the View window's menu. NetMon displays the Network Monitor Experts window, as shown in Figure 23-10.

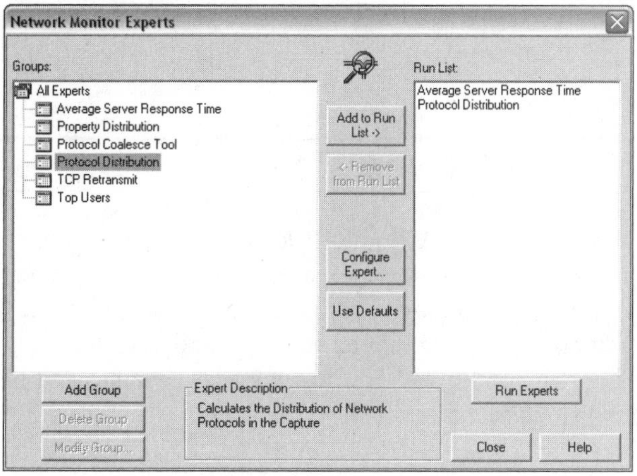

Figure 23-10   *Selecting experts to run*

NetMon's experts can help you determine which protocols are in use on your network and which computers are generating the most traffic. NetMon displays the results in a tabbed dialog box, as shown in Figure 23-11, enabling you to examine the experts' results in detail.

Figure 23-11 *Examining expert results*

REVIEW

Done!

In this session, you learned how Network Monitor (NetMon) can be used to capture and analyze network traffic. You learned how to apply pre- and post-capture filters, automate NetMon's capture process with triggers, and use experts to analyze the data you capture. You also learned how your network's infrastructure can affect NetMon's operation, and you learned how to work with switches and hubs to make NetMon an effective troubleshooting tool.

QUIZ YOURSELF

1. How can you prevent NetMon from discarding packets when it is capturing data overnight? (See "Using triggers.")

2. How can you reduce the amount of data on the View window to focus on certain protocols? (See "Filtering captured data.")

3. How can you quickly determine which computer on your network is creating the most traffic? (See "Running analysis experts.")

4. How can you ensure that NetMon will work in a switched network environment? (See "NetMon obstacles.")

Performing Disaster Recovery Operations

Session Checklist

✔ How to back up and restore data

✔ How to install the Recovery console

✔ How to use Automatic System Recovery

**30 Min.
To Go**

Windows Server 2003 includes a number of features that help you recover from hardware and software failures without losing data. In this session, you'll learn how to use Windows Backup to create backup files in case your servers fail. You'll also learn to install the Recovery console to help recover from system failures and use Windows Automated System Recovery (ASR) to help in the event of a total operating system failure.

Make sure you take the time to understand and perform disaster recovery tasks while your servers are in normal operating condition. Once your servers fail, you can do little to recover them if you haven't taken the appropriate disaster recovery steps in advance.

Never allow production servers to operate without a disaster recovery plan in place. Test and document your recovery procedures to be sure they work *before* disaster strikes.

Backup and Restore

Windows Server 2003 includes a basic backup and restore application called Windows Backup. The application enables you to back up the files on any computer on your network, and to back up the *system state* of the local computer to a backup file on disk or tape (if you have a properly-configured tape backup device).

 System state is a special set of data that includes the system Registry, Active Directory (on domain controllers), and critical system files. You should regularly back up the system state of all your Windows Server 2003 computers.

The built-in backup application provides only basic backup and restore functionality. You need to purchase a third-party backup application like Veritas' BackupExec if you want to perform advanced backup and restore operations:

- Back up the system state of computers across the network (the built-in application can back up only the local computer's system state).

- Schedule backups that include several computers across the network (while you can do this with the built-in application, it's cumbersome and time-consuming).

- Manage a large set of backup media, such as tapes or optical disks.

Backing up data

Windows Backup enables you to back up files and the local computer's system state. When you launch Backup for the first time, it runs in Wizard mode and walks you through the task of backing up your computer's data. If you prefer not to use the Wizard, you can cancel it and use Windows Backup in Advanced mode, which is shown in Figure 24-1. Advanced Mode allows you to begin selecting files for backup, select files to restore, and so forth.

In Advanced mode, you indicate the items you want to back up by placing checkmarks next to them. You then click Start Backup to begin backing up the selected data.

Windows Backup can back up data either to a disk-based file or to a backup tape. The backup tape device must be attached to your computer, and the correct drivers must be installed, before Windows Backup can detect the device. If you do not have a properly configured tape device attached, Windows Backup enables you to back up data only to a disk-based file.

Figure 24-1   *Windows Backup in Advanced mode*

Do not rely on a disk-based backup file. If your computer's hard disk fails, then you'll lose your backup file along with the data the backup was supposed to be protecting!

Types of backups

Windows Server 2003 attaches an *archive bit,* or flag, to each file stored on disk. When the archive bit is cleared, it indicates that the file has not changed since it was last backed up. When the file is changed, Windows automatically sets the archive bit, indicating that the file needs to be backed up. The archive bit plays an important role in the different types of backups that Windows Backup supports:

- **Normal backup.** Also referred to as a Full backup, a Normal backup backs up all the files you select. It clears the archive bit on each file.

- **Daily backup.** Backs up only the files whose "last changed" dates match the current date. The backup does not modify the archive bit on each file that it backs up. The Daily backup is intended to catch all the files that have changed that day.

- **Incremental backup.** Backs up all files whose archive bits are set, and it clears the archive bits. The Incremental backs up any files that have changed since the last Full or Incremental backup.

- **Full backup.** When restoring, you need the most recent Full backup, and every Incremental backup performed since the Full backup, in order to restore all of the files on your server to their most recent condition.

- **Differential backup.** Backs up all the files whose archive bits are set, but it does not clear them. Subsequent Differential backups back up the same files, so Differentials grow progressively larger until a Full or Incremental backup is performed.

When restoring, you need only the most recent Full backup and the most recent Differential backup.

Managing backup tapes

20 Min. To Go

If you back up data to tape, you should establish a tape rotation schedule. A good rotation schedule enables you to keep several backup tapes on hand and additional tapes in an offsite storage facility (where they will be protected against fire and other disasters that can occur at your office), and the rotation schedule still minimizes the amount of money you have to spend on backup tapes.

For example, you might create a backup schedule that uses two basic sets of six tapes, as shown in Table 24-1.

Table 24-1 *Sample backup schedule*

Evening	Backup type	Using tape
Saturday	Normal (Full)	Use a fresh tape, and send it to offsite storage on Tuesday morning.
Monday – Friday	Daily	Use tape set A, which contains one tape per evening.
Saturday	Normal (Full)	Use a fresh tape, and send it to offsite storage on Tuesday morning.
Monday–Friday	Daily	Use tape set B, which contains one tape per evening.

Keep 26 weeks of Saturday evening tapes offsite. Each week, have the offsite facility bring back the oldest tape on Tuesday morning, when they come to pick up the new tape. Reuse the tape they bring back the following Saturday night.

This sample schedule requires you to have a total of 37 tapes. Of the 37, 10 are used for the midweek Daily backups, 26 are stored offsite, and 1 is used for the

Saturday night backup. You'll always have a full backup tape on hand Monday morning in case you need to perform a file restore, and you'll have a rolling two weeks of daily backup tapes in case you need to restore a file that was last changed on a particular day.

Restoring data

Windows Backup enables you to restore data that you backed up earlier. You need to make sure you have all of the appropriate backups available, such as the most recent Full backup, and any Incremental or Differential backups, as appropriate.

Don't wait until you need to restore files to test your restore process. Periodically perform a test restore to make sure your backups are working and that your backup tapes are reliable. You can restore files to a non-production server to test the restore process.

When you perform a restore, you can have Windows Backup restore files to a different location than they were backed up from. This technique is useful when you need to examine the restored files to make sure they're the ones you want.

The Recovery Console

The Recovery console is a special command-line interface that you can use to help perform troubleshooting and recovery tasks on your server. The Recovery console is not installed by default, although you should install it on every Windows Server 2003 in your organization.

To install the Recovery console, insert the Windows Server 2003 CD into the server. From the Start menu, select Run, and type d:\i386\winnt32.exe /cmdcons, replacing d:\ with the letter of the CD-ROM drive on your server.

The Recovery console appears as an additional operating system selection on the server's startup menu. When you select the Recovery console, Windows Server 2003 starts with a minimum configuration, no graphical user interface, and a limited set of tools. You have to log on to the Recovery console using the password of the server's local Administrator account.

Once you log on to the Recovery console, you can perform a number of useful tasks:

- Repair the Boot.Ini file, which contains the list of operating systems available on the server and is the source for the operating system selection menu.

- Copy files from the Windows Server 2003 CD to replace corrupted or missing operating system files.

- Copy files from the server's hard disk to floppy disks, even files which are located on an NTFS partition.

- Repair the server's master boot record or modify the server's partition table.

- Perform administrative tasks to restore or modify Active Directory.

The Recovery console enables you to perform powerful, complex tasks using command-line tools. Do not attempt to use any Recovery console tools unless you fully understand how they work and what they will do to your server. Consult the Windows Server 2003 documentation for more information.

Automatic System Recovery

Windows Automatic System Recovery (ASR) is a last-resort process you can use to restore your server's operating system to full functionality. ASR does not restore your data files, and ASR does require that you perform a special ASR backup before ASR can be used.

ASR backup

**10 Min.
To Go**

You use Windows Backup to perform an ASR backup. Open Windows Backup and, if you're in Advanced mode, select ASR Wizard from the Tools menu. If Windows Backup is in Wizard mode, select ASR Backup from the Wizard's selection screen.

ASR backups require a blank, formatted, high-density floppy disk. ASR backups should be performed only to a tape device; backing up to a disk file is useless because you probably won't have access to the backup file if you actually need to use ASR restore.

The ASR Backup Wizard automatically backs up the files required to perform an ASR restore. ASR *does not include your data files,* so make sure you perform a regular backup of those files once the ASR backup is complete.

Perform a new ASR backup any time something changes on your server, such as when you install new hardware or software. You don't need to perform daily or weekly ASR backups, and you should always save the most recent two ASR backups (save two in case one of them becomes corrupted).

ASR restore

If your server fails and all attempts to restore it to operation also fail, you can resort to an ASR restore. Keep in mind that you must have your ASR backup tape, ASR floppy disk, and a Windows Server 2003 CD-ROM in order to perform an ASR restore. Also, ASR does not restore your server's data files. Once ASR is finished performing the restore, you need to restore your data files from a separate backup tape.

To perform an ASR restore, follow these steps:

1. Insert the Windows Server 2003 CD into your server's CD-ROM.

2. Restart the computer and allow it to boot from the CD.

3. While Windows Setup is initializing, watch the bottom of the screen. When you are prompted to press F2 for Automated System Recovery, press F2.

4. When prompted, insert the ASR floppy disk in the server's floppy disk drive.

5. Follow the onscreen instructions to complete the ASR restore.

After you make your first ASR backup, try restoring it to a test server that uses the same hardware as the server you backed up. The test confirms that your ASR backup is reliable and that you understand the restore procedures completely.

Done!

REVIEW

In this session, you learned about the importance of disaster recovery preparation, and you learned how to use Windows Server 2003's built-in tools for backup and restore, system snapshots, and Automatic System Recovery (ASR). You also learned how to install and log on to the Recovery console.

Quiz Yourself

1. How does ASR handle your data files? (See "Automatic System Recovery.")

2. What must you do to back up a remote computer's system state data over your network? (See "Backup and Restore.")

3. How do you install the Recovery Console? (See "The Recovery Console.")

4. How does a Daily backup affect files' archive bits? (See "Types of backups.")

Managing Hardware

Session Checklist

✔ How to install device drivers

✔ How to configure driver signing options

✔ How to recover from driver problems

✔ How to manage device drivers

**30 Min.
To Go**

Windows Server 2003 is designed to run on modern, complex computer hardware. That means one of the biggest tasks of administering a Windows Server 2003 computer is dealing with the actual computer hardware and how that hardware interacts with the Windows operating system.

In this session, you'll learn about device drivers, how to install them, and how to configure Windows driver security features. You'll also learn how to recover from problems caused by installing new drivers and how to manage device drivers and hardware profiles within Windows.

Never modify your computer's hardware or driver settings unless you know what effects your changes will have. Also, make sure you always back up your computer's operating system and data before modifying the hardware or drivers, in case your changes cause the computer to fail.

Device Drivers

Windows Server 2003 uses small software applications called *device drivers* to communicate with the hardware devices in a computer. For example, when you install a network interface card (NIC) in a computer, you also have to install a device driver that tells Windows how to communicate with the NIC. Device drivers are sometimes provided by Microsoft (the Windows Server 2003 CD contains thousands of device drivers), but most drivers are provided by the manufacturers of the hardware devices.

More so than any other type of software, device drivers must be programmed by thorough, careful programmers to very stringent specifications. That's because device drivers have special privileges under Windows and are allowed to perform tasks that no other software is allowed to perform. Those special privileges are required for device drivers to do their job, but they also allow poorly written drivers to crash the operating system very easily.

Microsoft contends that the majority of operating system crashes under older versions of Windows were caused by poorly written device drivers, not by bugs in the operating system software itself.

Because device drivers play such a critical role in a server's operations and reliability, Windows Server 2003 includes features to help you manage drivers efficiently. The most important features relating to device drivers are driver signing and device management.

Driver signing

Microsoft introduced the concept of driver signing in Windows 2000, and Windows Server 2003 continues to use driver signing as a means of improving the reliability of device drivers.

When a hardware manufacturer creates a device driver to go with a hardware device that they sell, they can submit the driver software to Microsoft for testing. Microsoft charges a fee for the testing process and tests the driver to make sure it is well written and will not cause problems with the operating system. If the driver passes the test, Microsoft modifies the driver software slightly by adding a digital signature. The signature includes information about the code within the driver and serves as proof that the driver software hasn't changed since Microsoft tested it.

When you install a device driver that has a Microsoft digital signature, Windows Server 2003 examines the signature and the driver software to make sure they match.

If they do, Windows installs the driver with no complaints. The signature gives you some assurance that the driver won't crash your server later on down the line.

Many manufacturers don't submit their drivers to Microsoft for testing, though. They choose not to do so for a couple of reasons:

- The testing process is expensive, and some manufacturers operate on thin profit margins. They can't afford to submit their driver software for testing.

- The testing process is also time-consuming. Many manufacturers prefer to release their hardware products, and the accompanying drivers, without waiting for Microsoft to test the drivers. Some manufacturers release products with unsigned drivers and then include a signed driver in a later version of the product, after Microsoft's testing is complete.

- Some manufacturers don't take a lot of time when programming their device drivers and know that the drivers won't pass Microsoft's tests.

Whatever the reason, you're likely to run across plenty of unsigned drivers as a Windows Server 2003 administrator. When you attempt to install an unsigned driver, Windows either warns you, prevents you from installing the driver altogether, or allows you to install the driver without even a warning. You can configure your server's behavior by following these steps:

1. Right-click My Computer and select Properties.
2. On the hardware tab, click the Driver Signing button.
3. Select the behavior you want your server to use when unsigned drivers are installed, as shown in Figure 25-1.

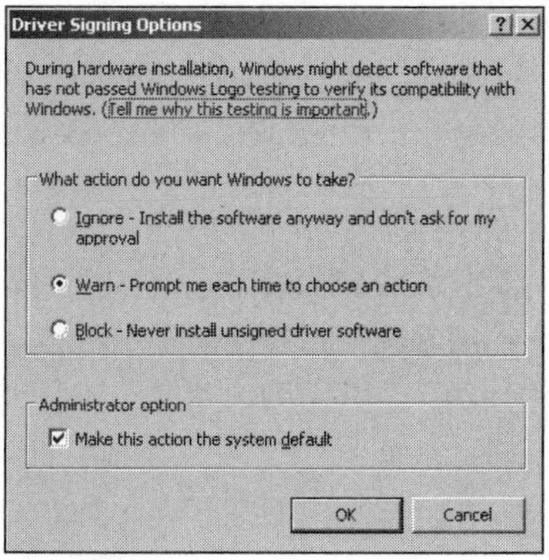

Figure 25-1   *Configuring driver signing options*

Who Cares about Driver Signing?

Unsigned drivers are not necessarily bad, despite what Windows' warning messages would have you believe. As I've outlined, there are valid reasons for a device manufacturer to not submit their drivers to Microsoft for testing. And, let's face it, Microsoft has certainly missed a bug or two in their own products, so their testing process is definitely not foolproof.

I use some common-sense guidelines regarding unsigned drivers. If they're from a reputable company that's been making Windows-compatible devices for a long time, I use the drivers. If the drivers are from an obscure company, or if I've had problems with the company's drivers in the past, I don't use their drivers until they get them signed.

Choosing not to use an unsigned driver also means choosing not to use the hardware that the driver goes with. A good time to make the "use or not use" decision is *before* you buy the hardware in question. Use manufacturer's Web sites and pre-sales phone numbers to determine whether or not their drivers are signed. If you can't check ahead of time, make sure you understand your options for returning the product if it comes with unsigned drivers that you're not willing to use.

If you do install hardware that includes unsigned drivers, don't install any other hardware for at least a week. That'll help you narrow down any new problems to the new hardware, rather than trying to decide which device is causing the problem. Make sure you use every feature of the new hardware so that its driver is thoroughly exercised on your server. And be prepared to remove the hardware — and its driver — if it causes problems on your system.

The behavior you select affects only your user account. If you want the behavior to apply to all users, select the "Make this action the system default" check box.

**20 Min.
To Go**

Device management

Windows Server 2003 offers a graphical interface for managing hardware devices. To access the interface, right-click My Computer and select Properties from the pop-up menu. On the Hardware tab, click the Device Manager button. Windows displays the Device Manager, which is shown in Figure 25-2.

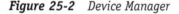

Figure 25-2 *Device Manager*

Device Manager lists all the different types of hardware attached to your computer. Under each type, Device Manager lists the actual hardware components that are installed. Device Manager changes the device's icons to represent their condition:

- A device with a regular icon is installed, enabled, and working correctly.
- A device with a yellow exclamation mark is not working correctly and requires your attention. Device Manager automatically expands the hardware type list to display icons with an exclamation mark.
- A device with a red "X" has been manually disabled. Device Manager automatically expands the hardware list to display icons with a red "X."

You can use Device Manager to troubleshoot, modify, and enable or disable devices. To enable or disable a device, right-click its icon and select Enable or Disable from the pop-up menu. To work with a device's properties, double-click the device (or right-click it and select Properties from the pop-up menu). When you do so, Device Manager displays the device's properties. The Drivers tab of the Properties dialog box, shown in Figure 25-3, enables you to manage the device driver associated with the device.

Figure 25-3 *Managing a device's drivers*

The Driver tab enables you to accomplish the following tasks:

- Examine details about the device's driver software, such as the version number and physical filenames. These details can help you determine whether you are using the most recent version of a driver.

- Replace a driver with a newer version. Clicking the Update Driver button enables you to provide a newer driver than the one that is currently installed.

- If you've updated a device driver and the new driver is causing problems, click the "Roll back driver" button to revert to the previous version of the driver. This feature is very useful, enabling you to quickly remove a bad device driver and restore your system to normal operations more easily.

- If you want to completely remove the driver, click the Uninstall button. Windows walks you through the process of removing the driver.

If you uninstall a device driver because you don't want to use it any more, make sure you also remove the related hardware. Otherwise, Windows just redetects the hardware and reinstalls the driver.

Device Driver Recovery

Because device drivers can so easily crash a server, Windows Server 2003 includes some special features to help recover from those crashes. Your two best tools are Safe Mode and the Last Known Good configuration. Both of these tools interact with device driver rollback, and you should be aware of how that interaction can affect your ability to recover from a server failure.

Safe Mode

When you start a Windows Server 2003 computer, the computer prompts you to select an operating system. You normally just choose Windows Server 2003. But the menu also provides options for selecting an alternative startup mode called Safe Mode. Safe Mode starts the operating system and enables only core device drivers that are absolutely critical for Windows to function, like the keyboard, hard drives, and mouse. If your computer crashes and you suspect a device driver, try starting the computer in Safe Mode. You'll be able to access the computer's hard disk and most of the operating system's features, and you'll reduce the chance of a driver causing another crash.

Windows also offers Safe Mode with Networking Support, which enables additional device drivers necessary to permit network connectivity. If Safe Mode seems to work OK, try Safe Mode with Networking Support. If the computer crashes, then you know one of your network-related device drivers is causing the problem.

Last Known Good configuration

Every time you log on to Windows Server 2003, the operating system copies a portion of its Registry into a backup location. By logging on, you've let Windows know that the system's hardware seems to be functioning correctly, and so Windows assumes that the current configuration is "good."

When you install a new device driver, any really bad problems are likely to occur the next time you restart the computer. A totally incompatible or malfunctioning driver often crashes the computer before Windows finishes starting, let alone before you log on. When this happens, select the Last Known Good option from Windows' operating system selection menu. Windows copies that "good" Registry configuration from its backup location and overwrites the current Registry.

The effect is to undo whatever changes the driver installation made to the Registry, which means Windows won't know the driver exists. It won't try to start the driver, and so the operating system won't crash when it starts. You'll be able to access the computer and troubleshoot the problem.

Some drivers don't finish starting until after Windows displays the logon screen. For safety, wait several minutes before logging on when you restart after installing a new device driver. That way, your Last Known Good configuration is still be available as a recovery option.

Last Known Good can be a real lifesaver when you restart your computer and it suddenly crashes before you can even log on. Last Known Good should be the first troubleshooting step you try whenever your computer crashes during the startup process.

Device driver rollback

As I described in the previous section, "Device Management," you can use the Device Manager to roll back drivers to a previous version. Here are some tips for making the driver rollback feature work best:

10 Min. To Go

- The most reliable drivers are on the Windows Server 2003 CD. When you install new devices, let Windows use a driver from the CD if it finds one. Even if that driver doesn't support all of your hardware device's functionality, the driver can serve as a guaranteed-to-function starting point. You can always update the driver to a more functional version, and you always have the original CD-based driver to roll back to in the event of a problem.

- Your second-best bet for device drivers is the Windows Update Web site (windowsudpate.microsoft.com). Microsoft usually posts signed drivers only to the Update site, so check there first for the latest versions of drivers for your hardware. As with the CD-based drivers, drivers from Windows Update serve as a good starting point because you can roll back to them if necessary.

- Device driver rollback does not occur automatically when you select Last Known Good. Last Known Good restores a previous copy of the server's Registry, but it doesn't affect the actual device driver files on disk. If you experience a problem with a new device driver and it crashes your system, you may still need to roll the driver back to a previous version to correct the problem.

Hardware Profiles

Windows Server 2003 supports hardware profiles, just as previous versions of Windows do. You may ask yourself why a server product would need hardware profiles, though, when the primary use for them on previous versions was to accommodate users with laptop computers.

Hardware profiles enable you to specify a set of hardware devices that are enabled on the computer. When the computer starts, you select a hardware profile (the default profile is selected automatically after a brief period of time), and Windows attempts to start only the devices listed in the profile. In a way, hardware profiles resemble customizable versions of Safe Mode.

For mobile users, profiles are a great way to disable devices that weren't used or present when the computer was undocked, for example. For servers, hardware profiles can be valuable troubleshooting tools.

Creating hardware profiles

To manage your server's hardware profiles, right-click My Computer. Select Properties from the pop-up menu, and click on the Hardware tab. Then click on the Hardware Profiles button to display the Profiles Manager, shown in Figure 25-4.

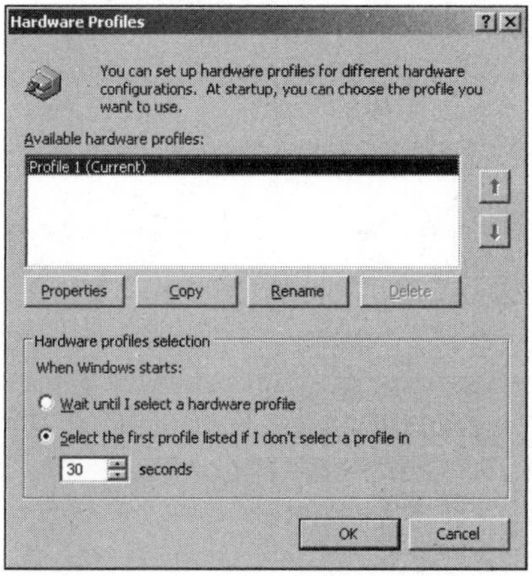

Figure 25-4   *Hardware Profiles Manager*

The Profiles Manager enables you to create new profiles by copying an existing one. You can also reorder the profiles because the first profile listed is treated as the default. The first profile listed should be your normal hardware profile that your server uses every day.

Once you create a new profile, you can restart your server and select that profile. The profile starts with the same settings as the profile it was copied from, but you can start making changes from there. Use the Device Manager to disable devices in the new profile, and you can start creating a custom hardware profile to fit your specific needs.

Make sure you give your hardware profiles descriptive names that help identify what the profile is used for.

Using hardware profiles

One use for hardware profiles is to create customized Safe Modes. For example, you might create a profile that enables only hardware devices that are using Microsoft-signed device drivers. That profile could become a troubleshooting option when you install a new driver and it crashes the computer, or when you think you're having problems with a particular device.

In a test lab, hardware profiles can be used to create different hardware configurations for testing purposes. Profiles enable you to easily test the interactions between various device drivers. Always make sure you have a default profile that enables only the drivers that you know work correctly together, so that you can restart the computer and troubleshoot problems that occur in your testing profiles.

Done!

REVIEW

In this session, you learned about the importance of device drivers to Windows Server 2003. You learned how Windows seeks to protect itself by using driver signing, and how Windows enables you to manage drivers using the Device Manager. You also learned how to recover from driver failures using Safe Mode, Last Known Good, and device rollback. Finally, you learned how hardware profiles can be used to create test and recovery environments on your servers.

QUIZ YOURSELF

1. How can you help prevent anyone who uses a computer from installing unsigned drivers? (See "Driver signing.")

2. How can hardware profiles help you recover from a device driver failure? (See "Using hardware profiles.")

3. When is it safe to use unsigned device drivers? (See "Who Cares about Driver Signing?")

4. Why are poorly written drivers a frequent cause of operating system crashes? (See "Device Drivers.")

Managing and Maintaining Servers

Session Checklist

✔ How to use the Event Viewer

✔ How to manage hotfixes and service packs

✔ How to perform regular server maintenance

**30 Min.
To Go**

Like any complex machine, servers must be regularly monitored and maintained. You (hopefully) wouldn't drive your car for thousands of miles without changing the oil and checking the tire pressure; Windows Server 2003 computers require the same basic monitoring and preventative maintenance.

Windows Server 2003 includes tools for monitoring and maintaining the server. Unfortunately, too many administrators ignore these tools in the face of everyday problems and challenges. Always keep in mind that while your servers may *appear* to be running normally, you'll never know what's going on "beneath the hood" unless you check.

In this session, I'll introduce you to Windows' Event Viewer. I'll also show you how to manage the inevitable hotfixes and service packs provided by Microsoft, and how to perform regular preventative maintenance using Windows Server 2003's built-in tools.

The Event Viewer

Windows Server 2003 uses a set of log files to track important system, application, security, and other events. These logs are collectively referred to as *event logs,* and you can examine them with Windows' built-in Event Viewer. The Event Viewer is part of the Computer Management console, which you can access by right-clicking My Computer and selecting Manage from the pop-up menu.

Viewing events

Windows Server 2003 includes three default event logs:

- **The Application Log.** Contains events logged by applications running on your server.
- **The Security Event Log.** Contains security events. This log also contains audit messages if you have enabled security auditing.

 You can learn more about security auditing in Session 3.

- **The System Log.** Contains events relating to the operating system itself.

As you install additional applications and services, they may create their own event logs. For example, when you install the Microsoft Domain Name Service (DNS), it creates an event log specifically for DNS-related events.

The Event Viewer is shown in Figure 26-1. Each line in the log is a single event, and you can view the detail of the event by double-clicking it. Each line also includes an icon, which identifies the severity of the event.

The three severity levels of events are

- **Informational.** Represented by the lowercase letter "i." Informational events are not errors and usually track when services are started or stopped.
- **Warning.** Represented by a yellow exclamation point. Warning messages usually mean something isn't working correctly but the server will continue to function. You should examine the event's details for information on what's wrong and how to fix it.

- **Error.** Represented by a red "X." Errors indicate that something is wrong and that some portion of the operating system — usually a service — cannot continue to function.

Figure 26-1   The Event Viewer

Make a regular habit of checking the event logs on your servers. If you don't, you'll never know when something goes wrong.

Event logs can contain a lot of events, and so the Event Viewer contains a filtering feature that enables you to focus on certain types of events. To enable the filter, right-click the event log and select Properties from the pop-up menu. Then select the Filter tab, as shown in Figure 26-2.

You can select the exact type of events you want to view, click OK, and the Event Viewer displays only events matching your criteria.

Events that do not meet your filter criteria are not deleted. Event Viewer simply hides those events as long as the filter is active.

Application Properties

General | Filter

Event types

☑ Information   ☐ Success audit
☑ Warning   ☐ Failure audit
☑ Error

Event source: Active Server Pages ▾
Category: Network ▾
Event ID: 1057
User:
Computer:

From: First Event ▾ 11/ 3/2001 ▾ 5:36:36 PM ▾
To: Last Event ▾   11/ 3/2001 ▾ 12:58:06 PM ▾

Restore Defaults

OK | Cancel | Apply

Figure 26-2   *Filtering events*

Managing the logs

By default, Windows restricts the event logs to a maximum size, so that they don't
grow and fill up your hard drive space. Windows automatically discards events older
than seven days to make room for new events, if necessary. You can configure this
behavior by right-clicking an event log and selecting Properties from the pop-up
menu. As shown in Figure 26-3, you can adjust the properties of the log to change
the log's maximum size and to change when Windows overwrites old events.

One log that you need to be especially careful of is the Security Event Log. If
you enable security auditing, the Security Event Log can fill up quickly. If
Windows is unable to overwrite old events, it won't log new security events. Not
logging security events is a security problem in and of itself, and so to prevent
that problem, *Windows automatically shuts down*. Windows logs an error to the
System Log indicating that the shutdown was due to a Security Event Log that was
full and could not be overwritten.

**If you plan to use security auditing, configure the Security Event
Log so that it is large enough and can overwrite events as necessary. Doing so prevents your server from shutting down unexpect-
edly due to a full Security Event Log.**

Figure 26-3 *Changing event log properties*

Hotfixes and Service Packs

Nobody's perfect, and the programmers at Microsoft are no exception. When they discover a problem (or "bug") with the Windows software, they usually correct it by releasing a hotfix. Hotfixes are designed to correct specific problems, and Microsoft does not always have the opportunity to test the hotfixes in every possible situation that they may be used. For that reason, you should apply hotfixes only if they correct a problem that you are experiencing.

Microsoft periodically gathers up all of the hotfixes and any other bug-fixes they have created into a service pack. Service packs are tested in a wide variety of situations and are generally more reliable and stable than the hotfixes they contain. Service packs are often quite large and can usually be obtained from Microsoft on a CD if you don't want to spend the time to download them.

Applying hotfixes and service packs

Hotfixes and service packs usually come with their own instructions for applying them. Service packs generally include an Update.exe program, which you can double-click to apply the service pack. Hotfixes are often self-contained and simply double-clicking the hotfix applies it.

**20 Min.
To Go**

Part V — Sunday Morning
Session 26

You can also apply hotfixes and service packs using the Windows Update Web site (windowsupdate.microsoft.com). Windows Update analyzes your server and determines which hot fixes or service packs are available and not already present on your server. The Web site can then download the fixes to your computer and install them automatically.

Slipstreaming service packs

Many administrators copy the contents of the Windows Server 2003 CD to a file server, enabling them to install Windows over a network connection on new computers. If you use this technique, you can *slipstream* service packs onto your copy of Windows Server 2003, which enables you to install new servers with the latest service pack built right in.

Imagine that you've copied the \i386 folder from the Windows Server 2003 CD to a share folder named \\Server1\WinNET. If you obtain the latest Windows Server 2003 service pack, you can apply it to your copy by executing update.exe /s:\\Server1\WinNET. Update automatically looks for the i386 folder in \\Server1\WinNET and applies the service pack files. The next time you install a server using the files in \\Server1\WinNET\i386, that server will automatically contain the latest service pack's files.

Removing hotfixes and service packs

If you install a hotfix or service pack and it causes problems, you can remove it. Just open the Add/Remove Programs application from the Control Panel. As shown in Figure 26-4, select the appropriate hotfix or service pack and then click the Remove button.

You should be aware of some cautions when removing hotfixes or service packs:

- Hotfixes and service packs create uninstall folders on your hard drive. These folders usually have a name like C:\Windows\$NTUninstallQ123456$. If you delete the folder a hotfix created, you cannot uninstall the hotfix.

- Once you install a service pack, you cannot uninstall any hotfixes that preceded the service pack unless you *first* uninstall the service pack.

- Because hotfixes sometimes modify the same files, you should uninstall them in the reverse order that you installed them. In other words, if you installed HotfixA, HotfixB, and HotfixC, and now you want to remove HotfixB, you should first remove HotfixC.

- Some hotfixes cannot be uninstalled. Before you install a hotfix, check the documentation that comes with each hotfix to determine if there are any restrictions on later removing the hotfix.

Add or Remove Programs

	Currently installed programs:	Sort by:	Name	
	NTI CD-Maker 2000 Professional	Size	16.56MB	
	One-Touch Buttons			
	Palm Desktop	Size	2.75MB	
	PocketMirror 3.0.2 (Standard Edition)	Size	5.12MB	
	PowerQuest PartitionMagic 7.0	Size	1.27MB	
	RiadaHeadline	Size	2.27MB	
	SnagIt 5	Size	8.75MB	
	Technical Information and Utilities October 2001	Size	20.58MB	
	Virtual PC	Size	8.32MB	
	Windows XP Hotfix (SP1) [See Q307274 for more information]			
	Windows XP Hotfix (SP1) [See Q309521 for more information]			
	Windows XP Hotfix (SP1) [See Q309691 for more information]			
	Windows XP Hotfix (SP1) [See Q310507 for more information]			
	To change this program or remove it from your computer, click Change/Remove.		Change/Remove	
	WinZip	Size	3.04MB	

Change or Remove Programs / Add New Programs / Add/Remove Windows Components

Figure 26-4   *Removing a hotfix*

Using Automatic Update

If your servers have access to the Internet, you can configure Windows Server 2003 to automatically download important updates and service packs, and to alert you when they are ready to be installed. To enable this feature, right-click My Computer and select Properties from the pop-up menu. Then click on the Automatic Updates tab, and select the behavior you want your servers to use, as shown in Figure 26-5.

Automatic Update usually downloads only critical updates that Microsoft feels all administrators should install. Hotfixes meant to address less common problems won't usually be applied by Automatic Update.

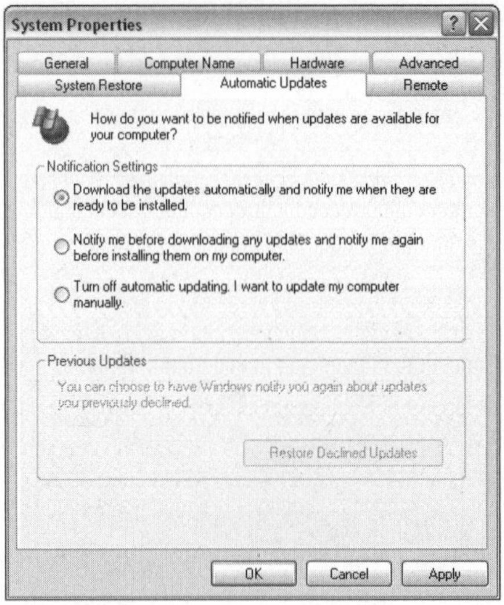

Figure 26-5   *Configuring Automatic Update*

Regular Maintenance

Even when there's nothing wrong with your servers, you should still perform certain regular maintenance tasks. The two most important tasks are disk defragmentation and checking disks for errors.

Disk defragmentation

Windows Server 2003 stores files in small blocks on your hard disk. Large files can take up hundreds or thousands of these blocks. On a new server, new files are written to the disk in a series of contiguous blocks, which can be later read from disk very quickly, just as you can read the contiguous words of this book very quickly.

When you delete a file, Windows Server 2003 tries to reuse the blocks the file occupied. If a new file won't fit within the reusable space, Windows writes what it can and then writes the rest of the file to free space elsewhere on the disk. When the file is later read from disk, the disk drive has to jump around to find all of the file's blocks. It's as if the "book words in this printed were order in random." As more and more files are deleted, and new files written, the files on the disk become *fragmented*. Severe fragmentation can significantly reduce the performance of a server.

**10 Min.
To Go**

Every couple of months or so, you should use Windows' built-in disk defragmentation tool to check your disks for fragmentation and, if necessary, defragment the files. You can access the defragmentation tool from the Computer Management console. As shown in Figure 26-6, the tool displays a graphical representation of your disk's fragmentation status. Red lines indicate fragmented files, and a large number of red lines means you should defragment your disk.

Figure 26-6   *Disk defragmentation*

> **Defragmenting a large hard disk can take a long time — several hours if the disk is badly fragmented. While the server can continue to operate during the defragmentation process, the server's performance will be much slower than usual. Schedule disk defragmentation for times when the server won't be heavily needed by users.**

Checking disks for errors

You should also periodically check your hard disks for errors. Errors can include

- **Cross-linked files.** Often caused by improperly shutting down the server or improperly ending applications.
- **Bad sectors.** Tend to occur as a disk drive grows older.

- **Bad directory entries.** Can result from poorly written applications or improperly shutting down the server.

Windows includes a disk error checker. To access it, right-click My Computer and select Properties. On the Tools tab, shown in Figure 26-7, click the Check Now button.

Figure 26-7 *The Tools tab*

You can also access Windows Backup and the disk defragmentation tool from the Tools tab.

Windows displays a small dialog box to enable you to customize the error checker's behavior, as shown in Figure 26-8. I recommend checking both check boxes and allowing the error checker to detect and repair as many errors as it can. Error checking usually takes only a few minutes, and the server can continue to operate while the check is in progress.

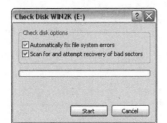

Figure 26-8   *Configuring error checking*

Done!

REVIEW

In this session, you learned about the importance of regular server maintenance, and you learned about Windows Server 2003's maintenance tools: Event Viewer, disk defragmentation, and others. You also learned how to manage the hotfixes and service packs on your system, including how to configure your server to automatically download and apply fixes.

QUIZ YOURSELF

1. How can you prevent an event log from filling up? (See "Managing the logs.")
2. How can you ensure that your Internet-connected servers always have the latest Microsoft updates? (See "Using Automatic Update.")
3. How can you remove service packs or hotfixes if necessary? (See "Removing hotfixes and service packs.")
4. How can you speed up the performance of your server's hard disks? (See "Disk defragmentation.")
5. How can you correct cross-linked files or bad sectors on a hard disk? (See "Checking disks for errors.")

PART

V

Sunday Morning Part Review

1. What VPN protocol offers a more secure tunnel by encrypting more of the transmitted data?
2. Which VPN protocol provides both tunneling and encryption?
3. What Windows Server service accepts VPN connections?
4. How can firewalls affect a VPN?
5. What protocols allow RRAS to talk to network routers and exchange routing information?
6. What server platforms do not include Internet Connection Sharing?
7. How can RRAS act as a basic port-filtering firewall?
8. How can RRAS act as an Internet gateway?
9. How can you quickly obtain statistics about your network based on data that you capture with Network Monitor?
10. How can you obtain the full version of Network Monitor?
11. What data can you capture with Network Monitor?
12. How can Network Monitor be used as a troubleshooting tool?
13. When does Windows Server perform a system snapshot or checkpoint?
14. What files does Automatic System Recovery restore for you?
15. Where can you back up system state data using Windows Backup?
16. What type of backup includes all of the files on your computer that have changed that day?

17. If your computer crashes before you log on, what is a good first step in troubleshooting the problem?

18. How can you revert to a previous version of a device driver?

19. How can you create a customized Safe Mode startup environment that includes only drivers known to work correctly on your server?

20. How can you enable or disable drivers in a hardware profile?

21. What effect does a full Security Event Log have on your server?

22. How can you remove a hotfix from your server?

23. How can you deploy new copies of Windows Server that include the latest service pack?

24. How does disk defragmentation improve system performance?

PART

VI

Sunday
Afternoon

Working with Windows Clusters

Session Checklist

✔ Different types of Windows clusters

✔ How clusters work

✔ How to create a cluster

✔ How to install clustered applications

**30 Min.
To Go**

As you learned in Session 1, Windows Server 2003 adds clustering capabilities to the Enterprise Server and Datacenter Server editions of the product. These clustering capabilities enable you to create more scalable and reliable server-based applications by helping to load-balance client traffic across multiple servers and provide backup servers in case one should fail.

In this session, you'll learn about the different types of Windows clusters and how they work. You'll also learn how to create a cluster, how to install clustered applications, and how to determine if an application can be successfully clustered.

Windows Clusters

Windows Server 2003 supports two different types of clusters: failover clusters and load-balancing clusters. Each type serves a very different purpose and enables you to achieve different scalability or reliability needs within your environment.

Scalability vs. Reliability

Scalability refers to a solution's ability to accommodate more work. Imagine that you have a file server that can handle about 1,000 users at once. Once it reaches that limit, though, there's no way to make the data it contains easily available to more people. In other words, the file server isn't scalable.

Reliability refers to a solution's ability to survive failure. Imagine a phone center with 200 representatives. If five of those representatives call in sick, it's no problem because the other 195 can handle the workload. The call center is said to be reliable because it can survive the failure of some of its components. The call center would be scalable, too, because if call volume increased, more representatives could be added to handle the additional workload.

Scalability and reliability are often a trade-off. Not all server applications can be both, and some can be made more reliable than scalable, or vice versa. Clustering is designed to address both issues, and the different types of clusters address reliability and scalability in different ways.

Failover clusters

In a Windows failover cluster, two servers (referred to as *nodes*) are connected to a single external disk storage subsystem. They also have their own internal storage subsystem. Both servers have application software installed, such as Microsoft Exchange Server. The application stores its data on the external shared storage subsystem. The application runs on only one node at a time. However, if that node experiences a hardware failure, the other node takes over. To users, the two nodes appear to be one giant server. This is referred to as *active-passive* clustering, where one node is active and the others are passive, waiting for the active node to fail.

Enterprise Server supports two-node clustering, while Datacenter Server supports four-node clustering.

The primary disadvantage of a failover cluster is that the passive nodes aren't doing useful work. They're usually expensive hardware, which makes it frustrating to have them sitting around just waiting for the first node to fail. A technique called *active-active clustering* allows both nodes to run an application. When one node fails, the remaining node continues doing its own work and picks up the work the failed node was handling. The surviving node effectively acts as two servers, although it may perform somewhat slower because of the additional work. Active-active clustering allows both nodes to perform useful work and still act as backups to each other.

Active-active clustering requires a physically separate storage subsystem, which is attached to all cluster nodes, for each active node in the cluster.

Windows achieves failover clustering through the Windows Cluster Service, which is a separately installed component under Enterprise Server and Datacenter Server. The service defines shared resources, which only one cluster node can own at a single time. For example, a two-node active-passive cluster (in which only one node is active at a time) might have the following shared resources:

- A shared name and IP address. Clients access the server using this name and address, rather than the names and IP addresses of the individual nodes. This behavior allows the clients to connect to whichever node is active because that node responds to the shared name and IP address.

- A shared storage subsystem.

- Other shared services, such as file shares or printer shares.

Shared resources can be grouped, and only one node can own a shared resource or a shared group. For example, in a two-node active-passive cluster, one node owns all of the shared resources. If that node fails, the other node seizes control of the shared resources and becomes the active node, responding to client requests and running the cluster's applications.

Nodes monitor one another through a private network connection. The active node periodically sends a *heartbeat* signal over the network connection. The heartbeat simply informs the passive node that the active node is running normally. If the heartbeat signal stops, the passive node knows that the formerly active node has failed and can begin taking control of the cluster's shared resources. The process of taking control is known as *failover*.

Figure 27-1 shows a sample two-node, active-passive cluster responding to client requests.

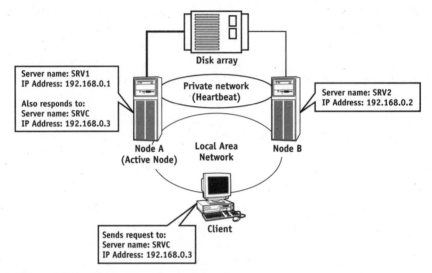

Disk array

Server name: SRV1
IP Address: 192.168.0.1

Also responds to:
Server name: SRVC
IP Address: 192.168.0.3

Private network (Heartbeat)

Server name: SRV2
IP Address: 192.168.0.2

Node A (Active Node)

Local Area Network

Node B

Client

Sends request to:
Server name: SRVC
IP Address: 192.168.0.3

Figure 27-1   *Two-node active-passive cluster*

Load-balancing clusters

Load-balancing clusters work somewhat differently than failover clusters. They use the Network Load Balancing (NLB) software included with Enterprise Server and Datacenter Server. The nodes of an NLB cluster are called *members,* and the only thing they share is a network connection and one or more virtual IP addresses. The virtual IP addresses allow clients to communicate with the entire cluster, rather than with an individual member.

Cluster members communicate with one another over the network, exchanging information about how busy they are. When clients send data to the cluster's virtual IP address, all of the cluster members "see" the data. However, only the least-busy cluster member — as determined by the members' exchange of information — responds to the request.

Clients see the cluster as one giant computer, although it may contain dozens of computers. Because an administrator has no way of knowing which member will handle individual requests, each server must contain identical software and data. That way, clients receive the same type of response no matter which cluster member handles their request.

**20 Min.
To Go**

Figure 27-2 shows an NLB cluster. A client on the network uses DNS to resolve the computer name CLSTR to the cluster's virtual IP address. The client then sends requests to that virtual IP address, and the request is handled by the cluster member least busy at the time.

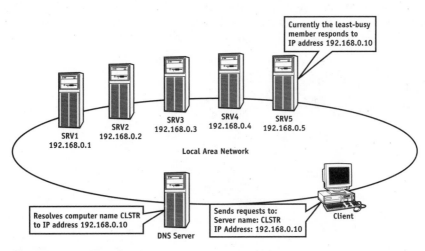

Figure 27-2   *NLB cluster*

NLB is available on Windows Server 2003 standard edition. It is also included with Microsoft Application Center 2000.

Creating a Cluster

Before you begin installing and configuring the clustering software, make sure your server hardware is cluster-compatible.

- Load-balancing clusters require that each member contain at least two network interface cards (NICs). One is used to handle client requests with the NLB software, while the other is used for the cluster members to communicate with one another.

- Failover clusters must conform to a special Cluster Hardware Compatibility List published by Microsoft. You can find the list in the Windows Server 2003 documentation or online at www.microsoft.com/windows.

Failover clusters

Failover clusters rely on the Microsoft Cluster Service. The service is installed, but not configured, by default on every Enterprise Server and Datacenter Server installation. To actually create a cluster, open the Cluster Administrator console on the computer that will become the first node in the cluster. When prompted, select the option to create a new cluster, as shown in Figure 27-3.

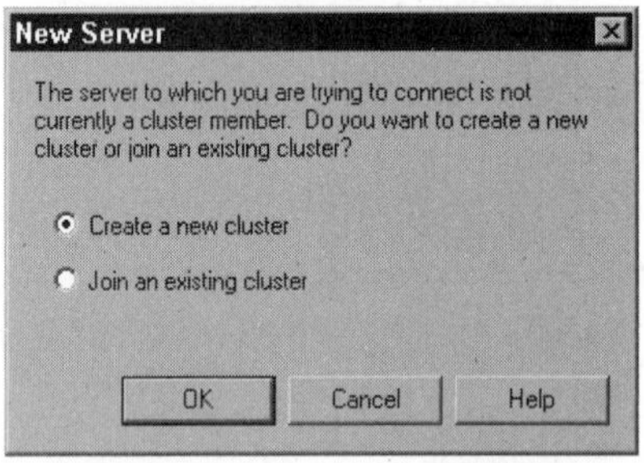

Figure 27-3 *Creating a new cluster*

Cluster Administrator launches a Wizard, which prompts you to create a name for the new cluster. You also have to identify the domain in which the cluster will be created, as shown in Figure 27-4. Each cluster node must belong to the domain you specify.

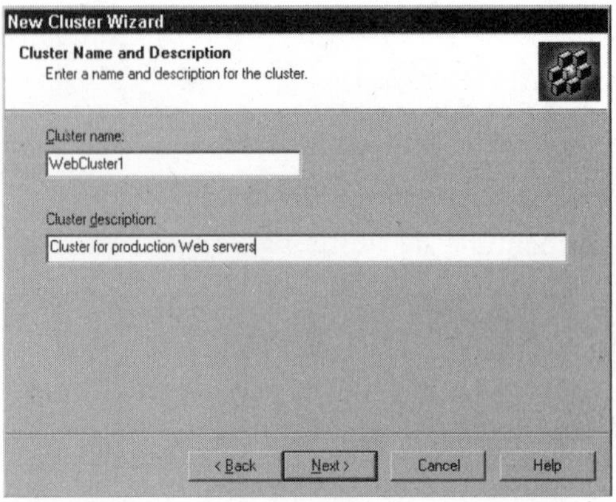

Figure 27-4 *Identifying the new cluster*

Complete each screen of the Wizard to identify the NICs that will be used for client and private cluster communications, which drive letter will be used to store cluster data, and so forth. Once the Wizard is complete, repeat the process on the other cluster nodes, selecting the option to join an existing cluster.

 You can test clustering without having two nodes. Just create a new cluster on a test computer, and don't bother adding any additional nodes. The result is a one-node "cluster" that you can use to become familiar with the clustering software and the Cluster Administrator console.

Load-balancing clusters

Load-balancing clusters rely on the Network Load Balancing (NLB) software, which is installed by default on Enterprise Server and Datacenter Server. To configure NLB, follow these steps:

1. Open Network Connections from the Control Panel.
2. Right-click the connection that represents the local area network connection that the NLB software will run on.
3. Select Properties from the pop-up menu.
4. Place a checkmark next to Network Load Balancing.

 If Network Load Balancing isn't listed, click Install. Then, double-click Services, and select Network Load Balancing from the list of services.

5. Specify a name and IP address for the new cluster, as shown in Figure 27-5.
6. Click OK to close the dialog boxes, and repeat these steps on each member of the cluster. Make sure you specify the same IP address and name for the remaining members.

Figure 27-5   *Configuring NLB properties*

Clustered Applications

There are three basic types of applications in the world, at least as far as the Microsoft Cluster Service is concerned:

- Applications that are cluster-aware
- Applications that are clusterable but not cluster-aware
- Applications that are not clusterable

The third type of application isn't worth discussing here, but in the next two sections I show you how to determine if an application is cluster-aware or clusterable, and what the differences are.

**10 Min.
To Go**

Cluster-aware applications

Cluster-aware applications are programmed to understand the Microsoft Cluster Service. These applications often provide simplified cluster setup, and are designed to integrate closely with the Microsoft Cluster Service. Microsoft SQL Server

Enterprise Edition and Microsoft Exchange Server Enterprise Edition are examples of cluster-aware applications. Microsoft SQL Server Enterprise Edition detects when you are installing it on a cluster node automatically installs itself on both cluster nodes, creates its data files on the cluster's shared storage subsystem, and sets up the necessary resource information in Cluster Administrator.

Cluster-aware applications are usually the easiest to install and run on a cluster.

Clusterable applications

Clusterable applications don't necessarily provide specific support for Microsoft Cluster Service but should run on a cluster anyway. You must install the application software on each node, configure the software to store its data on the external shared storage subsystem, and manually configure resource information in Cluster Administrator. In order for an application to qualify as clusterable, it must exhibit the following behaviors:

- The application's clients must communicate with the server over TCP/IP.

- The application's clients must tolerate a delay in responses, in case a request is sent while the application is failing over from one node to another.

- The application must allow its executables to be stored on each node, and its data to be stored on a separate physical drive.

- The application must not attempt to store any client-related data on the node's local storage subsystem.

Many Internet-based applications meet these criteria, and most companies have very little trouble writing their internal business applications to meet these criteria.

Load-balancing applications

Any TCP/IP-based application is potentially compatible with Network Load Balancing clusters. The only requirement is that the application not rely on any local server resources, such as local databases, to serve clients. That requirement makes sense when you remember that clients may be load-balanced to several different members over the course of a single session, and all of the client's data must be accessible to all of the members. Back-end databases that each member has access to makes the most sense for load-balancing applications.

Managing a Cluster

Whenever you manage a cluster, you have to remember that you're effectively managing more than one server at once. Always keep that in mind because the consequences of your actions are broader than just a single computer.

Failover clusters

Failover clusters are managed with the Cluster Administrator console. You should always instruct the console to connect to the cluster's shared name or IP address, which causes the console to connect to the cluster's active node. You can, however, direct the console to connect to a specific node by specifying that node's IP address or name. This technique is useful if one node is not responding and you want to connect directly to a different node in the cluster.

Cluster Administrator enables you to manage cluster resources and even perform failovers on demand. On-demand failover is useful, for example, when you need to perform maintenance on the active cluster node. You can direct the passive node to take over, enabling you to perform your maintenance tasks without impacting users.

You can also configure failback policies, which cause the cluster to try to return ownership of the cluster's shared resources to a specific node. Failback enables you to use cluster nodes that don't have identical hardware. For example, you might use a smaller, less expensive server as your passive node. If the main node fails, you can fix it and configure failback policy to automatically return cluster operations to the main node in the evening, when no users will be impacted by the failback.

Load-balancing clusters

Load-balancing clusters cannot be centrally administered using the tools in Windows Server 2003. However, if you have a large NLB cluster, you can purchase Microsoft Application Center 2000, which provides a way to centrally manage and control NLB-based clusters and the applications they run.

Done!

REVIEW

In this session, you learned about the two different types of Windows clusters. You also learned how those clusters work, and how you can create and manage them. You learned about cluster-aware applications and how to determine whether an application can be clustered.

This session provides only an overview of the complexity of Windows clustering. Be sure to read and understand the Windows clustering documentation before configuring or managing any clusters in your production environment.

QUIZ YOURSELF

1. What type of cluster uses a shared disk storage subsystem? (See "Windows Clusters.")

2. What type of cluster uses many different servers that share no hardware? (See "Windows Clusters.")

3. What server name should you connect to when attempting to manage a cluster? (See "Managing a Cluster.")

4. What installation steps are usually required for a cluster-aware application? (See "Clustered Applications.")

Managing Certificate Services

Session Checklist

✔ How certificates work and what they are used for

✔ How to install and configure Certificate Services

✔ How to manage Certificate Services

✔ How users interact with Certificate Services

**30 Min.
To Go**

I n today's world, digital certificates are becoming more and more important because they help bring a level of security to the Internet, and to computers in general, that isn't otherwise available. In this session, you'll learn how certificates work and how they can be used. You'll also learn how to install, configure, and manage Microsoft Certificate Services, which enables you to issue your own digital certificates.

How Certificates Work

Digital certificates are used to encrypt data. However, creative use of encryption means that certificates can also be used to verify data, guarantee identity, and much more. Understanding how certificates work is critical to understanding many Internet-based protocols and to understanding Microsoft Certificate Services.

Digital encryption

Encryption is the process of scrambling information so that only the sender and recipient can read it. You probably remember the secret decoder rings you owned as a child, that let you encode and decode messages to and from your friends. Those rings were a very simplistic form of encryption. Modern encryption involves mathematical algorithms so complex that they are often patented. Modern encryption techniques typically are so powerful and complex that it would take thousands of computers working nonstop several months — or even years — to crack the code and decrypt the data.

The simplest way to encrypt data is to use a password. The password is used as an *encryption key*, a starting point for the encryption algorithm. The creator of the password sends a copy of it to the recipient. The recipient can then use the same encryption algorithm, together with the password, to decrypt the information. In this example, the password serves as a symmetric key because both halves of the key — the half used to encrypt it and the half used to decrypt it — are the same.

Symmetric keys pose several obvious problems, not the least of which is how to securely transmit the key. After all, if the key is intercepted, then the entire encryption process is worthless.

Public/private keys

Asymmetric keys, also called public/private key pairs, solve the problems created by symmetric keys. In an asymmetric key, someone sending information obtains the recipient's public key. That key is used to encrypt the information. Anyone can access the public key because it can be used only to encrypt information. The recipient uses their private key, which only she has access to, to decrypt the information.

Asymmetric keys are ideal for the Internet because the Internet provides a way for users to access each others' public keys. The keys generally are created by commercial *certificate authorities,* who maintain a database of public keys. The keys are issued in the form of digital certificates, and users' private keys are stored in certificate repositories on their computers.

Certificates for encryption

Certificates are always used to encrypt data — they really have no other purpose. Encryption is always performed with one key, and decryption with another. When the purpose of encryption is just to protect data while it is transmitted to the recipient, then the recipient's public key is used for the encryption, and his private key for decryption.

When you stop to think about it, the fact that *only the holder of the public key* can decrypt the data, certificates can become incredibly flexible.

Certificates for identification

One common use of certificates is for identification. For example, the Windows Server 2003 authentication protocol, Kerberos, can use certificates for identification purposes. Imagine that you need to contact an Internet server, and you plan to download some information from it. You're not concerned about the information being intercepted on its way to you, so encryption isn't necessary. You are concerned that the information actually comes from the server you intend to contact. On the Internet, it's very easy to misdirect users so that they are using a different server than the one they intended to use. Certificates can provide positive identification — here's how:

1. You contact the server and request an identity check.
2. The server takes its identity information, along with the current date and time, and encrypts them with the server's private key.
3. The server transmits the encrypted "ID card" to your computer.
4. Your computer obtains the public key of the server you intended to connect to from a certificate authority and attempts to decrypt the "ID card." Keep in mind that the public key can only decrypt something that was originally encrypted with the server's private key.

   - If your computer cannot decrypt the "ID card," then the identity check fails. You obviously aren't connected to the server you had intended to connect to.
   - If your computer can decrypt the "ID card," then the server you are connected to must be the one you intended because it used the correct private key. The identity check is a success.

Your computer can ensure that the date and time on the "ID card" is recent, which prevents someone on the Internet from capturing a previously transmitted packet and trying to reuse it to fool you.

Certificates for verification

Certificates can also be used to verify data. For example, suppose you visit a Web site, and it offers to transmit a special Web browser plug-in to you. The plug-in enables you to view multimedia content on the Web site. You'd like to accept the plug-in, but you know that viruses are everywhere on the Internet. How can you be sure that the plug-in you receive is safe?

The Web server can use a certificate to *digitally sign* the plug-in before transmitting it. The Web server performs a mathematical calculation on the binary code of the plug-in to create a *checksum*. The checksum is a unique value that corresponds to the binary code of the plug-in. The Web server can then encrypt the checksum with the server's private key.

When your browser receives the plug-in, it obtains the server's public key from a certificate authority. Your browser then performs the same checksum calculation on the plug-in and verifies that the checksum it calculates matches the decrypted checksum sent from the server. If the two checksums match, then you know two things:

- The server you intended to contact really did send you the plug-in (identity check).
- The plug-in code hasn't been modified since it left the server (verification). If the code had changed, your browser would have come up with a different checksum.

So long as you trust the owners of the Web site not to deliberately send you a virus-infected plug-in, you can be reasonably sure that the plug-in you received is safe.

**20 Min.
To Go**

How Certificate Services Works

Microsoft Certificate Services is a special service that accepts requests for certificates and then issues certificates in accordance with policies you define. By default, Certificate Services can be configured to automatically issue a certificate to anyone who requests it or to accept requests and wait for an administrator to approve each one before issuing the certificate. Certificate Services is extensible, so that a software developer can write policy modules that define how Certificate Services issues certificates. For example, you might install a policy module that verifies a person's identity in your company's human resources database and then automatically issues a certificate.

Certificate Services is capable of acting as a certificate authority, or CA, just as commercial CAs like VeriSign or Thawte. You can use Certificate Services to implement your own *public key infrastructure,* where Certificate Services, instead of a commercial CA, maintains your company's public keys. Using Certificate Services can be much less expensive than a commercial CA, which may charge hundreds of dollars annually for each certificate you request.

Setting Up Certificate Services

You install Certificate Services just like any other Windows Server 2003 component: Open Add/Remove Programs on the Control Panel and select Add/Remove Windows Components. Select the Certificate Services check box and click OK.

Once Certificate Services is installed, you still have to configure it. Open the Add/Remove Windows Components window again, and you'll see an option to configure Certificate Services. Click the Configure button to launch the Certificate Services Wizard.

The first screen of the Wizard, shown in Figure 28-1, enables you to select the type of CA you want to create.

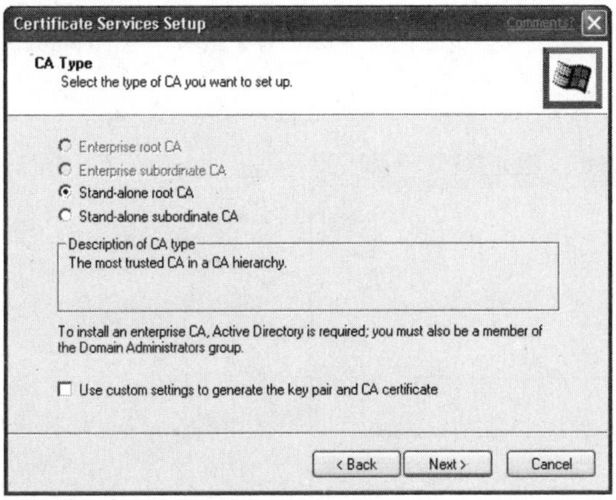

Figure 28-1   *Selecting a CA type*

You can create four types of CAs:

- **Enterprise Root CA.** Can be installed only on a domain controller and acts as the ultimate certificate authority in your domain.

- **Enterprise Subordinate CA.** Can be installed only on a domain controller. Subordinate CAs are given authority by a root CA to issue certificates, which helps divide the workload of issuing certificates.

- **Standalone Root CA.** Performs the same function as an Enterprise Root CA but is installed on a computer that isn't a domain controller.

- **Standalone Subordinate CA.** Performs the same function as an Enterprise Subordinate CA but is installed on a computer that isn't a domain controller.

Enterprise CAs store certificate information in Active Directory, which takes advantage of Active Directory's built-in replication and fault tolerance.

All CAs must have a certificate that allows them to issue certificates. Your root CAs can issue their own certificate, which is called a *self-signed* certificate. Your root CAs can also use a certificate-issuing certificate that is issued by a commercial CA, which is usually quite expensive. The advantage to using a commercial CA to authorize your own CAs is that most Windows computers are preconfigured to trust the common commercial CAs. I'll talk more about the issue of trust in the last section of this session, "Certificates and Internet Explorer."

Once you select the type of CA to create, the Wizard prompts you to name your CA, as shown in Figure 28-2. Select a unique name that fits into your domain naming convention.

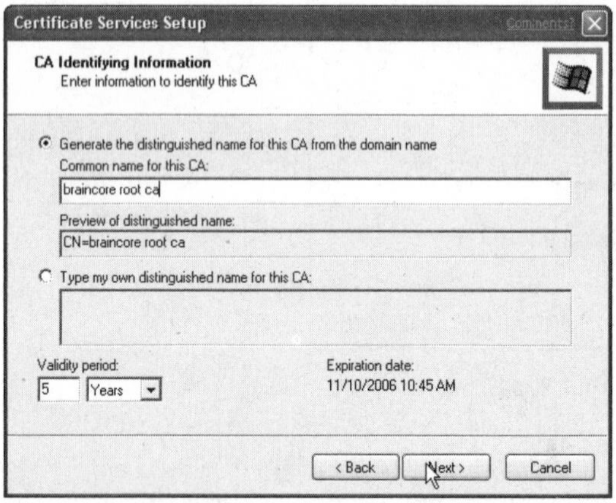

Figure 28-2   *Naming the CA*

Next, the Wizard asks you to select the folders that certificate information will be stored in, as shown in Figure 28-3. Enterprise CAs will use the default Active Directory folders for some of the certificate information.

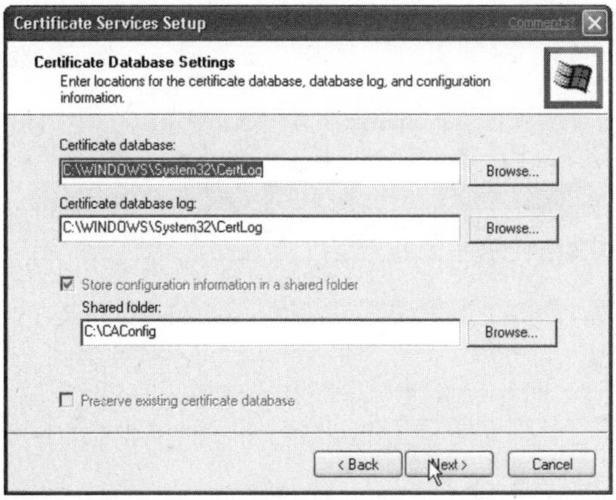

Figure 28-3 *Configuring the CA storage folders*

Once the Wizard finishes, you can begin using Certificate Services right away.

Using Certificate Services

Certificate Services sets up a virtual folder under your server's Default Web Site on Internet Information Services. The virtual folder provides access to a Web-based certificate interface, which users can use to manage their certificate requests from Certificate Services.

Requesting certificates

After installing Certificate Services, users can point their Web browsers to http://*servername*/certsrv to access a Web-based Certificate Services end-user interface. As shown in Figure 28-4, users can request a new digital certificate right from their Web browsers.

Issuing certificates

Once a user has requested a certificate, Certificate Services (by default) treats the request as pending until an administrator does something about it. You can use the Certificate Services console to view pending requests, validate the identity of each requestor, and issue certificates. As shown in Figure 28-5, you can right-click each pending request and use the pop-up menu to issue the certificate or deny the request.

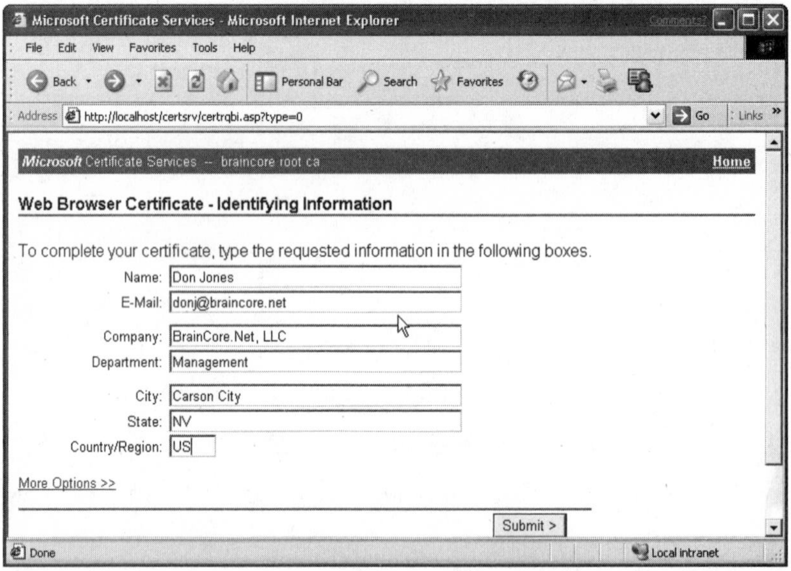

Figure 28-4   *Requesting a certificate*

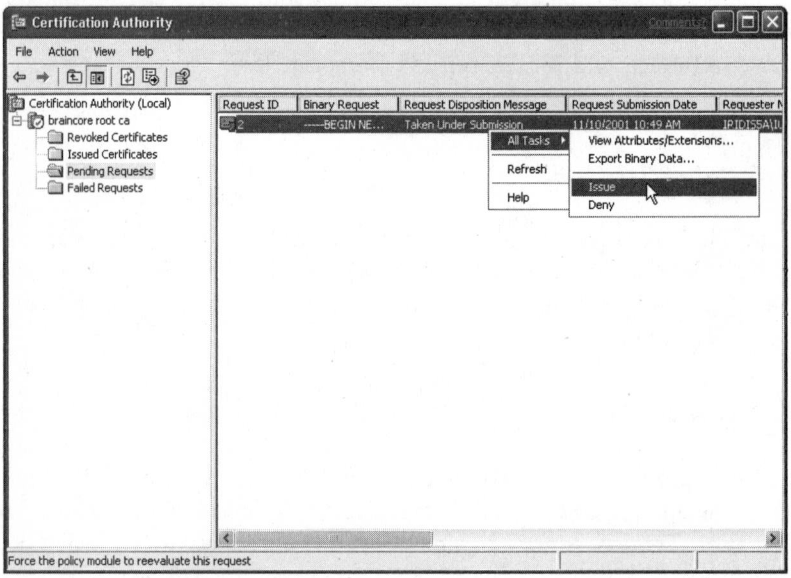

Figure 28-5   *Issuing certificates*

Approved certificates disappear from the pending list and reappear in the console's list of issued certificates, as shown in Figure 28-6. You can right-click any issued certificate to view its details or even revoke the certificate.

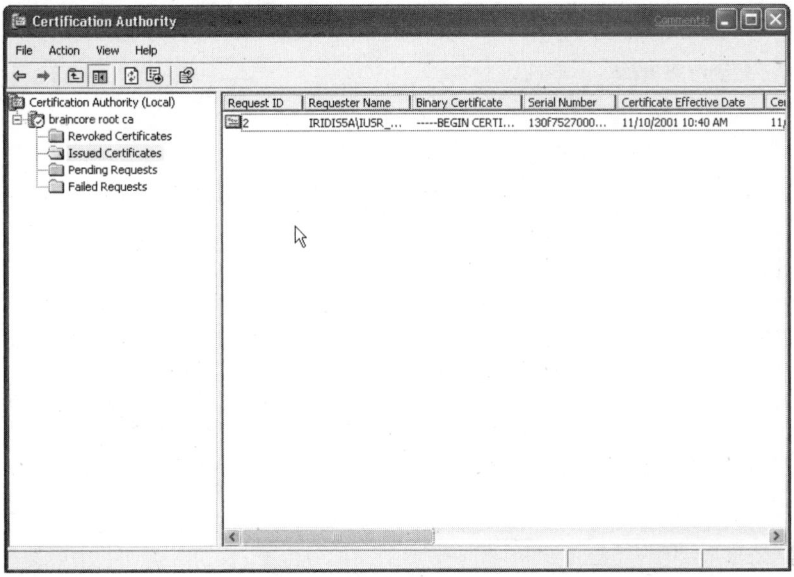

Figure 28-6 *Viewing issued certificates*

Users can use their Web browsers to view the status of their certificate requests. Once approved, users can download their certificates directly into their Web browser or e-mail application, as shown in Figure 28-7.

Certificates and Internet Explorer

Internet Explorer (IE) is preconfigured to trust certificates that are issued by the major commercial CAs. You can access the list of trusted root authorities in IE by selecting Internet Options from the Tools menu, clicking the Content tab, and then clicking the Certificates button. As shown in Figure 28-8, the preconfigured list, called a Certificate Trust List (CTL) is quite extensive.

**10 Min.
To Go**

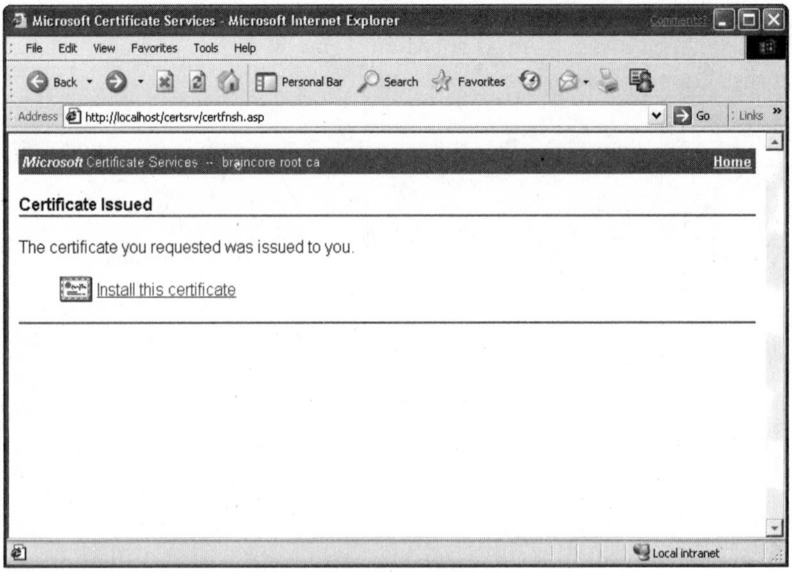

Figure 28-7 *Picking up an issued certificate*

Figure 28-8 *IE's preconfigured list of trusted root CAs*

Certificate Uses and Revocation

Certificates have to be issued for a specific purpose, and the certificate itself contains a list of purposes it may be used for. Certificate Services' Web interface enables users to request certificates that their Web browsers can use to identify the users, or that the users can use within e-mail applications to encrypt and digitally sign e-mail messages.

Once you revoke a certificate, Certificate Services no longer provides access to its matching public key. However, users can continue using the certificate. You should periodically update a Certificate Revocation List (CRL), which can be distributed to your users by Active Directory Group Policy. The CRL lists certificates that you have issued and later rejected, enabling users' computers to automatically reject the revoked certificates should they encounter them.

Any certificate issued by those CAs is automatically accepted by IE, provided the certificate has not expired and does not appear on a Certificate Revocation List (CRL). Also, IE automatically trusts any certificate that can be traced back to a trusted CA. For example, if you establish a root CA and obtain a certificate-signing certificate from VeriSign, then IE will trust your certificates, too, because IE trusts VeriSign and VeriSign, through the certificate-signing certificate they issued, trusts your root CA.

If you establish your own root CA and create a self-signing certificate, IE does *not* automatically trust the certificates the CA issues. When IE receives a certificate issued by your CA, IE displays an error message and asks the user whether or not she trusts you. You can prevent IE from displaying that error by adding your root CA's certificate to IE's CTL. The easiest way to accomplish that in a domain environment is to use an Active Directory Group Policy to modify the CTL on every computer in your domain.

REVIEW

In this session, you learned how digital certificates work, and how they can be used to enhance computer security and provide identification services. You also learned how to install, configure, and manage Microsoft Certificate Services, and

Done!

Part VI — Sunday Afternoon
Session 28

how to issue certificates to your users. You learned how to configure Internet Explorer to trust the certificates you issue, and you learned how Certificate Services can be extended to meet your organization's needs.

QUIZ YOURSELF

1. What can certificates be used for? (See "How Certificates Work.")
2. What kinds of certificates are used most frequently on the Web? (See "Certificates for encryption.")
3. How can users request a certificate from Certificate Services? (See "Requesting certificates.")
4. How can you revoke a certificate that you've issued? (See "Issuing certificates.")
5. How do you configure Internet Explorer to trust the certificates you issue? (See "Certificates and Internet Explorer.")

Understanding Performance Management

Session Checklist

✔ How to define acceptable performance

✔ How to use the Performance console

✔ How to create a performance baseline

✔ How to document performance trends

✔ How to optimize performance

**30 Min.
To Go**

Windows Server 2003 is a complex operating system with hundreds of features and literally thousands of performance characteristics. Of course, you want your servers to be in top condition — but what *is* "top condition," and how can you tell whether or not your servers are there?

In this session, you'll learn to understand the basics of performance management, including how to define acceptable performance levels. You'll also learn to use Windows Server 2003's tools for performance monitoring, and how to create performance baselines and trends in an effort to optimize overall system performance.

Defining Performance

One question new administrators always ask me is, "How can I tell when my servers are performing at their best?" My answer is always, "What level of performance is acceptable for your organization?"

Always remember that the servers on your network were placed there to serve some business need, whether as a file server, a print server, an application server, or in some other capacity. When you or your boss made the decision to buy the servers, you had certain expectations, which may have included:

- How many users can utilize this server at the same time?
- What is the longest response time users can expect when using this server?
- How much data can this server store?
- How long will this server last before we have to upgrade it?

Those expectations define your lowest level of acceptable performance. If you don't have written expectations, take the time to write them down. Clearly define what you expect your servers to do and how well you expect them to do it. Your minimum standards might not be hard for your servers to meet initially, but as demand on the servers grows, your servers will have to work harder to meet your minimum performance standards. At some point, even working as hard as they can, your servers won't be able to meet your standards, and it'll be time for an upgrade.

The two best indicators generally are the number of users you want a server to support and the slowest response time that you are willing to accept from the server. Knowing both of those numbers helps you determine whether the server is meeting, exceeding, or failing to meet your expectations.

Once you've defined your expectations, you can start using Windows Server 2003's built-in tools to monitor your server's performance and determine whether or not your performance expectations are being met.

Using the Performance Console

Windows Server 2003's Performance console is your primary tool for monitoring system performance. The Performance console is installed by default and includes the System Monitor snap-in, which actually displays performance information.

You can also access the System Monitor snap-in from the Computer Management console, which provides a convenient place to monitor and manage many of your server's functions at the same time.

The Performance console enables you to perform three important performance-related tasks:

- Monitor performance data in real time
- Save performance data to log files for later use
- Set performance alerts to respond to specific performance conditions

You can use the Performance console on another computer to monitor the performance of a server. That's a good idea because simply running the Performance console can affect your performance readings.

Monitoring real-time data

The most common use of the Performance console is to monitor system performance in real time, by using a graph to display key performance counters. Figure 29-1 shows an example performance graph in progress.

Each line on the graph represents a single performance counter. Each counter measures a specific performance characteristic, such as processor utilization or free memory. Related counters are grouped together into performance objects, which often represent a single subsystem, such as processor or memory.

Click the + button on the toolbar to add a new counter to the graph. As shown in Figure 29-2, you can select a performance object and then select any of its counters. If a counter applies to more than one *instance,* you can select the instance you want to monitor. For example, a dual-processor computer has two instances of the Processor performance object. You can also select a special "Total" instance that averages all available instances for the object.

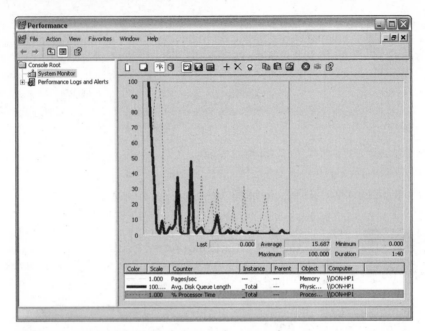

Figure 29-1 Monitoring real-time performance data

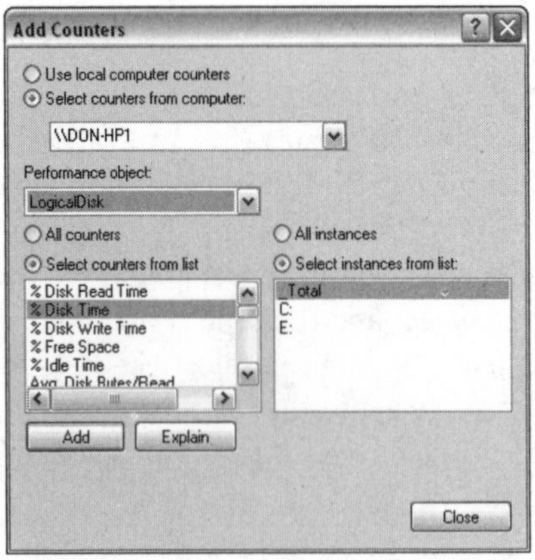

Figure 29-2 Adding counters to the graph

**20 Min.
To Go**

Setting performance alerts

Performance alerts allow the Performance console to act as your assistant, alerting you and taking actions whenever specified performance thresholds occur. Alerts can be set on any performance counter and can either simply alert you by sending a pop-up message to your workstation or take action by executing a command line.

To create a new alert, open the Performance console and right-click on the Alerts item in the left pane. Select "New alert setting..." from the pop-up menu. As shown in Figure 29-3, the console displays a three-tabbed dialog box.

Figure 29-3   Creating a new alert

Configure the dialog box as follows:

- Use the Add button to add new performance counters to the alert.

- Configure a threshold for each counter. For example, in Figure 29-3, the Disk Space Free counter is configured with a threshold of "Less than 1000." The threshold indicates that the alert will be fired when the available free disk pace falls below 1,000 bytes.

- On the Action tab, shown in Figure 29-4, specify the action you want the Performance console to take when the alert is fired. For example, you can configure the alert to write an event log entry, send a message to a workstation, or execute a command-line task.

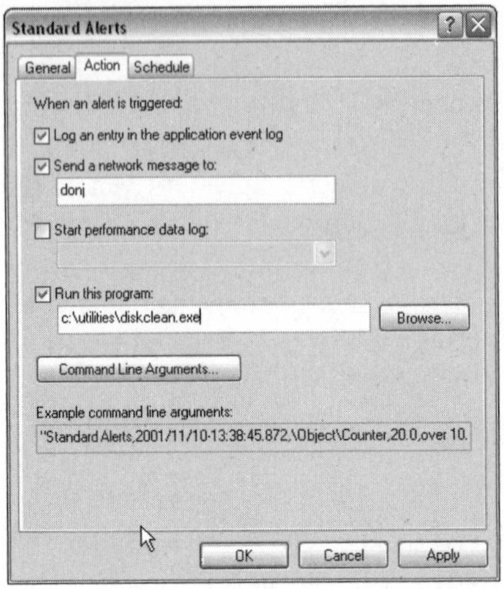

Figure 29-4   Configuring alert actions

- Finally, use the Schedule tab to indicate when the alert should be active. The schedule enables you to have the Performance console scan the alert's counters periodically rather than constantly, which reduces the alert's performance impact. Figure 29-5 shows a sample schedule.

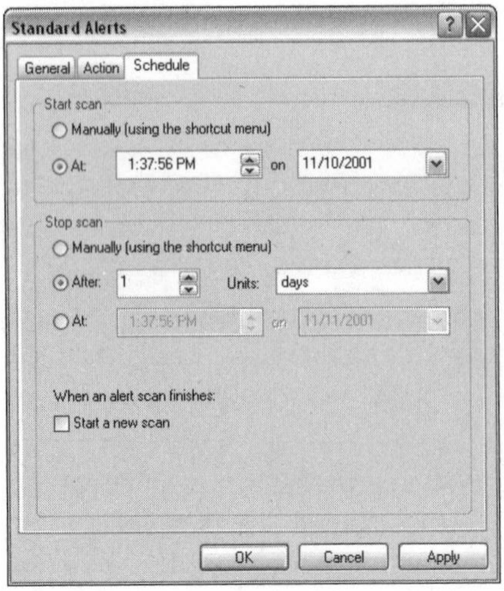

Figure 29-5   Configuring an alert schedule

Don't configure alerts to scan constantly because doing so actually imposes a negative performance impact on your server. Have the alert scan on a regular schedule depending on how often the counters you are monitoring change their values.

Creating performance logs

Performance logs enable you to collect performance objects data into a log file without monitoring the data in real time. You can use the Performance console to create a new log, and then stop and start that log as necessary. When started, the log collects data; it stops collecting data when you stop the log. Once you stop a log, you can view the performance data on a graph, just as if you were viewing the data in real time.

Performance logs enable you to monitor performance data even when you can't sit in front of the Performance console. Simply use the log to collect the data and then review it later.

Performance logs are your best tool for creating performance reports. To create a new log in the console, right-click Performance logs and select "New Log Settings..." from the pop-up menu. The console displays a three-tabbed dialog box similar to the one used for configuring alerts. The General tab is shown in Figure 29-6, and enables you to configure the counters that are included in the log. You can also configure the interval that the console waits in between performance value checks.

Don't configure your performance logs to use an interval of less than five minutes or so. More frequent intervals negatively impact server performance and create more performance data than you need for most purposes.

The dialog's Log Files tab, shown in Figure 29-7, enables you to configure the physical files that will store the performance data. You can configure a maximum log file size, and you can configure the naming convention that will be used to name the log files.

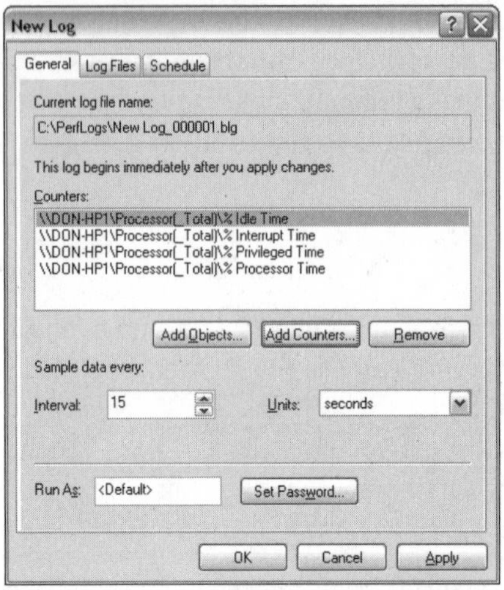

Figure 29-6   *Configuring a performance log*

Figure 29-7   *Configuring log file parameters*

Performance Reporting

Performance reporting should be a proactive task, one that you perform on a regular basis to ensure that your servers are meeting your documented performance expectations. Don't wait until your servers are obviously slowing down to check their performance; create a performance report once a month, or more frequently in a fast-growing environment.

Performance baselines

Performance reporting starts with a baseline. After you configure a server, but before you place it into production, analyze its performance. Specifically, analyze its memory, processor, disk, and network subsystems. The result is an *idle baseline,* which shows you the server's performance when it isn't doing any work.

Take another baseline, called a *production baseline,* after you place the server into normal operation. Also measure the number of users that are utilizing the server, the average response times they are receiving, and any other measurements that match your documented performance expectations.

If your server's key performance areas — processor, memory, disk, and network — are struggling to meet your initial performance expectations, then either your expectations are too high or your server's hardware isn't powerful enough. Remember that your performance expectations should include room for growth. If your server is struggling to meet your initial performance expectations, what will happen when additional users start placing more data on the server?

Performance trends

Every month (or more frequently in fast-growing environments), take another measurement of your servers' performance. Also document the number of users who are utilizing the servers and the response times they're receiving. Each month's report helps you build a trend, which you can represent as a graph. The trend helps you predict when your server will fall below your performance expectations *before* it actually does so.

For example, suppose you take trend reports for six months after placing a file server into operation. Your performance expectations were for the server to always provide no more than a one-second response time for up to 2,000 users. The server's idle baseline shows a 5 percent network utilization and 2 percent processor utilization. When the server was placed into production, you had only 100 users, and they received a response time of less than one-tenth of a second. Over the past six months, you've added more and more users, and response time has gone up slightly each month. Your trend reports indicate that every 100 users adds 10 percent processor utilization at 12 percent network utilization, as well as a one-tenth increase in response time.

If you carry the trend forward, your server will be able to handle only 300 more users and maintain a one-second response time. In fact, 300 more users will push the processor utilization to over 90 percent and network utilization to over 108 percent! If you continue adding 100 users every month, you'll need to upgrade or replace the server within two months.

> **Carefully monitoring performance trends can make you the hero that prevented a problem, rather than the poor guy who has to deal with it.**

Optimizing Performance

Windows Server 2003 has four primary subsystems that have the biggest impact on overall system performance. In the next four sections, I'll briefly describe how to optimize each of these subsystems.

> **Performance optimization is more meaningful when you can talk about optimizing a server for a specific task. I'll show you how to do that in Session 30.**

Memory subsystem

The memory subsystem consists of the Random Access Memory, or RAM, installed in your server. Windows Server 2003 can handle up to 4GB of RAM (64GB for Datacenter Server) in a single server. When memory utilization approaches 80 percent, the server begins relying more and more on slower virtual memory, which is created by using disk space. To improve memory performance:

- Install the fastest memory that your server's hardware will work with.
- Install error-correcting memory, which helps correct any single-bit errors that occur in memory and speeds up overall memory operations.

Storage subsystem

Your server's storage subsystem consists primarily of hard drives and is one of the first subsystems to show signs of poor performance. Here are some tips for improving disk performance:

- Use RAID 5 arrays whenever possible, with as many physical drives in the array as possible. These arrays are faster than single disks because all of the drives in the array work together to store data.

- Buy drives with a high Rotations Per Minute (RPM) speed. Low-end drives run 5,400 RPM, and high-end desktop drives run 7,500 RPM. High-end server drives can run 10,000 RPM or faster and are able to read and write data much more quickly.

- Spread Windows' paging file across multiple physical drives, or place the file on a RAID 5 array. Doing so improves the performance of virtual memory.

Processor subsystem

A server's processor subsystem consists of 1 or more microprocessors (up to 4 in Server and Enterprise Server and up to 32 in Datacenter Server). Here are some tips for improving processor performance:

- Use bus-mastering accessories like drive controllers, video adapters, and network interface cards (NICs). These accessories can access memory without using the processor, thus freeing up the processor for other tasks.

- Use processors designed for server use. Processors designed for desktop use may include enhanced multimedia features that don't provide a benefit to a server.

- Use multiple processors only if your server is running applications like Microsoft SQL Server that are designed to work well with multiple processors. While Windows Server 2003 can theoretically run any application on multiple processors, poorly written applications can actually run slower on multiprocessor systems.

- Use the fastest processors you can get, particularly if they contain server-enhanced features like pipelining or a large L1 or L2 cache.

Network subsystem

Along with the disk subsystem, the network subsystem is usually the first culprit in poor performance. The network subsystem is limited to the overall speed of your network. Here are some tips for optimizing network throughput:

- Install servers on networks that don't use collision avoidance. Fiber Distributed Data Interface (FDDI), for example, is a 100 Mbps network that uses fiber-optic cables and a token-passing scheme that allows more network throughput. Collision-based networks like Ethernet can rarely maintain a network utilization higher than 70 percent, whereas token-based networks like FDDI can often maintain 90 percent utilization or better.

- Connect servers directly to switch ports, which can allow the server to carry on multiple network conversations at once.

- Install multiple NICs in a server to allow it to communicate with multiple network segments at once. Windows Server 2003 has an effective network throughput in excess of 800 Mbps, which means you could theoretically connect one server to six or seven different 100 Mbps networks and achieve close to maximum throughput for the server.

Done!

REVIEW

In this session, you learned how to define performance levels that are acceptable in your organization. You also learned how to create performance baselines and trends, which enable you to predict when performance will fall below acceptable levels. Finally, you learned how to optimize the primary subsystems of your server computers to improve and optimize performance conditions.

QUIZ YOURSELF

1. What are the four primary subsystems that require performance tuning? (See "Optimizing Performance.")

2. How can you use the Performance console to create performance baselines and trends? (See "Using the Performance Console.")

3. How can performance trends help you prevent performance problems? (See "Performance trends.")

4. How can you use performance alerts to automate system performance tuning? (See "Setting performance alerts.")

Performance Tuning and Optimization

Session Checklist

✔ How to optimize file server performance

✔ How to optimize application server performance

✔ How to optimize Terminal Services performance

**30 Min.
To Go**

I n Session 29, you learned about some of the key factors that affect server performance, and you learned how to monitor and report on server performance. In this session, I'll show you how to optimize your servers' performance for specific tasks and which performance counters to watch closest in your quest for a top-performing server.

In Session 29, I mentioned that performance optimization depends on the task you're using your servers for. In this session, I'll focus on performance optimization for specific types of tasks. What if you use your servers for more than one type of task, though? For example, what if you use a domain controller — technically an application server — as a file server also? In that case, combine the techniques used for an application server and a file server.

Optimizing a server that fills two roles can be difficult because the roles often have contradictory optimization techniques. Therefore, one overriding optimization technique is to use your servers for a single purpose whenever possible.

Optimizing File Server Performance

A file server's job is to accept network data and write it to disk and, more frequently, pull data off of disk and onto the network — all as quickly as possible.

Optimization goals

File serving makes heavy use of both disk and network subsystems. As you learned in Session 29, those subsystems are the two most likely to cause performance problems in any situation, and that goes double for a file server. File serving requires relatively little processor power and the fastest possible network and disk subsystems. Here are some general optimization tips for file servers:

- Attach as many physical disks to your server as possible, and configure them in one or more RAID 5 arrays. For example, if you need 100GB of storage space on the server, buy ten 10GB drives instead of two 50GB drives. In a RAID 5 array, drives work together to perform the file server's work, so the more drives you have helping out, the better your storage subsystem's performance.

- Go somewhat heavy on memory. Windows Server 2003 is smart about caching information in memory, where it can be served faster than reading it directly from disk.

- Optimize your server's network connectivity. While Windows Server 2003 can read data from disk at megabytes per second, it can send that data across the network at only mega*bits* per second — one-eighth as fast. Use multiple network connections, fast networks, and switches to optimize network performance.

Key performance counters

The performance counters to watch are those relating to your storage and network subsystems. Specifically, watch the following:

- **Disk Bytes/sec, from the LogicalDisk object.** This counter shows you how many bytes your disks are dealing with. The higher the number, the harder they're working. This is a good counter to give you an idea of overall workload.

- **Avg. Disk Queue Length, from the LogicalDisk object.** This counter shows the number of disk requests waiting to be serviced. If this number ever gets higher than 2 for a prolonged period of time, your server is seriously strapped for disk throughput. You can help combat the problem by installing additional drive controllers, so that more controllers are pulling data from disks. Ultimately, though, the way to correct long disk queues is to add another file server to your network and move some of the workload to it.

- **% Idle Time, from the LogicalDisk object.** This counter shows how much time the disks spend idle. You want this counter to be at least 5–10 percent at all times (although it may briefly dip to zero from time to time). Idle time allows Windows to "catch its breath" and perform basic housekeeping.

All of the LogicalDisk counters have a _Total instance that represents an average of all installed logical disks. If you have multiple logical disks, monitor the _Total instance, or monitor the instance that represents your busiest disk.

- **Bytes Total/sec, from the Network Interface object.** This counter shows the total number of bytes transmitted across the network. On a file server, this number should roughly match the amount of data passing to the disk subsystem. If your server has multiple NICs, monitor all of the instances of this counter.

- **Output Queue Length, from the Network Interface object.** This counter shows the number of packets waiting to be sent to the network. If this number is higher than 1 for more than a millisecond or so, then your network interface is creating a performance bottleneck.

Where's the Network Interface Object?

Your server's Performance console may not include a Network Interface object. If it doesn't, install Network Monitor (see Session 23). Network Monitor's installation includes the Network Interface performance object.

You'll notice additional performance objects as you install additional services. For example, WINS, Active Directory, DHCP, and DNS all install additional performance objects along with their primary software components. Most Microsoft software, in fact, installs additional performance objects that enable you to monitor that software's specific performance characteristics.

Optimizing Application Server Performance

**20 Min.
To Go**

Application servers perform work on behalf of client computers located on your network. That means they work a server a bit harder than a file server. Application servers usually have high processor requirements, moderate to high disk requirements, and moderate network requirements. Well-written applications send only small amounts of data to their clients, which means they don't need the robust network subsystem that a file server does.

Optimization goals

Optimization differs depending on the exact applications you're using. For example, Microsoft SQL Server is processor-heavy, disk-heavy, and memory-heavy; Internet Information Services is primarily a memory and disk application, placing less load on the processor than SQL Server. In general, though, application servers need the following optimizations:

- Processor power is key for most application servers' performance. Multiple, fast processors with server-enhanced features like large L1 and L2 caches are your best bet.

- Memory is important because applications often utilize memory in lieu of slower disk space when they can. Every application on a Windows Server 2003 is allocated 2–3GB of memory; if you have less physical memory than that, the application will use slower disk space to make up the difference. Try to install enough physical memory to accommodate your applications.

Since Windows Server 2003 and Enterprise Server can handle only 4GB of memory, and since the operating system itself uses up to 1–2GB, try not to run more than one major application on a server. If you need to run multiple large applications, consider using Datacenter Server, which can access up to 64GB of memory.

- Disk throughput is important for most applications because they store their data on disk. As with file servers, multiple disks in RAID 5 arrays provide the best performance.

- Network throughput is important for an application server, but less critical than it is for a file server. Application servers don't usually bottleneck their network interfaces before bottlenecking in the memory or processor subsystems.

Key performance counters

Keep an eye on the following performance counters when you're optimizing your application servers:

- **% Processor Time, from the Processor object.** The instances of this counter show how hard each processor is working. In a multiprocessor system, you'll notice that the first processor (instance zero) works a bit harder than the others. That's because the operating system tends to use the first processor more than the others.

- **Multiprocessor use.** If your first processor is working *significantly* harder than the others, then your server applications aren't utilizing multiple processors very well. Contact the application vendor to see if they can provide a newer version or a version that is tuned for multiprocessor use.

- **Individual processor use.** Individual processors should not exceed 75 percent utilization for extended periods of time, although they will peak to 100 percent from time to time. If a processor is maintaining more than 75 percent utilization, you need to add more processors or reduce the server's workload.

- **Queue Length, from the Server Work Queues object.** This counter shows the number of requests waiting for the server's attention. If this counter maintains a value of more than four for any period of time, the computer's processor is definitely overworked.

- **Pages/sec from the Memory object.** This counter indicates the number of memory pages that had to be retrieved from the system paging file, rather than from physical memory. If this value gets too high, the server may start *thrashing*, which is a process where the server spends so much time reading from the page file that it is unable to effectively fulfill client requests. If this counter maintains a value of more than a couple of dozen for long periods of time, you need to add memory to your server or reduce its workload.

- **Available Bytes, from the Memory object.** This counter shows how many bytes of memory are currently available for processes running on the server. This value may fluctuate a lot under normal conditions. A troubleshooting tip: Shut down the various applications and services on a server, and this counter's value should increase. If it doesn't, you may have an application or service that *leaks memory*, or fails to report it to Windows as available once the application ends. Contact the application's vendor to discuss the application's behavior because memory leaks can seriously degrade application server performance.

Optimizing Terminal Services Performance

10 Min. To Go

Terminal Services has many of the same performance issues as an application server. Often times, the server is running regular desktop applications, such as Microsoft Office, rather than server applications like Microsoft Exchange Server. So your optimization goals are slightly different:

- Multiple processors are definitely called for because they allow more users to run desktop applications, even though those applications expect to be run only on a single processor.

- Network throughput is perhaps the least important subsystem because only the visual interface is sent to the client, and even that is sent in a highly optimized, compressed format that can use less than 15 Kbps of bandwidth.

- Memory is incredibly important. You wouldn't configure a desktop computer with less than 64 to 128MB of memory these days, and each user logging onto a Terminal Services session needs at least that much. Like other applications, Terminal Services can use disk space to emulate memory, at a cost in access time.

- Disk throughput is important when you don't have enough physical memory to handle users' needs. Disk throughput is used primarily for the operating system's paging file, which provides virtual memory when the server's real memory runs out. The applications run on a Terminal Server are typically designed to work with the slow, single hard drive found in a desktop machine, so running on a server-class hard drive or RAID 5 array is more than fast enough.

Optimize your Terminal Services servers much as you would an application server, with extra focus on the processor and memory subsystems. Don't concentrate too much on the disk subsystem, but do keep an eye on it because it likely will be used to provide virtual memory to the server.

REVIEW

In this session, you learned about the key goals when optimizing a server's performance and the key performance counters to watch. You learned how performance optimization changes depending on the tasks you're asking a server to perform, and you learned how to optimize for the three most common server roles: file server, application server, and Terminal Services server.

Done!

QUIZ YOURSELF

1. What performance counters indicate that you don't have enough RAM in your server? (See "Optimizing Application Server Performance.")

2. How can you install a performance object that exposes network performance data? (See "Optimizing File Server Performance.")

3. Why is the network subsystem less important to a Terminal Services server? (See "Optimizing Terminal Services Performance.")

PART

VI

Sunday Afternoon
Part Review

1. What advantage does a failover cluster provide?

2. What technique allows the two nodes in a failover cluster to be productive at the same time?

3. What are two examples of Microsoft server applications that are cluster-aware?

4. What are the basic requirements for an application to be cluster-compatible?

5. What server name should you connect to in order to manage a cluster?

6. What service provides clustering appropriate for Web servers?

7. What is the difference between a certificate authority that you create and a commercial certificate authority like VeriSign?

8. What basic certificate-issuing policy is included with Certificate Services?

9. What are digital certificates used for?

10. What is the difference between a symmetric key and an asymmetric key?

11. When should you conduct a performance baseline?

12. What is the purpose of performance trending?

13. What are the four main areas of a computer that create performance bottlenecks?

14. What are the key elements in fine-tuning a file server's performance?

15. What are the key elements in fine-tuning an application server's performance?

16. What are the key elements in fine-tuning Terminal Services performance?

What's on the CD-ROM

✔ System requirements

✔ Using the CD

✔ What's on the CD

✔ Troubleshooting

This appendix provides you with information on the contents of the CD that accompanies this book. For the latest and greatest information, please refer to the ReadMe file located at the root of the CD.

System Requirements

Make sure that your computer meets the minimum system requirements listed in this section. If your computer doesn't match up to these requirements, you may have a problem using the contents of the CD.

For Windows 9x, Windows 2000, Windows NT4 (with SP 4 or later), Windows Me, or Windows XP:

- A PC with a Pentium or faster CPU.
- Windows 95, Windows 98, Windows 2000, Windows NT 4.0, Windows Me or Windows XP installed.
- At least 32MB of RAM (64MB is recommended for Windows NT 4.0, Windows 2000, and Windows XP).
- A minimum of 100 MB of disk storage.
- A CD-ROM drive.
- A Windows-compatible monitor and graphics card capable of displaying at least 256 colors.

Using the CD

To install the items from the CD to your hard drive, follow these steps:

1. Insert the CD into your computer's CD-ROM drive.
2. A window appears with the following options: Install, Browse, eBook, and Exit.

   Install: Gives you the option to install the supplied software and/or the author-created samples on the CD-ROM.

   Browse: Allows you to view the contents of the CD-ROM in its directory structure.

   eBook: Allows you to view an electronic version of the book.

   Exit: Closes the autorun window.

If you do not have autorun enabled or if the autorun window does not appear, follow the steps below to access the CD.

1. Click Start ➪ Run.
2. In the dialog box that appears, type **d:\setup.exe**, where *d* is the letter of your CD-ROM drive. This brings up the autorun window described above.
3. Choose the Install, Browse, eBook, or Exit option from the menu. (See Step 2 in the preceding list for a description of these options.)

What's on the CD

The following sections provide a summary of the software and other material you'll find on the CD.

Self-assessment test

A self-assesssment test on the CD enables you to evaluate your knowledge of Windows Server 2003. In case you need a review, each answer refers you to the appropriate session in *Windows Server 2003 Weekend Crash Course*.

Windows Interface Tutorial

The CD includes a bonus chapter on the Windows interface. This focused tutorial shows you how to use Windows' interface themes, how to select a theme, and how to launch applications.

eBook version of Windows Server 2003 Weekend Crash Course

The complete text of this book is on the CD in Adobe's Portable Document Format (PDF). You can read and search through the file with the Adobe Acrobat Reader (also included on the CD).

Troubleshooting

If you have difficulty installing or using any of the materials on the companion CD, try the following solutions:

- **Turn off any anti-virus software that you may have running.** Installers sometimes mimic virus activity and can make your computer incorrectly believe that it is being infected by a virus. (Be sure to turn the anti-virus software back on later.)
- **Close all running programs.** The more programs you're running, the less memory is available to other programs. Installers also typically update files and programs; if you keep other programs running, installation may not work properly.
- **Reference the ReadMe:** Please refer to the ReadMe file located at the root of the CD-ROM for the latest product information at the time of publication.

If you still have trouble with the CD, please call the Wiley Customer Care phone number: (800) 762-2974. Outside the United States, call 1 (317) 572-3994. You can also contact Wiley Customer Service by e-mail at techsupdum@wiley.com. Wiley provides technical support only for installation and other general quality control items; for technical support on the applications themselves, consult the program's vendor or author.

Answers to Part Reviews

Friday Evening Part Review Answers

1. **What are the four editions of Windows Server 2003, and what are their major differences?**

   The four editions are Standard Edition, Web Edition, Enterprise Edition, and Datacenter Edition. The primary difference is in the amount of physical RAM and number of processors that can be utilized by the operating system. Web Edition also has major feature differences from the other versions.

2. **What does the term *multitasking* mean?**

   The ability to run more than one task, or process (such as an application), at the same time.

3. **What are three methods you can use to install Windows Server 2003?**

   CD-ROM, over the network, or from a Remote Installation Services (RIS) server.

4. **How would you set up and start an unattended upgrade of Windows Server 2003 using a CD-ROM?**

   Unattended upgrades can be started by running `Winnt32.exe /upgrade` from the i386 folder of the Windows Server 2003 CD-ROM.

5. **What capability allows Windows Server 2003 to run on servers that have no mouse, monitor, keyboard, or video card?**

   Support for headless servers.

6. **What are the built-in local users included with Windows Server 2003? How about the built-in users installed with Active Directory? What can these users do?**

   The two built-in local users are Administrator and Guest. The built-in domain user accounts installed with Active Directory also include Administrator and Guest. In both cases, the Administrator user has full control over the local computer (or domain), and the Guest user is disabled by default.

7. **What are some of the built-in local groups included with Windows Server 2003? How about the built-in groups installed with Active Directory? What can these groups do?**

   The built-in local groups include Administrators and Users. Members of the Administrators group have full control over the computer. All new user accounts are automatically added to the Users group by default. Built-in Active Directory domain groups (and their capabilities) include Domain Admins (full control over the domain), Enterprise Admins (full control over a forest), Domain Users (which contains all domain user accounts by default), and Schema Admins (control over Active Directory's schema).

8. **How can you determine who has been logging on to your servers and accessing resources?**

   By enabling auditing on logon events and by enabling auditing on the appropriate resources. Audit events are written to the Security Event Log.

9. **How can you force users to select passwords with at least ten characters?**

   Establish a local computer (or domain) policy that requires passwords to have a minimum length of ten characters.

10. **How can you prevent users from changing their passwords and then immediately changing back to their old passwords?**

    Establish a local computer (or domain) policy that specifies a minimum password age.

11. **What are the three roles a server can play on your network?**

    Standalone, member server, or domain controller.

12. **What is the difference between a standalone server and a member server?**

    A member server belongs to a domain and can assign permissions to domain users and groups. A standalone server does not belong to a domain and can use only its local users and groups for permissions.

13. **When is a single domain appropriate for an organization?**

Whenever the users and groups in the organization are administered by a single individual or department.

14. **Why might an organization choose to include all of their users in a single organizational unit (OU)?**

When all of the organization's users have identical security and policy requirements.

15. **How can two independent domains be brought together into a forest?**

By establishing an explicit trust between the two domains.

16. **What must a DNS server provide in order to be compatible with Active Directory?**

Support for SRV records and for dynamic DNS updates.

17. **How can you remove Active Directory from a domain controller and make it a standalone server again?**

Run Dcpromo.exe and demote the domain controller.

18. **What is the best method or methods to install Windows Server 2003 on a dozen identical computers that are attached to your network?**

Create an installation image using unattended setup and a Remote Installation Services (RIS) server.

19. **What advantages does Active Directory offer over using local user accounts on standalone servers?**

Active Directory allows many servers to share a common set of user and group accounts and enables users to access all of the resources in an organization with a single username and password.

20. **What must you do to reactivate a user who has mistyped her password too many times and has become locked out?**

Use Active Directory Users and Computers to unlock her account.

Saturday Morning Part Review Answers

1. **What file system supports file and folder permissions?**

NTFS is the only file system that supports permissions.

2. **What file system is compatible with Windows Server 2003 and Windows 98?**

   Both FAT16 and FAT32 are compatible.

3. **How can you make the files on a Windows Server 2003 computer available to users on the network?**

   Share the folder containing the files.

4. **How can you control access to files that are located on a FAT32 volume?**

   Share the folder containing the files and then apply share permissions, or convert the volume to NTFS and use file and folder permissions.

5. **What is the minimum number of hard disks required for a RAID 5 array?**

   Three.

6. **What are the two components of a UNC?**

   The server name and the share name: \\Server\Share.

7. **What does DFS stand for?**

   Distributed File System.

8. **How do you add new UNCs to DFS?**

   Use the DFS Administrator to add a new link to an existing DFS tree.

9. **How does DFS enable you to load-balance access to shared files?**

   By adding multiple replicas to a single DFS link. Each replica must point to a UNC containing identical files and folders.

10. **How can you compress an encrypted file?**

    You cannot. Files can be compressed, or encrypted, but not both.

11. **Who can access an encrypted file?**

    The owner of the file, anyone the owner places on the access list, and any designated Recovery Agents.

12. **How can you prevent users from using too much disk space on a server?**

    Implement disk quotas and create a quota for the users that limits that amount of space they can utilize.

13. **If a user compresses a file, how does it count against his disk quota?**

    The original, uncompressed file size counts against their quota.

14. How does a printer relate to a print device?

A printer is a software queue that sends print jobs, one at a time, to a physical print device, such as a laser or inkjet printer.

15. How can you control the hours that users can print documents?

Modify the properties of the printer so that the printer is active only during the desired hours.

16. How does Terminal Services send screen images to a client?

By intercepting the Graphical Device Interface (GDI) commands and transmitting them to the client.

17. Who is allowed to log on to Terminal Services in Remote Administration mode?

Members of the server's local Administrators user group.

18. How long will Terminal Services operate in AppServer mode without a Licensing server?

90 days.

19. What map-back capabilities are provided by the Terminal Services 5.1 client software?

Sound, communication ports, printers, and storage devices.

20. How can users send faxes using a centralized Windows Server 2003 computer?

Install a fax device, install Fax Services, and share the fax printer that Windows creates.

Saturday Afternoon Part Review Answers

1. What are some of the common configuration options that DHCP can configure on a client computer?

Default router, DNS server, WINS server, and domain name.

2. How can you use DHCP and still ensure that a computer always uses the same IP address?

By creating a DHCP reservation for the computer.

3. **How can you use DHCP to configure client computers to use a WINS or DNS server?**

   By configuring the addresses of the WINS or DNS servers as global or scope options on the DHCP server.

4. **How do you configure two WINS servers to exchange name-to-IP address mappings with each other?**

   By configuring them as replication partners.

5. **How can you use the WINS snap-in to manage more than one WINS server at once?**

   By configuring the snap-in to connect to the other WINS servers and display their information.

6. **How do you ensure that WINS clients can look up the IP addresses of servers that aren't compatible with WINS?**

   By creating static WINS entry for the non-WINS servers.

7. **What type of DNS record allows another computer to determine the IP address of your company's e-mail server?**

   An MX record.

8. **How can your DNS server help resolve Internet host names that are not contained within its database?**

   By forwarding the request to another DNS server.

9. **What type of DNS record allows a computer to have a nickname?**

   A CNAME record.

10. **How does a computer decide whether or not data should be sent to the computer's default gateway?**

    By examining the network ID portion of the destination IP address. If it is the same as the computer's own network ID, then the default gateway is not used. If the network IDs are different, then the default gateway is used.

11. **What protocol does a computer use to determine the physical address of another computer?**

    The Address Resolution Protocol, or ARP.

12. **What TCP/IP protocol does a computer use when it wants to ensure that data transmissions are received by the destination computer?**

    The Transport Control Protocol, or TCP, which allows the destination computer to confirm receipt of individual packets.

13. **What piece of information allows a computer to determine which portion of an IP address identifies a network and which identifies a computer?**

The subnet mask.

14. **What tool enables you to apply a security template to a computer by using a batch file?**

Secedit.exe.

15. **Why are security templates better than configuring security on individual computers?**

Because templates can be centrally configured and then applied to computers, enabling you to create a consistent security policy across all of your computers.

16. **How does the Security Configuration Manager enable you to analyze the result of applying several security templates?**

By showing you the effective policies after analyzing the templates you want to apply.

17. **How do you configure domain security policies?**

By configuring the local security policy of a domain controller.

18. **What are three major classes of security policies?**

Account policy, lockout policy, and security options.

19. **What effect does a policy have when it is undefined?**

Undefined policies have no effect.

20. **How can you create your own security templates?**

By using the Security Configuration Manager, or SCM, to define the policies in the template and then saving the template to a file.

Saturday Evening Part Review Answers

1. **What three properties can IIS use to distinguish between multiple virtual Web sites on a single server?**

IP address, host header, and port number.

2. **What four types of sites can you set up in IIS?**

Web sites (HTTP), FTP sites, NNTP sites, and SMTP sites.

3. **What is the primary use for an IIS SMTP site?**

   To allow Web applications running on the IIS server to send e-mail.

4. **How can you prevent anonymous users from accessing a particular file on an IIS Web site?**

   Configure NTFS permissions on the file and specify the users and groups that should have access to it.

5. **What is the default TCP port for an IIS Web site?**

   Port 80.

6. **Why are FTP sites used when HTTP offers similar file download capabilities?**

   FTP sites offer upload capability and are more easily used by automated upload and download scripts that many organizations use to exchange data on a regular basis.

7. **What client software enables users to interact with an NNTP site?**

   Any newsreader software, including Outlook Express and Outlook.

8. **What client software enables users to interact with an FTP site?**

   Any FTP client software. Microsoft includes a command-line FTP client with Windows, and third-party vendors offer graphical FTP clients, such as CuteFTP.

9. **How can you configure a Web site to save information about user activity to a log file?**

   On the Web site's properties, ensure that the Enable logging check box is selected.

10. **What happens if a user tries to access a Web site that is uniquely identified by a host header, but the user's proxy server removes the HTTP 1.1 headers from the request?**

    The Web server will not be able to identify the intended site and will direct the user to the Web site that uses the same IP address but does not have a host header configured. That generally means that the user will be directed to the Default Web site.

11. **What two types of remote connections are most commonly used with RRAS?**

    Dial-up and VPN (virtual private network).

12. **What two VPN protocols does RRAS support?**

    Point-to-Point Tunneling Protocol (PPTP) and Layer 2 Tunneling Protocol (L2TP).

13. **What two protocols are necessary to create an encrypted VPN with clients who are not PPTP-compatible?**

    L2TP is used to create the virtual connection, and IP Security (IPSec) is used to encrypt the contents of the tunnel.

14. **How can you monitor the users who are currently dialed in to an RRAS server?**

    By using the RRAS console to monitor remote client connections.

15. **How can you centralize the remote access policies for several RRAS servers?**

    By configuring RRAS to use a RADIUS server instead of the default Windows authentication method.

16. **What standard protocol does IAS use?**

    Remote Authentication Dial-In User Service, or RADIUS.

17. **How does RRAS authenticate users through IAS?**

    By forwarding the user's logon credentials and other information to IAS and asking IAS if the user is permitted to connect.

18. **What service must already be present in order for IAS to operate?**

    IAS reads remote access policies from the local server, which requires RRAS to be installed. IAS also works with Active Directory (AD) and uses AD user accounts in its authentication process.

19. **How can IAS be used to forward RADIUS requests to another RADIUS server?**

    IAS can act as a RADIUS proxy, receiving RADIUS requests from a remote access server and forwarding those requests to another RADIUS server based on certain information about the user who is attempting to connect.

20. **How can IAS help monitor your remote access utilization?**

    IAS supports accounting, which can create log files that detail the remote access activity on your RRAS servers.

Sunday Morning Part Review Answers

1. **What VPN protocol offers a more secure tunnel by encrypting more of the transmitted data?**

   The Layer 2 Tunneling Protocol (L2TP), combined with IP Security (IPSec), makes it impossible for eavesdroppers to determine what VPN protocol is in use by encrypting more of the transmitted data.

2. **Which VPN protocol provides both tunneling and encryption?**

   The Point-to-Point Tunneling Protocol (PPTP).

3. **What Windows Server 2003 service accepts VPN connections?**

   Routing and Remote Access Service (RRAS).

4. **How can firewalls affect a VPN?**

   Firewalls can block the TCP ports required by VPNs. They can also block the General Routing Encapsulation (GRE) protocol that VPNs use, and firewalls using Network Address Translation (NAT) can defeat GRE's encapsulation techniques.

5. **What protocols allow RRAS to talk to network routers and exchange routing information?**

   Routing protocols, including Routing Information Protocol (RIP) and Open Shortest Path First (OSPF).

6. **What server platforms do not include Internet Connection Sharing?**

   Web Server, Enterprise Server, and Datacenter Server.

7. **How can RRAS act as a basic port-filtering firewall?**

   You can configure input and output filters to permit or deny only specific traffic on a server's network interfaces.

8. **How can RRAS act as an Internet gateway?**

   By configuring RRAS in Internet Server mode.

9. **How can you quickly obtain statistics about your network based on data that you capture with Network Monitor?**

   By running one or more analysis Experts within Network Monitor.

10. **How can you obtain the full version of Network Monitor?**

    It is included with Microsoft Systems Management Server and certain Microsoft Official Curriculum training courses.

11. What data can you capture with Network Monitor?

Any information that is transmitted on the network segment that your server is connected to. The version of Network Monitor included with Windows Server 2003 captures only traffic that is sent to or from the server or that is broadcast to the entire segment.

12. How can Network Monitor be used as a troubleshooting tool?

Network Monitor enables you to capture and analyze network traffic. If you know how the various protocols on your network should work, you can use Network Monitor to determine which ones are not working correctly and why.

13. When does Windows Server 2003 perform a system snapshot or checkpoint?

On a regular basis, when you perform a manual checkpoint, or when you install new software or device drivers.

14. What files does Automatic System Recovery restore for you?

Only operating system files.

15. Where can you back up system state data using Windows Backup?

Either to a disk-based file, or to a locally attached tape device.

16. What type of backup includes all of the files on your computer that have changed that day?

A Daily backup.

17. If your computer crashes before you log on, what is a good first step in troubleshooting the problem?

Restart by using the Last Known Good configuration.

18. How can you revert to a previous version of a device driver?

By using Device Manager to perform a device driver roll back.

19. How can you create a customized Safe Mode startup environment that only includes drivers known to work correctly on your server?

By creating hardware profiles and disabling any questionable drivers in the new profile.

20. How can you enable or disable drivers in a hardware profile?

By starting the server with that profile and then using Device Manager to enable or disable the appropriate drivers.

21. **What effect does a full Security Event Log have on your server?**

    By default, Windows does not overwrite events in the Security Event Log until they are at least seven days old. If the log fills and Windows cannot overwrite any events, Windows shuts down.

22. **How can you remove a hotfix from your server?**

    By using Add/Remove Programs on the Control Panel to uninstall the hotfix.

23. **How can you deploy new copies of Windows Server 2003 that include the latest service pack?**

    By using the service pack's slipstream option to update a disk-based copy of the Windows Server 2003 CD's contents.

24. **How does disk defragmentation improve system performance?**

    By arranging files so they occupy contiguous spaces on disk, which makes it easier for the disk drive to read a file into the server's memory.

Sunday Afternoon Part Review Answers

1. **What advantage does a failover cluster provide?**

   If one node in the cluster fails, the other node or nodes can continue doing the work the failed node was doing.

2. **What technique allows the two nodes in a failover cluster to be productive at the same time?**

   Active-active clustering allows both nodes to perform useful work. In the event that one node fails, the remaining node picks up the entire workload of both.

3. **What are two examples of Microsoft server applications that are cluster-aware?**

   Microsoft SQL Server and Microsoft Exchange Server.

4. **What are the basic requirements for an application to be cluster-compatible?**

   It must use TCP/IP to communicate with its clients; it must allow its data to be stored separate from its executable files; and its client software must tolerate brief timeouts during a cluster failover.

5. **What server name should you connect to in order to manage a cluster?**

   The virtual server name that the cluster uses, rather than the individual names of the cluster nodes.

6. **What service provides clustering appropriate for Web servers?**

   Network Load Balancing (NLB) provides a form of clustering and load balancing suitable for Web servers.

7. **What is the difference between a certificate authority that you create and a commercial certificate authority like VeriSign?**

   Users' Web browsers are preconfigured to trust certificates issued by VeriSign. They are not preconfigured to trust certificates issued by your own CA.

8. **What basic certificate-issuing policy is included with Certificate Services?**

   The basic policy can be configured to immediately issue certificates or to wait for an administrator to approve a certificate before issuing it.

9. **What are digital certificates used for?**

   Digital signatures, identification, and encryption.

10. **What is the difference between a symmetric key and an asymmetric key?**

    A symmetric key's two halves are identical and must be protected in order for the key to remain secure because either half can be used to encrypt or decrypt. An asymmetric key's halves are different, and the public half does not need to be protected.

11. **When should you conduct a performance baseline?**

    When your servers are first configured and placed into a normal production environment.

12. **What is the purpose of performance trending?**

    To monitor performance over time so that you can predict when performance will fall below acceptable levels before it actually happens.

13. **What are the four main areas of a computer that create performance bottlenecks?**

    Memory, network throughput, hard disk throughput, and processor speed.

14. **What are the key elements in fine-tuning a file server's performance?**

    Hard disk throughput and network throughput.

15. **What are the key elements in fine-tuning an application server's performance?**

    Memory, network throughput, hard disk throughput, and processor speed.

16. **What are the key elements in fine-tuning Terminal Services performance?**

    Memory, processor speed, and, to a lesser degree, hard disk throughput.

Index

Continued

K

Continued

Wiley Publishing, Inc.
End-User License Agreement

READ THIS. You should carefully read these terms and conditions before opening the software packet(s) included with this book "Book". This is a license agreement "Agreement" between you and Wiley Publishing, Inc. "WPI". By opening the accompanying software packet(s), you acknowledge that you have read and accept the following terms and conditions. If you do not agree and do not want to be bound by such terms and conditions, promptly return the Book and the unopened software packet(s) to the place you obtained them for a full refund.

1. **License Grant.** WPI grants to you (either an individual or entity) a nonexclusive license to use one copy of the enclosed software program(s) (collectively, the "Software" solely for your own personal or business purposes on a single computer (whether a standard computer or a workstation component of a multi-user network). The Software is in use on a computer when it is loaded into temporary memory (RAM) or installed into permanent memory (hard disk, CD-ROM, or other storage device). WPI reserves all rights not expressly granted herein.

2. **Ownership.** WPI is the owner of all right, title, and interest, including copyright, in and to the compilation of the Software recorded on the disk(s) or CD-ROM "Software Media". Copyright to the individual programs recorded on the Software Media is owned by the author or other authorized copyright owner of each program. Ownership of the Software and all proprietary rights relating thereto remain with WPI and its licensers.

3. **Restrictions On Use and Transfer.**

   (a) You may only (i) make one copy of the Software for backup or archival purposes, or (ii) transfer the Software to a single hard disk, provided that you keep the original for backup or archival purposes. You may not (i) rent or lease the Software, (ii) copy or reproduce the Software through a LAN or other network system or through any computer subscriber system or bulletin- board system, or (iii) modify, adapt, or create derivative works based on the Software.

   (b) You may not reverse engineer, decompile, or disassemble the Software. You may transfer the Software and user documentation on a permanent basis, provided that the transferee agrees to accept the terms and conditions of this Agreement and you retain no copies. If the Software is an update or has been updated, any transfer must include the most recent update and all prior versions.

4. **Restrictions on Use of Individual Programs.** You must follow the individual requirements and restrictions detailed for each individual program in the About the CD-ROM appendix of this Book. These limitations are also contained in the individual license agreements recorded on the Software Media. These limitations may include a requirement that after using the program for a specified period of time, the user must pay a registration fee or discontinue use. By opening the Software packet(s), you will be agreeing to abide by the licenses and restrictions for these individual programs that are detailed in the About the CD-ROM appendix and on the Software Media. None of the material on this Software Media or listed in this Book may ever be redistributed, in original or modified form, for commercial purposes.

5. **Limited Warranty.**

   (a) WPI warrants that the Software and Software Media are free from defects in materials and workmanship under normal use for a period of sixty (60) days from the date of purchase of this Book. If WPI receives notification within the warranty period of defects in materials or workmanship, WPI will replace the defective Software Media.

   (b) WPI AND THE AUTHOR OF THE BOOK DISCLAIM ALL OTHER WARRANTIES, EXPRESS OR IMPLIED, INCLUDING WITHOUT LIMITATION IMPLIED WARRANTIES OF MERCHANTABILITY AND FITNESS FOR A PARTICULAR PURPOSE, WITH RESPECT TO THE SOFTWARE, THE PROGRAMS, THE SOURCE CODE CONTAINED THEREIN, AND/OR THE TECHNIQUES DESCRIBED IN THIS BOOK. WPI DOES NOT WARRANT THAT THE FUNCTIONS CONTAINED IN THE SOFTWARE WILL MEET YOUR REQUIREMENTS OR THAT THE OPERATION OF THE SOFTWARE WILL BE ERROR FREE.

   (c) This limited warranty gives you specific legal rights, and you may have other rights that vary from jurisdiction to jurisdiction.

6. **Remedies.**

   (a) WPI's entire liability and your exclusive remedy for defects in materials and workmanship shall be limited to replacement of the Software Media, which may be returned to WPI with a copy of your receipt at the following address: Software Media Fulfillment Department, Attn.: *Windows Server 2003 Weekend Crash Course*, Wiley Publishing, Inc., 10475 Crosspoint Blvd., Indianapolis, IN 46256, or call 1-800-762-2974. Please allow four to six weeks for delivery. This Limited Warranty is void if failure of the Software Media has resulted from accident, abuse, or misapplication. Any replacement Software Media will be warranted for the remainder of the original warranty period or thirty (30) days, whichever is longer.

(b) In no event shall WPI or the author be liable for any damages whatsoever (including without limitation damages for loss of business profits, business interruption, loss of business information, or any other pecuniary loss) arising from the use of or inability to use the Book or the Software, even if WPI has been advised of the possibility of such damages.

(c) Because some jurisdictions do not allow the exclusion or limitation of liability for consequential or incidental damages, the above limitation or exclusion may not apply to you.

7. **U.S. Government Restricted Rights.** Use, duplication, or disclosure of the Software for or on behalf of the United States of America, its agencies and/or instrumentalities "U.S. Government" is subject to restrictions as stated in paragraph (c)(1)(ii) of the Rights in Technical Data and Computer Software clause of DFARS 252.227-7013, or subparagraphs (c)(1) and (2) of the Commercial Computer Software - Restricted Rights clause at FAR 52.227-19, and in similar clauses in the NASA FAR supplement, as applicable.

8. **General.** This Agreement constitutes the entire understanding of the parties and revokes and supersedes all prior agreements, oral or written, between them and may not be modified or amended except in a writing signed by both parties hereto that specifically refers to this Agreement. This Agreement shall take precedence over any other documents that may be in conflict herewith. If any one or more provisions contained in this Agreement are held by any court or tribunal to be invalid, illegal, or otherwise unenforceable, each and every other provision shall remain in full force and effect.